ILLINOIS CENTRAL COLLEGE
A12901 605704

W9-ASJ-218

How Safe Are Our Skies?

How Safe Are Our Skies?

Assessing the Airlines' Response to Terrorism

Rodney Wallis

Westport, Connecticut
London

Library of Congress Cataloging-in-Publication Data

Wallis, Rodney, 1933–
How safe are our skies? : assessing the airlines' response to terrorism / Rodney Wallis.
p. cm.
Includes bibliograhical references and index.
ISBN 0–275–97847–8 (alk. paper)
1. Hijacking of aircraft—Prevention. 2. Aeronautics, Commercial—United States—Security measures. 3. Aeronautics, Commercial—Passenger traffic. 4. Airports—Security measures. 5. Terrorism—Prevention. I. Title.
HE9779.W35 2003
363.12'4—dc21 2002193039

British Library Cataloguing in Publication Data is available.

Library of Congress Catalog Card Number: 2002193039
ISBN: 0–275–97847–8

First published in 2003

Praeger Publishers, 88 Post Road West, Westport, CT 06881
An imprint of Greenwood Publishing Group, Inc.
www.praeger.com

Printed in the United States of America

The paper used in this book complies with the Permanent Paper Standard issued by the National Information Standards Organization (Z39.48–1984).

10 9 8 7 6 5 4 3 2 1

This book is dedicated to the memory of my mother.
She loved to fly.

Contents

Acknowledgments

My deepest thanks go to my editors, Heather Ruland Staines at Greenwood Publishing and to Emma Bailey at Westchester Books whose guidance I found invaluable when finalizing my text.

I also thank my friend Neville Roberts, a guru in the world of computers, who led me through the maze of information technology opportunities that proved so helpful in the preparation of this book.

CHAPTER 1

The Personal Risk: How Safe Is It to Fly?

"How safe is it to fly?" This question has been asked ever since Wilbur and Orville Wright first persuaded a heavier-than-air machine to leave the ground. Debates subsequent to the events that unfolded at Kitty Hawk on December 17, 1903, were about safety. Today, the horrendous airborne attacks by al-Qa'eda terrorists on multiple targets in America on September 11th, 2001, have put issues of airline security uppermost in most people's minds. Whether contemplating a journey on a commercial airliner or simply viewing one passing overhead, the question that might now be asked is, "How safe are our skies?"

This question is not new. In 1986, George Bush, then Ronald Reagan's vice president, studied the subject of terrorism from the perspective of the United States. The first half of the decade had seen an escalation in savage acts perpetrated by terrorists against aviation and land-based installations all around the world. People from many different countries had been killed, but U.S. citizens appeared to be most frequently targeted. Aviation drew particular attention from terrorists. They saw U.S. flag carriers, primarily Pan American World Airways (Pan Am) and Trans World Airways (TWA), as easy surrogates for the country whose flag they carried on the tail of their aircraft. In 1985, TWA had suffered a prolonged aircraft seizure at the hands of Shiite Muslims. One of their Boeing 737s had been hijacked after it had taken off from Athens airport. During the seizure, a young U.S. navy diver was killed and a number of other American passengers were taken hostage and spirited away to secret destinations in the Lebanon after the aircraft had landed at Beirut. At the end of that same year, the Abu Nidal terror gang turned its attention to land-based targets and launched simultaneous gun and grenade raids on Rome and Vienna airports. Five Americans were killed, one a young girl of eleven. They had not even boarded their plane.

The daily news coverage afforded such incidents helped swell public opinion against terrorism and was central to President Reagan's decision to establish a task force under his vice president.[1] The president knew that U.S. citizens viewed terrorism as one of the most serious problems facing the government. He believed they rated the subject alongside budget deficits and strategic arms control. In fact, it is most probable that since personal safety was involved, it demanded much higher consideration in the thinking of the average air passenger than even Ronald Reagan afforded it.

Armed with the president's mandate, George Bush set out to review the terrorism scene. He was aided by a task force of 14 senior government officials, each with a major responsibility within the national program to combat terrorism. Together, they sought to reassess the government's priorities and policies and to satisfy themselves that the national program was properly coordinated to achieve the most effective results. It was to be discovered only a few short years later that "proper coordination" had not resulted from the task force's activities. Nor were the "most effective results" achieved. Federal Aviation Administration (FAA) monitoring failed to identify failures in Pan Am's implementation of mandated security procedures. The airline's delinquency left its passengers vulnerable to saboteurs in December 1988. As the result of a bomb detonating in the baggage hold of flight 103, the *Maid of the Seas,* 270 people died. But this jumps too far ahead, too fast. The vice president had much to offer on the topic of the eponymous question when he reported back to Ronald Reagan on the findings of his task force.

The United States, the United Kingdom, France, Germany, and indeed most industrialized and developed nations pay a heavy toll in lives cut short by motoring accidents. George Bush told President Reagan that in the United States, there were 40,000 highway deaths every year. It could not be contemplated that at any time deaths of

American citizens resulting from acts of airborne terrorism would ever reach such appalling figures. Thus, in North America—as elsewhere—it was an incontrovertible fact that air passengers were exposed to greater risks driving in their cars to an airport than they were from the actions of criminals on board an airplane or from the evil activities of ground-based saboteurs bent on destroying a commercial aircraft. That was so when the vice president reported to his boss in 1986. It was just as correct in 1997 when another U.S. vice president, Al Gore, told his president, Bill Clinton, "The danger of an individual becoming a victim of a terrorist attack—let alone an aircraft bombing—will doubtless remain very small."[2] Even with the horrendous loss of life when the Twin Towers of the World Trade Center were destroyed and the Pentagon damaged on September 11th, 2001, the number of Americans who died in that year as a result of an aviation cause was less than one tenth of the number slaughtered on U.S. roads. Taken as a percentage of the numbers of air passengers worldwide, the figure becomes infinitesimal.

George Bush quoted another statistic back in 1986. He said 18,000 people were murdered each year in the United States. Given the frequency with which those unfortunate people were killed by persons known to them, sometimes family members, once again domestic dangers to life far exceeded those resulting from chance encounters with terrorists at home or abroad.

It is, of course, easy to quote statistics to prove a point, but figures alone tend to become valueless when emotions are involved. Al Gore said, "We fear a plane crash more than we fear a car crash." If one air passenger in a hundred million was, statistically, likely to suffer as the result of an airborne terrorist action, the intending traveler might still reasonably ask, "What if that one person is me?" One purpose of this book is to enable its readers to assess for themselves the potential for personal danger when making an air journey. Another is to suggest how to minimize any doubts that might remain after such self-analysis. Armed with the facts, those contemplating making a flight in a commercial airliner may be best able to settle their own misgivings.

One last set of figures drawn from George Bush's report on the activities of his task force showed that 25 Americans were killed by terrorist action in 1985, not all as a result of attacks on civil aviation targets. American service personnel were killed in a restaurant in Madrid; another was murdered in El Salvador, and one citizen was killed on board a cruise liner. Of the twenty-five, only two died as a result of terrorist action within the mainland United States.

An easy conclusion to draw from the vice president's study was that Americans traveling by air within the continental United States were safer than those traveling abroad. American skies might be deemed to be safer than foreign ones. Since in 1985 only a very small percentage of U.S. citizens traveled outside of the mainland United States, the pressure on the Federal Aviation Administration to protect air operations focused on overseas services of U.S. air carriers. This thinking dominated aviation policy making in the United States for a decade and a half after George Bush's team had finished their work. Indeed, until the first attempt to destroy the World Trade Center towers in 1993 and the bombing of the Federal Building in Oklahoma City in 1995, few in the United States believed that sites or people on their continent were vulnerable to any form of terrorist attack. Nothing would convince domestic airline management in America that any threat was posed to their operations. Naively they believed it was only foreign operations that had to be protected. Domestic services did not—in their view—require similar attention or a similar expenditure of capital. The traumatic events in New York City, Washington, D.C., and Pennsylvania in 2001 should have ended such thinking once and for all. The skies above the United States can no longer be considered beyond the reach of those intent on harming the country or its residents. The skies have to be made safe, and they have to be seen as safe, before air transport resumes its normal place in the travel plans of Americans. It can be done, as the following pages will attempt to show, but it will require commitment from the government and from airport and airline management.

One person recognized the immensity of such a task long before September 11th, 2001. Four years earlier, Victoria Cummock, a member of the White House Commission on Aviation Safety and Security, wrote a dissenting addendum to the commission's report on the loss, in unexplained circumstances, of a TWA Boeing 747, off the eastern seaboard of the United States. She claimed, "History has proven the aviation industry's lack of sincerity and willingness to address safety and security on behalf of their customers." Cummock was writing in the context of the U.S. aviation industry. There, a lack of sincerity and willingness was a matter of record, as the commissioner pointed out. She knew then that it would require strong motivation to move U.S. domestic carrier thinking on security matters to a new level. The

2001 attacks, when domestic as opposed to international aircraft were deliberately selected by the terrorists, should have been motivation enough. However, doubtless the strong arm of government will still be required if security for domestic air passengers is to be maximized.

Of course, the White House Commission considered safety as well as security, although the commission failed to reach a final conclusion on what brought down the aging 747 that was the initial subject of its deliberations. The National Transportation Safety Board (NTSB) did conclude that the aircraft's central fuel tank had exploded, but the board could not determine the source of the ignition energy. Of the possibilities considered during their investigation, board members believed the most likely was a short circuit outside the tank, which "allowed excessive voltage to enter it through electrical wiring associated with the fuel quantity indication system." Could an improvised explosive device (IED), small enough to leave little or no trace, have been positioned adjacent to the central fuel tank and set to go off at a predetermined altitude or time? We will probably never know. Two months after the al-Qa'eda attacks, America was faced with another mysterious crash. This time, a ten-year-old Airbus 300 aircraft belonging to American Airlines (AA) was the victim. It plunged out of the skies almost immediately after takeoff from New York's Kennedy Airport, the same departure point as TWA flight 800. (The crashes of TW 800 and AA 63 and others are considered separately later in chapter 7, Unexplained Crashes.) Such losses raised anew the question, "How safe is it to fly?" But for now, for most people those still unbelievable events of September 2001 link safe skies with freedom from terrorism. The events did, after all, generate a global war on terror.

The Western world's commitment to an open society and its reliance on a sophisticated infrastructure to manage its affairs was identified by George Bush as one cause of the West's vulnerability to terrorism. Small rather than big government is a political aim of his son, President George W. Bush, but for skies over America to become as safe as the general public demands, government will have to become involved.

This leaves unanswered the question "How safe are our skies?" As has been shown, flying is safer than traveling by road, but such a response would hardly be the reassurance an air traveler is seeking. If the question had been, "Are our skies safe enough?" the simple answer would have been no. In the year prior to the Bush task force meeting, more than 10,000 people died in America from accidents in the home. The question asked then might have been, "Where are we safe?" To promise safety in any area of life is just not possible. However, flying as a commercial passenger within the United States can be considerably safer than it was shown to be in 2001. No one should have been able to board aircraft in the United States with sufficient weapons to effect a series of coordinated hijackings. That this was possible four times on a single morning at different airports demonstrates most clearly that the security in place was woefully lacking. Yet it had been considered adequate by the airport and airline management and accepted as sufficient by the Federal Aviation Administration. Congress moved swiftly to effect very necessary repairs to the system, but did they do enough? The reader is offered a response to this and related questions in chapter 3, Governments Response to Air Terrorism.

Safety and security are, in some ways, matters of perception. In an aircraft flying 30,000 above the surface of the earth, passengers have no control over their environment. They are dependent for their safety on the pilot and on the engineers who maintain the aircraft. In these uncertain times, passengers are dependent on the performance of ground staff and security personnel to ensure that no malcontent is able to harm the aircraft and its human payload. Because all these activities are outside the control of passengers, for travelers uncertainty will always exist. But it is within the capability of airline and airport managements to assuage the fears and misgivings of the air traveler. Air companies can raise the perceived level of security to a point where customers accept it as sufficient. Governments may need to push the air carriers in the right direction, although the fiscal penalties resulting from passengers opting not to travel where uncertainty exists may well be motivation enough. As this text develops, perhaps a beginning will have been made in widening the understanding of just what is needed and what can be achieved. In the meantime, it is necessary to fall back on statistics: Figures still confirm that air transport is the safest form of travel.

It is worth noting that outside the United States, air travel did not diminish nearly as much as it did in North America following the September 11th attacks. In the United Kingdom, where the drop in tourist receipts resulting from the shortfall of transatlantic travelers was very marked—low-budget operators such as Easyjet and Ryanair, who carry British vacationers to sun spots on the European continent, reported increased passenger loads. Whatever threat appeared to be posed against American operators was not deemed to exist as far as the average European holiday flight was concerned. Passengers on these aircraft saw their skies as safe. They would have been exposed to very visible security controls at their departing airports, and such visibility clearly afforded them peace of mind. They did not believe terrorists bent on harming them could have boarded their vacation aircraft. Nor did they fear an attack from the ground. Faced with the question, "How safe are our skies," they had answered, at the very least, "safe enough!" There is a lesson here for U.S. airport and airline managements and for Congress.

In 1989 and again in 1996, eminent commissions[3] were established by successive U.S. presidents to study air terrorism. Both had followed fatal accidents when large numbers of Americans had died. The first was the bombing over Lockerbie, Scotland, of Pan American (Pan Am) flight 103. The second was the loss of the TWA Boeing off the east coast of America. The findings of the second commission had motivated Commissioner Cummock to decry the efforts of the airlines to protect their charges. "How safe are our skies?" was asked after both incidents. It was asked once more in September 2001. This book began with that very question.

Dr. Assad Kotaite, president of the Council of the International Civil Aviation Organization (ICAO), spoke on air safety in an address given in Montreal just days after the al-Qa'eda attacks. He said, "The tragic events of 11 September in the United States sharpened the resolve of Contracting States and other members of the international community present at the Assembly[4] to ensure that air transport remains the safest and most efficient system of mass transportation ever created." Such reassurance was to be expected from an ICAO president, but the wheels of ICAO move slowly. For Americans to quickly regain confidence in flying, unilateral action was required. First efforts came in the form of the Aviation and Transportation Security Act, which gave new mandates to the Federal Aviation Administration and changed the shape of aviation security operations in the United States. Flying *can* be made safer in the skies above America and elsewhere. It *must* be made safer, and the traveling public must be able to judge the level of safety for themselves. American citizens contemplating journeys by air should have the same assurance in flying as a safe and secure means of transportation as their European counterparts when the latter jet off to the sun.

How safe are our skies? There can be no definitive answer to such a question, but when the perception of all air travelers allows them to answer, "safe enough," the issue will no longer have relevance. Failure for Americans, in particular, to achieve such confidence would be a victory for terrorism. President George W. Bush would then have lost a major battle in his war on terror.

CHAPTER 2

Air Terrorism

What is terrorism? "Sheer bloody murder," according to one noted Scottish academic, Professor Paul Wilkinson, the author of a range of books on global terrorism, and head of the Centre for the Study of Terrorism at Scotland's St Andrew's University. He moved from his usual prose style to offer this simplistic but apt definition after years of studying terrorist incidents in many parts of the world. It undoubtedly described how people felt following the Lockerbie disaster in December 1988 and doubtless similarly defined for many people the events that unfolded in New York City, Washington, D.C., and Pennsylvania in September 2001. But is it enough? Lockerbie certainly resulted from the actions of murderers bent on taking the lives of innocent victims. For the aircraft to be destroyed, however, the terrorists had to rely on the failure of Pan Am's security and the ineffectiveness of the U.S. Federal Aviation Administration's own enforcement policies. To be successful, the terrorists also needed failures in the German and British aviation security programs. There was no conspiracy involving civil servants of the three nations, merely an understanding on the part of the terrorists that defense mechanisms, defined and mandated by the ICAO (the International Civil Aviation Organization), were missing.

The September 11th attacks also required ineffective security programs at the airports from which the hijackers seized the four aircraft used in the assault. The hijackers had to be able to reach their targeted aircraft without baggage handlers and screeners detecting any weapons they were carrying. Standards relating to international civil aviation operations are developed within the working chambers of ICAO, and once adopted, their implementation is mandated worldwide. To become effective, however, the ICAO rules have to be incorporated into national laws and then be employed. As the Lockerbie tragedy had shown, written words are meaningless unless governments enforce their implementation. But no matter what rules ICAO develops, none of them has application to U.S. domestic operations. Rules to protect U.S. and other passengers who fly on the some of the world's busiest routes are made in Washington and are enforced, or should be enforced, by the Federal Aviation Administration. The administration is, of course, free to incorporate the international standards into domestic rules. In the context of a state's freedom to decide on national levels of aviation security, a high-level ministerial aviation security conference held in the Montreal offices of ICAO in February 2002 had relevance. Policy makers there debated the applicability of international security standards to domestic services. The declaration at the conclusion of the two-day meeting included a commitment to "apply within national territories appropriate additional aviation security measures to meet the level of threat." The conference had balked at the idea of mandating international standards on domestic services.

Those who flew the two airliners into World Trade Center towers and their co-conspirators who attacked the Pentagon in Washington and caused a fourth aircraft to crash in Pennsylvania had to know that in 2001, U.S. domestic aviation security programs fell short of the international levels called for by ICAO. They would have known that domestic aviation security in the United States was inadequate and ineffective. To achieve their wretched ends, the terrorists would have relied on failure of the domestic carriers to protect their operations. They would have known too that there was no adequate government oversight of airport security. "Sheer bloody murder" is too simplistic a description of the tragic events that marked 2001.

A noted Canadian scholar, Dr. David Charters of the Department of Strategic Studies at the University of New Brunswick had offered a different definition of terrorism to the International Air Transport Association (IATA) security experts some years earlier. He told the airlines, "Terrorism is a violent process of social change involving the premeditated use of criminal techniques by agents of a state or a clandestine political organization to achieve political ends." He added, "Terrorism becomes transnational when the process involves the violation of national properties or attacks on foreigners or foreign property at home or abroad."

This definition was offered following an upsurge in terrorist activity around the time George Bush was preparing for President Reagan his report on combating terrorism. It perfectly encapsulated the beliefs widely held at that time. Dr. Charters did not go on to define *air* terrorism. There was no need. The international air carriers recognized only too well that acts of violence against their companies and their passengers were unquestionably political in their concept. They were certainly carried out by clandestine political organizations. Some incidents may even have been state sponsored. IATA members also knew that attacks were aimed at particular aircraft because the planes were seen to represent the government of registry, not the shareholders of the company. Vice president Al Gore recognized this fact. He wrote in the report of the White House Commission on Aviation Safety and Security, "When terrorists attack an American airliner, they are attacking the United States." Acts of unlawful interference—the terminology used by ICAO to describe terrorism directed against civilian aircraft—are political. Responses by governments frequently reflect this fact.

Dr. Charters' definition talked of "premeditated use of criminal techniques by agents of a state or a clandestine political organization to achieve political ends." The world has witnessed aircraft seizures where the goal was to secure the release of fellow militants held in prison. Sometimes the seizure was to bring emphasis to a particular cause. With such motives, there was always the probability that those unfortunate passengers held hostage during an aircraft hijacking would be released unharmed. Certainly some passengers were brutally killed, but most hostages survived. Sometimes their survival depended on the skill of trained negotiators; other times they were saved because the government of the country to which the hijackers had elected to fly opted to grant the criminals safe passage to freedom in return for the safe handing-over of the aircraft and the people on board. At all times the terrorists wanted to escape with their lives. They and their hostages were most at risk from a bungled attempt to storm the aircraft by ill-trained militia.

Saboteurs in the 1980s had all made certain their lives were not at risk from the bombs they placed on aircraft. The bombers of an Air India Boeing 747 over the Atlantic in 1985 were safe in Vancouver when their device exploded. The criminals who attacked Pan Am flight 103 in 1988 were a continent away when the Lockerbie tragedy occurred. And it was similar with many other airborne bombings. The al-Qa'eda quadruple attacks in the United States on September 11th were very different. The terrorists elected to die to achieve their goal, which, it must be assumed, was simply the destruction of symbols of America's power, both fiscal and military. No one claimed responsibility for the assaults. It was sufficient for the terrorists that a statement had been made. Anarchy had entered the lexicon of airborne terrorism.

President George W. Bush quickly blamed Osama bin Laden, a Saudi dissident, for the September 11th outrages. Al-Qa'eda was his organization. Responsibility had been laid at bin Laden's door for a series of terrorist acts directed against U.S. targets. The U.S. government was satisfied he was behind the attacks on two U.S. embassies in Africa, where more than 200 people were killed. Government officials named him as the force behind a seaborne assault on a U.S. warship in the Yemen in which 17 service personnel died. His was said to be the hand behind the 1993 bombing of the World Trade Center in New York. There six people were killed. All acts of land- and sea-based terrorism were now attributed to bin Laden. With more than 3,000 additional deaths laid at his door, bin Laden had entered the realms of air terrorism.

It was natural to tie bin Laden to the September attacks. Ramzi Ahmed Yousef, one of the Islamic fundamentalists found guilty of the 1993 World Trade Center bombing, had previously planned to bomb 12 U.S. aircraft in the Asia-Pacific region, but he was caught before he could put his agenda into operation. He was arrested in Pakistan and deported to the United States, where he was tried, found guilty, and sentenced to life imprisonment for conspiracy. Yousef had forged the links between urban and air terrorism. If bin Laden was a co-conspirator in the 1993 bombing, the potential was there for him to have been associated, at the very least, with Yousef's plans for multiple bombings of U.S. aircraft. The switch to aircraft for a second assault on the World Trade Center fits into a scenario most likely to have originated from that same stable.

Terrorism in the new millennium has moved away from the goals that motivated earlier militants. Early acts of unlawful interference with civil aviation were normally claimed by or identified with known dissident groups. It is true that no one declared responsibility for bombing Air India's aircraft, the *Kanishka,* in 1985, but many believed that the horrendous loss of life had shocked the saboteurs who had planted the bomb and that shame and guilt had caused the silence. This thinking may not be too far from the mark.

The *Kanishka* exploded over the Atlantic when a bomb carried in an unaccompanied suitcase detonated. Investigators were led to this conclusion because simultaneously with the destruction of the aircraft, a suitcase had exploded in the baggage makeup area of Tokyo's Narita Airport. From the debris of that explosion, pieces of a Sanyo radio receiver were identified together with remnants of a suitcase known to have been carried on an incoming Canadian Pacific aircraft. The case was labeled for transfer to an Air India flight departing for the subcontinent. By this time investigators knew that the *Kanishka* had carried an unaccompanied suitcase. The tragedy was, the aircraft was operating behind schedule. Had it been on time, the bomb would have detonated on the ground in London. The terrorists, Sikh militants, may not have intended to destroy the aircraft in flight.

No one claimed responsibility for the Lockerbie bomb, but it is not suggested that those responsible did not intend to take the lives of everyone on board Pan Am's *Maid of the Seas.* Like the *Kanishka,* the *Maid of the Seas* was operating behind schedule. Had it been on time, the aircraft would have been over the Atlantic with little chance of investigators' recovering sufficient remnants of the wreckage to pinpoint the cause of the loss or of identifying the probable saboteurs. But in this incident there was an identifiable "political end." It is generally accepted that the Pan Am aircraft was destroyed in revenge for the shooting down of an Iranian Airbus, with more than 200 passengers and crew on board, by a U.S. warship, the *Vincennes,* earlier that same year.

Perhaps no definition is needed specifically for air terrorism. Certainly by late summer 2001 most Americans had, for 13 years, related this phenomena to the 1988 destruction of Pan Am's flight 103. The facts of that tragedy had been etched into their minds. The aircraft had been flying 30,000 feet above the small Scottish border town of Lockerbie when an improvised explosive device detonated in the baggage hold, killing all 259 passengers and crew on board the jet and 11 residents of Lockerbie when burning wreckage fell on their homes.

This was not the biggest loss of life from an act of airborne terrorism—that had occurred when the *Kanishka* was lost—but at the time, Lockerbie had seen the largest loss of American lives to a single act perpetrated by terrorists against a civil aviation target.

Few people could have contemplated a more horrendous scenario than that which befell the *Maid of the Seas.* Yet the events of September 11th were to supersede that traumatic happening. New Yorkers going about their routine business witnessed an act so evil in its conception and enactment that no writer of fiction would have dared include it in even his most outlandish manuscript. Two commercial aircraft, seized by Middle Eastern terrorists shortly after their takeoff from Boston's Logan Airport, American Airlines flight AA 011 and United Airlines (UA) flight 175, were deliberately flown into the Twin Towers of the World Trade Center in Lower Manhattan. Those who directly witnessed the assault on the Twin Towers were joined by many millions of television viewers around the world who watched unbelievingly as fire engulfed the two structures causing them to collapse with a loss of life exceeding 3,000. In Washington another hijacked American Airlines aircraft, flight 077, seized after it had taken off from that city, was flown into the Pentagon, the headquarters building of the U.S. armed forces. A fourth aircraft, this time United's flight 093, which had departed from Newark en route to San Francisco, was seized. The intention of the terrorists, it was believed, was to attack the White House. The plane crashed in an open field in Pennsylvania after passengers fought to overcome the Islamic militants who had seized the aircraft. These events comprised the most devastating terrorist onslaught in history. More people died that day in the four assaults than were killed during the attack on Pearl Harbor more than a half century earlier. It was an act that was to propel the United States into a fourth Asian war: Japan, Korea, Vietnam, and now Afghanistan. President George W. Bush threatened to expand the war against terror to other theaters.

The potential for an airborne strike by terrorists at the heart of a great metropolis had always existed. It had been considered and debated within aviation circles, but the scenario had always been of a seized aircraft being forced to crash randomly into a city center. In 1994, Islamic fundamentalists who seized an Air France A-300 airbus in Algeria had intended to bring the aircraft down over Paris. In the event, the aircraft landed in Marseilles en route to the French capital, and members of France's elite anti-terrorist squad successfully stormed the aircraft. All four terrorists were killed.

That there existed terrorists prepared to die for their cause was known by the dawn of the third millennium, but the air transport industry falsely believed it was cocooned against airborne suicidal militants. Industry experts judged as a land-based phenomenon the type of atrocity that saw so many U.S. marines killed when a terrorist, oblivious to his own destruction, drove a truck containing high explosive into their barracks in the Lebanon. It was believed that the intense psychological pressure needed to persuade men to undertake suicide missions could not be sustained beyond the time it took to board a vehicle and drive it to a predetermined destination just a short journey way. Similarly, it was held that those individuals who strapped bombs to themselves and walked to a selected spot where they detonated their devices would be confined to land-based targets. It was realized that airports fell into the area of possible targets for suicide bombers, but no one contemplated that such scenarios would translate readily into an airborne massacre. Yet history might have pointed to the Japanese kamikaze pilots in World War II. They had to sustain their hypnotic state for a period of time sufficient to fly to their target.

Debates continued within the International Civil Aviation Organization and the International Air Transport Association. Specialists had viewed the growing complexity of reservations, check-in, immigration, customs controls, and security screening and considered them a sufficient deterrent to the risk posed by a suicidal bomber. The state of mind required for a self-destruct saboteur to operate was not believed to be sustainable over the length of time needed to travel to the airport and complete predeparture procedures without someone along the way identifying unusual behavior patterns. The airlines had reason to believe their theory. For years they been suffering fraudulent attacks on their revenue through the use of counterfeit, forged, or stolen tickets. Systems developed to counteract this criminal activity and training given to passenger service staff had developed a sixth sense in many check-in agents. A multitude of passengers had been apprehended at check-in as the result of staff recognizing false documents; others had been detected simply because the agent sensed something was wrong. Something in the person's demeanor during check-in had triggered warning bells. It did so again on December 21, 2001, when American Airlines staff at

Charles de Gaulle Airport in Paris became concerned over a passenger, Richard Reid. He was attempting to register for a flight to Miami. The staff called the French border police. Reid passed whatever examination they undertook, but he was not cleared before the aircraft he had intended to take had departed. When Reid flew the next day, he was hiding an improvised explosive device in the heel of his shoes.

Airline check-in agents have become effective in identifying passengers who are posing as bona fide tourists but who are likely to claim refugee status on arrival at airports in Western Europe or North America. The numbers of such persons, deemed illegal immigrants by the immigration services, had escalated to epidemic proportions in the 1980s. They continue to grow. To stem the tide, targeted countries, led by the United States, imposed fines on air carriers bringing such persons to their shores. These penalties quickly exceeded seven figures for many of the major European and American airlines. The airlines reacted swiftly to stem this drain of capital. They worked with specialist government agencies to train staff at home and abroad to detect fraudulent travel documents, a problem associated with many illegal movements, and in some places took on a role that more correctly lay with the immigration services. Once again, training paid dividends. It showed that the airlines' first line of defense against those who sought to evade government controls was the check-in counter.

These experiences added to the faith most international carriers in developed countries had in their security programs and their staff. Carriers invested large sums of money in capital equipment for use at airports in addition to establishing relevant training programs for their staff. Several years of peaceful existence without experiencing the ravages of terrorism left the carriers with a reasonable, if fragile, sense of security. Similar investments were made by many of the major airports in Europe, Asia, and Australasia, adding to the carriers' and their passengers' belief that reasonable precautions were in place to preempt the hijacker or the bomber. These international security precautions were not adopted for U.S. domestic services. It was a deficiency the Islamic militants so ruthlessly exploited.

The tragedies that unfolded on September 11th showed America and the world that a new phenomenon had arrived. Men of an entirely different disposition had superseded the hijacker of the type so active in the 1970s and 1980s. Many of the aircraft seizures toward the latter part of the old millennium had been by young, educated men, often university graduates. They generally had an identifiable cause. They were either seeking publicity for their cause or had taken the aircraft and its human payload as a negotiating chip, often to be used to secure the release of colleagues held in Western prisons. They had one thing in common. They did *not* want to die during or as a result of their actions. Aviation defenses against hijackers and policies aimed at containing incidents once they occurred worked on the premise that the hijackers would want to live after their acts of unlawful interference. The September attacks were carried out by men who had chosen to die in order to achieve their mission. They had no negotiating objective. They had no message other than to express in the most terrible way their all-consuming hatred of the United States of America.

Thus the attacks on the Twin Towers and the Pentagon and the downing of United's flight 093 began a new era in air terrorism. The new and devastating phenomenon, which had arrived with the terrorists on that day, was the educated terrorist, trained to fly modern jet aircraft and with an anger against Western democracy and against the United States in particular so intense that death was of no consequence. It changed the world's concept of air terrorism. The world of the kamikaze had entered civil aviation operations. Anarchy was the new terror.

The new airborne anarchy took security services back to earlier discussions within ICAO's panel of aviation security experts. There, members had debated the possibility of terrorists using an improvised explosive device to cause an aircraft to explode over a city, resulting in mass destruction and loss of life. Like the earlier air bombings, this would have been without danger accruing to the perpetrators. Just as in the Lockerbie and Air India bombings, the saboteurs would be many thousands of miles away when their deadly weapons exploded. Safeguards were built in to a carrier's normal operation to make such sabotage difficult to achieve. Mandated security programs required by the ICAO were believed appropriate to meet such a threat making such a ploy impracticable.

However, the world has now been thrust into an age where biological and chemical weapons are used as offensive munitions. Not since the Great War in the early twentieth century has such evil ordnance been used against Western society. But Saddam Hussein, the leader of the rogue state Iraq, had developed such weapons and had used them against his own people. In an earlier book by this author,

Lockerbie: The Story and the Lessons, a warning against such weapons being used against civil aviation targets was raised. That text noted that in April 1995, a bomb containing the nerve gas Sarin had been detonated in the Tokyo Metro. The culprits were a far-out religious sect. A number of people had died and many were injured as a result of the attack. The question raised by the Tokyo attack was, could this tactic be used against air transport?

As far back as 1989, the Indian government's representative on the ICAO panel of aviation security experts had asked the members to consider the potential for the use of nerve gas against commercial airliners. Debate centered on the possibility of such weapons being used to seize the aircraft or simply to cause it to crash. The general consensus was that such an attack was too complex for terrorist use. Bombing was considered more simple and thus posed the greatest threat. Defenses were developed to minimize the danger from improvised explosive devices. Even so, forward thinking aviation managements noted the need to anticipate possible future changes in the modus operandi of fanatical groups of terrorists. It was, after all, only a short jump from ground transportation targets to civil aviation ones. Future airport security plans had to seek to contain such attacks should they be aimed against ground facilities. If nerve gas attacks could be mounted in subway stations, they could just as easily be mounted in an airport terminal, although the open spaces of the latter would not lend themselves to such use as easily as the confined tunnels of a metro system.

However, the threat posed by biological and similar weapons has to be considered again. Following the quadruple assaults in September 2001, anthrax spores were distributed by mail to addresses in the United States. As this book was being written, no one had been identified with this wicked action, but many believed the likely source would be found among dissidents within the United States. The public was mindful of the bombing of the Federal Building in Oklahoma City in 1995, a crime for which a young American, Timothy McVeigh, was found guilty and executed. But with a new breed of terrorist existing and with certain Middle Eastern regimes violently opposed to the West, the potential for such people to couple the use of biological or chemical weapons with an aircraft delivery system must be considered. An aircraft exploding over a city with the device releasing biological material is a scenario too horrendous to contemplate, yet those responsible for assessing future threats and for developing safeguards against acts of air terrorism must take such nightmare prospects into their considerations. As air terrorism has evolved, the conclusions of incidents have become more violent. Effective defense programs have to be developed and put in place to eliminate all possibilities. It can be done. Hi-tech responses to the saboteur have proved effective. Variants of equipment available today could safeguard not only the air transport industry and its customers but also ground based citizens of potential target countries as well. Governments and air companies must work together to forge a defensive capability so strong that terrorists will be deterred from using aviation as a method for their wretched deeds. The vigor shown when airborne terrorism first reared its head in the international arena must be reignited.

Governments have the key role in the war on terror. They control the intelligence services, and intelligence is vital if democracies are to be guarded against terrorism, whether land-based or airborne. There is every reason to believe that the intelligence services failed the American people over the September 2001 attacks. It became clear immediately after the events that information had been circulating but had not been acted upon. Names of the hijackers were known to the CIA and FBI, yet these criminals were able to move freely within the United States and board aircraft with little or no special attention paid to them. That the freedom abused by the hijackers exists is doubtless partly a result of the problem identified by George Bush 15 years earlier. He saw a commitment to an open society as one cause of the West's vulnerability to terrorism. The maxim "innocent until proven guilty" is a weakness in the defense against modern terrorists, who are not bound by codes of ethics. Rather, they use them as a weapon against democracy. Yet to move away from basic human rights beliefs would be a victory for evil over good. Somehow, governments have to find a balance that protects the innocent and safeguards against the guilty.

One deficiency of the intelligence and secret services in September 2001 was the failure to communicate. Had the names of the men responsible for the atrocities, already known to the intelligence services, been passed to the air carriers, a simple computer input could have highlighted the men's names at the time they checked in for their flights. Appropriate police action may then have prevented the men from boarding and thus seizing the aircraft used in the attack. An opportunity exists for those responsible for protecting Western society to work with the air carriers to coordinate defenses against air terrorism but communication is not on the resumé of many intelligence organizations. Consider again the bombing of Air India's *Kanishka.*

In the years following the aircraft's destruction by Sikh extremists, numerous stories arose about alleged lack of communication between the Canadian Security Intelligence Service (CSIS) and the federal police force, the Royal Canadian Mounted Police (RCMP). Claims and counter claims emerged in respect of surveillance tapes relevant to the bombers made by the CSIS but never handed over to the RCMP. They were mysteriously destroyed by the intelligence service. The missing tapes were telephone wiretap recordings of conversations between two Sikhs.

It is known that the CSIS had one prominent Sikh activist under surveillance for some time before the bombing. Agents of the intelligence service had on one occasion trailed him, together with a second cell member, to a wooded area outside Vancouver in British Columbia, where the two subsequently tested an explosive device. The agents initially believed the explosion to be a weapon firing, and they took no action. Later, RCMP officers found the remains of two blasting caps at the site, indicating that something more significant than a gun being fired had taken place. The conversations overheard by the CSIS could have been highly significant, perhaps even leading to action by the Canadian Mounties, which may have prevented the bombing. Thus in this instance too, failure to communicate may have had a significant part to play in a large loss of life.

If one lesson is to be learned from major assaults on civil aviation, it is that the intelligence services must work with those directly responsible for a nation's security. Equally they must recognize the important role airline staff can play in making the skies safe to fly. Air terrorism can be minimized, but doing so requires the combined actions of governments and their security agencies together with the carriers and airport managements.

Governments must add offensive action to defensive mechanisms if air terrorism is to be beaten. They must attack those who wage war on airline passengers and crews. Retroactivity is always too late. President George W. Bush's decision to carry the fight to terrorists wherever they exist can only be applauded. But it leaves a gap. Not all terrorist cells are of such stature that a state, even small military detachments of a state, can be sent into action against them. A defense system to protect against these people is as vital as action against states who sponsor terrorism. Just as the carriers put their staff into the front line against the fraudster, so too must they use their staff as agents in the war on terror. Suffice to say, action is essential if citizens of Western democracies are ever to take to the skies again in the numbers contemplated before September 2001.

Although air terrorism entered a new phase with the World Trade Center and Pentagon attacks, bringing anarchy and suicidal operatives into the security equation, many of the features of these incidents had been witnessed before. The simultaneous attacks caused many commentators to marvel at the ability of terrorists to coordinate their activities so that multiple aircraft seizures could be undertaken at the same time. This, they falsely claimed, was new. It was certainly not new. Almost 31 years to the day (and there may be great significance in this), in September 1970, four aircraft were seized at European airports. The attempted hijacking of an El Al aircraft failed and it was flown to London. The remaining three were directed to Middle Eastern destinations. A Pan Am 747 went to Cairo. Two, belonging to Swissair and TWA, were directed by the hijackers to Dawson's Field, a remote, former Royal Air Force strip in the Jordanian desert. They were joined some days later by a British Overseas Airways Corporation (BOAC) VC-10, seized as a bargaining chip to secure the release of the captured El Al hijacker. Before rolling cameras and the media of the world, the three aircraft were blown up. It had taken masterful planning and should have shown the world that terrorists could organize themselves and their actions. The Pan Am aircraft was firebombed at Cairo airport. Thus coordinating a series aircraft seizures was not innovative. The forerunners of the 2001 gangs had done so successfully, also taking aircraft from different points of origin. There was a difference, however. Passengers and crews were released before the explosions took place. No innocent civilian lives were taken. It was a different world.

Coordination and detailed planning came to the fore again in 1985 when simultaneous machine gun and grenade attacks were mounted at Rome and Vienna airports by factions of the Abu Nidal terrorist gang. Eighteen people died and more than a hundred were injured. Ramzi Ahmed Yousef must have intended similar coordination when he plotted to destroy 12 U.S. aircraft in one swoop.

Nor was the engagement of educated terrorists new. The seizure of a Kuwait Airways aircraft in April 1988, showed that college graduates frequently numbered among the terrorists just as they did among the passengers. On this occasion, several of the hostages were young British university students. They were able to tell graphic stories during a debriefing session held in London shortly after the event. One, a young female graduate, said she had gone to the toilet and when she returned just four minutes later, she saw a man whom she thought was a security officer. She believed that someone had been arrested. Then she turned and saw the passengers were sitting with their heads down and she realized there had been hijacking. The young woman went to return to her seat, but one of the hijackers stopped her and asked her to "please sit here." She did, and at that moment a grenade fell out of his pocket onto the floor!

Other British hostages on the aircraft confirmed that this air of polite non-hostility was maintained throughout the time they were on board. A young male hostage had been reassured by the fact that the hijackers all appeared well educated. It made him feel they were unlikely to do anything too precipitate. Others said that although being held prisoners, they were shown no hostility. When, eventually, they were debriefed in London following their return to the United Kingdom, they said it had come as a surprise when they learned after their release that two persons had been killed. They realized the terrorists were capable of killing because of the commitment they had shown to their cause, but the young British passengers, had not believed this would happen. The 22 British passengers on board had been released at Mashad in Iran, the terrorists telling them, "We have no quarrel with you." The aircraft flew on to Larnaca Airport in Cyprus, where the killings had taken place. Eventually the aircraft flew to Algeria, where the government negotiated the release of the aircraft and its crew and remaining passengers in return for safe conduct for the hijackers to a country of their choice.

The seizure of Kuwait Airways flight 422 provides extensive material for anyone wanting to understand the nature of air terrorism and human behavior under extreme stress. The aircraft had been seized after departing from Bangkok en route to Kuwait. It had an eclectic collection of nationalities among the 97 passengers and 15 crew. Apart from the Britons, there were three members of the very populous Kuwaiti Royal Family, several Thais, plus Australians, Saudis, Germans, Jordanians, Egyptians, and Japanese.

The decision to release the non-Kuwaiti prisoners and particularly the British may have affected the outcome of the hijacking. After leaving Mashad, the aircraft landed in Cyprus, where a large contingent of the British army was based. Throughout the seizure, the British passengers had comforted themselves with the thought that "Mrs. Thatcher would send in the SAS [Special Air Services] to release them," if this became necessary. The young British students had the utmost faith in this belief. If they were correct and had they still been on board when the aircraft reached Cyprus, SAS action may very well have ended the hijacking there and then. Interestingly, while they were on the ground at Larnaca, the hijackers monitored radio broadcasts covering the seizure. They were aware of the speculation that the island's government might call on the United Kingdom to help them regardless of the fact there were no longer any British passengers on board. They may have shared the young students' faith that Mrs. Thatcher would act. This may have been an influencing factor in their deciding to search for a less hostile environment.

Throughout their ordeal—the hijacking lasted 15 days, setting the elapsed time record for an aircraft seizure—none of the passengers had been subjected to ideological lecturing, and the captors repeatedly told their hostages that they were sorry they had been caught up in the incident. They had stressed that they believed in what they were doing, that *they did not want to die,* but that they would if it were necessary. Their aim was to ransom the aircraft and its passengers against the freedom of 17 of their comrades held in Kuwaiti prisons. The latter were being held for participating in a series of 1983 bombings in the Gulf state in which 6 people had been killed and 80 others wounded. The terrorists had attacked the U.S. and French embassies in Kuwait. The government of Kuwait refused to give in to the blackmail demands being made on them. They declined to release the prisoners. Iran had refused to assist the terrorists while they were in Mashad. The United Kingdom government had reiterated its well-known strong stance against terrorism, thus reflecting the position of its prime minister, Margaret Thatcher, and Cyprus took a similar position when the aircraft landed in its territory.

Larnaca had not been the airport of first choice for the terrorists. They had wanted to land in Beirut, but the authorities threatened to shoot the aircraft down if it did not leave Lebanese air space. When the plane did finally touch down at Larnaca, there was only minimal fuel remaining. A major disaster was averted by the Cypriot action.

A transcript of the conversation between the aircraft and the Beirut control tower when the aircraft tried to land at Beirut is of great interest. It was reported in the *New York Times* of April 9, 1988:

> TOWER: If you try to land by force, the plane will be fired on.
>
> PILOT: A gun is pointed at my head. I request landing permission to land to refuel.
>
> TOWER: We have been 14 years under gunfire.
>
> HIJACKER: I shall punish control tower officials if they don't allow us to land. The passengers are all in a panic now and many of them are vomiting. Among the passengers is a member of the Kuwaiti Royal Family with a heart condition.
>
> TOWER: With all due respect to all families permit me to say that all the Lebanese suffer heart ailments. Do not try to talk to me sentimentally.
>
> PASSENGER: I plead with you to allow us to land in Beirut. The hijackers insist on landing in Beirut and emphatically refuse to go to any other airport. There is no fuel left to take us to another airport.
>
> PILOT: Please inform the Ministers of Justice, Interior and Public Works that we are compelled to land at Beirut Airport. There is no other option for us.
>
> TOWER: There is no chance of landing. You will have to shoulder the responsibility of your action.
>
> PILOT: If you fail to clear the runway within a few minutes we will land in the sea.
>
> TOWER: Do whatever you want. Crash on the tarmac or in the sea. We shall not let you land here.

Given the complex nature of the politics of terrorism, many governments seek to divert aircraft from their airspace and territory. They want to avoid becoming involved. Blocking the airport runway is seen by such governments as one way to achieve this. The airline industry strongly opposes the closing of runways. It is a highly dangerous ploy. Used for the purpose of a state avoiding its treaty obligations, it is disgraceful. There can be only one safe place for a hijacked aircraft, and that is on the ground. Once there, it should be kept there.

Closing runways had been discussed many times within the ICAO. The airlines, through IATA and the world's pilots, through the International Federation of Airline Pilots Associations (IFALPA), had continually urged the United Nations to accept that a seized aircraft is an "aircraft in distress." Such an aircraft, by the terms of ICAO's own conventions, must be given every assistance including navigational aids and the right to land. The ICAO Council, the supreme body of that organization, had consistently declined to accept the industry's position on the grounds that a hijacked airliner fell outside the legal definition of "aircraft in distress." Eventually common sense was to eat into this ostrich-like adherence to legal terminology, but it hadn't happened in 1988. There can be little doubt that the passengers on board KU 422 felt in distress, especially at the beginning of the seizure when the young British woman had seen a grenade fall to the floor and a second had had a grenade fall in her lap. The passengers still on board in Cyprus would have been in distress when two of their number were murdered and their bodies dumped on the tarmac.

Three years earlier, the passengers of a seized TWA Boeing 737 with Captain John Testrake in command were doubtless similarly distressed when the Lebanese officials sought to stop that aircraft landing at Beirut. The captain's heroism and that of his senior stewardess, Uli Derikson, is now part of American aviation folklore. The stewardess's courageous actions probably saved the lives of many of the passengers on that unfortunate flight.

Shiite Muslim gunmen carrying the standard weaponry of the Middle East terrorist (guns and grenades) had seized flight TW 847 shortly after it had departed from Athens' Hellinikon Airport bound for Rome. It had previously begun its journey in Cairo and was on a routine shuttle service between the three Mediterranean cities. At Rome, the aircraft received passengers from and fed them into another TWA service operating across Europe and the North Atlantic to New York. It was a popular service heavily used by American tourists. On this day, there were 145 passengers plus eight crew on board. Captain Testrake was ordered to fly to Beirut. On his approach to the Lebanon, the captain encountered what many other pilots had experienced in previous hijacks in different parts of the Mediterranean—a blocked runway.

Testrake told the Beirut tower that the terrorists were "beating up" passengers, and he was given permission to land. Once on the ground, the aircraft was refueled and a number of women and children released by the gunmen before the aircraft took off again and headed for Algiers. The Algerians gave a repeat performance to that of their Lebanese counterparts. They closed the airport but subsequently relented, allowing the aircraft to land. More passengers were released, but after a five-hour stay, the aircraft left again for Beirut. Once there, the captain was again refused permission to land before

Testrake was able to put the aircraft on the runway. Influential to the authorities' decision to change their minds was the threat by the terrorists to crash the aircraft on the Presidential Palace if permission was not given to put down at the airport.

Once the plane was on the ground, a young American navy diver was murdered and his body thrown onto the tarmac. The hijackers demanded that all the lights at the airport to be switched off, and during this period, a number of armed gunmen boarded the aircraft as reinforcements for those who had originally seized it. At the same time, hostages were taken from the aircraft—selected on the basis of their Jewish sounding names. The hijack had become a political hostage-taking incident on a par with the earlier seizure of the U.S. embassy in Teheran. With the reinforcements on board and a fresh supply of fuel and food, TW 847 took off once more and headed for Algiers.

Prior to this second departure from Beirut, the terrorists demanded that a compatriot held at Athens airport, a man who, it was believed, was to have been the third gunman on board the flight, be released and flown to Algiers. The threat was that all Greek nationals on board would be killed unless this was done. The Greek government acceded to this demand. Negotiations conducted by the Algerian authorities on the second arrival of the aircraft on their soil led to the release of 61 passengers.

An earlier demand of the terrorists had been for the release of Shiite Muslims held in Israel. This was now repeated. Political pressure behind the scenes was mounting, and doubtless discussions had reached feverish pitch when the aircraft was allowed to leave Algiers once more. Again it headed for Beirut. Television and print media reporters from around the world converged on the Lebanese city to cover what had started as an act of air terrorism but was now a full-blown hostage incident. They were to show that a handful of determined men could hold to ransom the might of a major power—the United States. The terrorists were ultimately to succeed in many of their demands before the hostages were eventually released and allowed to return home.

Later in the same year as the TWA Boeing was hijacked, another aircraft belonging to the same company and flying a similar route pattern was bombed as it descended through 10,000 ft into Athens. It had left Cairo earlier that day and had passed through Athens on its way to Rome. The bomb detonated on its return to the Greek capital. One male passenger was killed instantly, and three others, including a mother and her small baby, were sucked from the aircraft and fell to their deaths. Following the earlier seizure, TWA were believed to have been applying the highest possible security to their Eastern Mediterranean operations, yet terrorists had beaten the carrier's defenses once more.

The aircraft's pilot was able to land the plane at Athens, where forensic investigation showed that an improvised explosive device had detonated under a seat in row 10 of the aircraft. It was not possible to identify the methodology used in constructing the bomb, but the trail led to Cairo. There attention centered on a Lebanese woman who had boarded the aircraft at that airport, leaving it at Athens. Attention was drawn to the suspect because she had been late boarding and had had to be hurried through the security controls. The nature of her itinerary also raised questions. She was traveling from Cairo to Beirut via Athens, where she had a lengthy transit stop. A more convenient route would have been a direct flight from Cairo to the Lebanon. She claimed she was planning to meet someone at the Greek airport during her transit.

Security screening at Cairo had identified among her belongings a Sony Walkman radio. Subsequently it was thought this had contained a detonating device. The plastic explosive material needed to turn the radio into a bomb was believed to have been worn by the woman underneath her outer garments, where a cursory body check, normal for women in Middle Eastern airports, was unlikely to have uncovered it. It was believed that she may have worn the material in the fashion of a sanitary napkin. It was agreed that the plastic explosive, harmless until armed, was unlikely to have been hidden in a fake lining of the bag she had with her, a method used in other incidents. In fact, the bag had contained little other than the Walkman and a change of underclothes.

The woman was known to have gone to the toilet compartment during the flight and changed her seat from the ill-fated row 10, where she had been sitting. The probability was that the device was assembled on board and the plastic explosive, complete with detonator and simple timing device, positioned by the suspect under her original seat before she changed seats. If the TWA security procedures had failed at Cairo, where the company had added supplementary screening to augment that provided by the airport, so too had they at Rome. The captain reported that the aircraft's cabin had been searched during its turn-round in Italy prior to departing again for Athens. Cabin searching was not an FAA-mandated procedure at the time of the incident. It had been. A rule had been introduced following two under-seat bomb incidents in 1982, both involving Pan Am. In one, a young Japanese boy had been killed. A second disaster had been averted when cleaners found the device during their routine duties. The Federal Aviation Administration introduced a rule requiring all U.S. airlines operating on international routes to have seat cushions lifted and the vicinity of the seats searched during stopovers and turn-rounds. United States air carriers had objected to the procedure and the cost penalties they said would arise from it. The airline lobby in Washington proved effective, and the rule was rescinded just two months after its introduction. Cabin searching had remained an option carriers could follow if they so wished. If, as the captain asserted, the procedure was implemented at Rome when his aircraft was prepared for its return to Athens, the quality of the search had been inadequate. This assumes the scenario mapped out by investigators was the right one.

One group with Middle Eastern origins claimed responsibility for the bombing saying it was hitting back at American arrogance toward Libya. Libya was quick to deny any complicity. Even so, political motivation clearly lay behind the attack. It fell within Dr Charters' definition of transnational terrorism.

The examples of air terrorism discussed in this chapter all occurred between 1985 and 1988, a truly black period in the history of civil aviation. But this same period brought appropriate responses from the international air carriers. Working under the direction of IATA, they developed new policies and procedures to preempt acts of unlawful interference. Coordinating their efforts with ICAO, they did succeed in making the skies safer. The degree of their success can be judged by the reduction in acts of air terrorism in the following decade. In more than ten years, only one significant hijacking was reported and this was clearly not an action of international terrorists. Three former prison inmates seized an Ethiopian Airlines Boeing 767 after it had taken off from Addis Ababa for Nairobi and ordered the captain to fly them to Australia. With insufficient fuel for such a transoceanic flight, the captain was forced to bring the aircraft down in shallow waters close to the Comoros Islands. The aircraft broke into three pieces as it hit the water, and although there was little depth to the Indian Ocean at this point, 127 people died. Many of them drowned while still strapped in their seats.

CHAPTER 3

Governments Response to Air Terrorism: An Effective Approach or a Dangerous Myth?

The response of the United States and its allies to the attack on U.S. targets in September 2001 was immediate and unconditional. President George W. Bush declared war on terror. His primary target was Osama bin Laden, the immensely rich Saudi exile who led the fanatical Muslim terrorist organization al-Qa'eda. Bin Laden had based his group in the mountain wastes of Afghanistan. His natural allies, the Taliban, an Islamic fundamentalist movement, had been the unofficial government of most of the country since 1996. To the president, war against bin Laden meant taking on the Taliban, a task he was prepared to accept. Thus for a third time in modern times, troops from a Western country moved into Afghanistan. The British had been there in the nineteenth century when they fought two wars with the Afghans, occupying Kabul on both occasions. It was the turn of the Soviets in the twentieth century, and now, at the start of the twenty-first, the Americans arrived with their British allies. The Russians also returned. This reaction to the destruction wrought on U.S. targets by the airborne agents of al-Qa'eda was well outside the responses normally associated with air terrorism. However, other actions were taken that more directly affected civil aviation. The first of these actions closed the skies above America. As a result, U.S. airports, including Washington's National Airport, were closed. No aircraft were allowed to take off or land. Aircraft already en route to U.S. cities were diverted, many to Canada, where they stayed on the ground for several days until normal service was allowed to resume. A further, more lasting action was the passing of a bill through the U.S. Congress to tighten domestic security operations.

President George W. Bush signed into law the Aviation and Transportation Security Act, believing it "should give all Americans greater confidence when they fly." New aviation laws hadn't achieved their objectives in the past, and those who listened to the president's words were entitled to wonder if they would do so on this occasion. The objectives were clear and concise. In future all checked baggage to be carried on domestic flights had to be screened. But the baggage of passengers traveling Pan Am flight 103 in December 1988 had been screened! The act did not require bags to be matched with passengers, however. Only this procedure ensures that no unidentified, unaccompanied bag travels on a passenger aircraft. The decision to exclude positive passenger bag match was taken during the bill's passage through Congress. Yet had this procedure been used by Pan Am either in Frankfurt, Germany, from where the feeder flight to England departed, or at London's Heathrow, the departure airport for the ill-fated Pan Am jumbo, the aircraft would not have been destroyed.[5] Could Americans have greater confidence when taking a flight now a new act was in force than when doing so prior to September 2001? International observers with an understanding of aviation security looked at the decision to drop the requirement to match bags with their owners and marveled at the power of the domestic airline lobby. The latter had fought for years to prevent legislation forcing them to add this vital procedure into their security programs. The motive for the air carriers' objection was a financial one. They did not want to spend money on a system they believed, wrongly, would adversely affect their domestic operation.

The American Air Transport Association (ATA), the U.S. carriers' trade body, had argued from the mid-1980s onward against positive passenger bag match. In 2001 as Congress debated the new bill, the association was still opposed. ABC News reported that the ATA retained the belief that matching bags with passengers would not stop suicide bombers who might pack explosive devices in their checked baggage. This method of attack had never been used against international civil aviation targets. Given the arrival of terrorists who were ready to forfeit their lives in an airborne assault, however, such a possibility can no longer be ignored. Airports that have in place passenger and baggage reconciliation systems—ICAO and IATA's terminology for positive bag match—and have introduced baggage screening in a multilayered security program have already moved to minimize the possibility of an improvised explosive device being carried in a suitcase.

The ATA contends that positive bag match is an unnecessary and disruptive inconvenience. Is this how the relatives of those who died at Lockerbie see it? Reconciliation is intended to prevent the occurrence of another Lockerbie tragedy. The baggage bomb has been the chosen weapon of the saboteur for more than two decades; surely every effort must be made to eliminate its future use against commercial aircraft.

Another argument used by the ATA against positive bag match is that the procedure would not prevent a saboteur from using an unwitting accomplice to transport an explosive device in a suitcase. Such a passenger would not know the device was there. But it was to preempt just such a situation that a security checklist was developed for use at international airports. "Is this your bag?" "Did you pack it yourself?" "Are you carrying anything for anyone else?" "Has the bag been out of your sight?" These questions are familiar to even the occasional traveler. There is no single silver bullet approach to aviation security. Aviation's defense against terrorism has to be a multilayered one, with one defense mechanism placed on top of another.

ABC News had been among the first to raise doubts about the new act. The network reported that passenger and baggage reconciliation had been standard practice on international flights for years. It had a long and trusted provenance. The procedure had been developed at a meeting of international security managers drawn from member airlines of IATA, the International Air Transport Association. They had come together in Montreal on June 28, 1985, just days after the bombing of Air India's *Kanishka*. They had acted immediately to meet the threat posed by the baggage bomber. The new procedure was designed specifically to prevent any repetition of the Air India attack. United States and Canadian government security officials joined the airline representatives from around the world, but notable absentees were the heads of security of the U.S. carriers, many of whom were based just a short flight away. Only TWA sent a delegate; the Air India bombings were "foreign" and deemed by the U.S. air operators to be of little relevance to their operations. The key terrorist event for most U.S. carriers was the TWA seizure and the ongoing saga of the hostages held in Lebanon. This, they believed, was a domestic issue to be discussed in Washington.

The importance the U.S. carriers gave to the TWA seizure was understandable. It was a major national and media event with pictures of the aircraft on the ground at Beirut being shown daily. The images dominated newspaper front pages and television news bulletins. A picture destined to become one of the most famous graphic examples of a hijacking showed the aircraft commander, Captain John Testrake, being held at gunpoint in the cockpit of the seized jet. With a number of American men taken and held hostage in Beirut, the level of emotion created in the United States was certain to give precedence of thought in that country to this criminal act rather than to the Air India bombing. Yet it was a gargantuan mistake for U.S. airlines to give the Air India disaster only secondary importance. From the loss of the *Kanishka* had come the most significant change in international aviation security standards in the 1980s—the mandatory requirement for passenger and baggage reconciliation. Pan Am's failure to implement this procedure was to claim 270 more lives just three years later. It is to be hoped that similar dire consequences will not result from the failure of Congress to mandate the procedure's use on national services.

The FAA representatives who had attended the airline gathering in Montreal did take note of the international carriers' recommendations. In 1986, the administration mandated that positive passenger bag match be used for all services coming under their registry and operating from overseas airports designated to be at extra-ordinary risk. Pan Am's failure to apply this rule was one reason a New York jury found the airline guilty of willful misconduct in respect of the bombing of their flight 103.

Those U.S. carriers opposed to the application of positive passenger bag match to domestic flights were doubtlessly influenced by the size of their home market. They considered the procedure to be time consuming and thus costly. This bottom-line attitude had much to do with the "lack of sincerity and willingness" noted by Commissioner Cummock. The U.S. carriers had been additionally opposed because in their opinion, there was no terrorist threat posed to flights operating nationally. The first attempt to destroy the World Trade Center in New York in 1993 should have warned them that foreign agents bent on harming the United States had arrived on their shores. They should have been warned by the bombing of the Federal Building in Oklahoma City in 1995 that urban terrorism of the type so frequently witnessed in Europe and the Middle East during the 1980s was now a matter of fact in the United States. Ramzi Ahmed Yousef, in prison in the United States for his part in the first World Trade Center bombing and for plotting to blow up 12 U.S.-registered aircraft in the Pacific, had shown the link between urban and aviation terrorism. Yousef had known links to bin Laden. The U.S. domestic airlines should have seen that a new threat existed and changed their policies. They should have listened to those commentators who urged them to focus attention on domestic airline vulnerability to the saboteur. The language of the Aviation and Transportation Security Act, 2001, suggested they had not done so.

Without any of the above, the terrible results wrought by bin Laden's attack on U.S. domestic targets should have driven home to American carriers that a new and terrible threat had arrived to menace their operations. The need to maximize air defenses against terrorism was so obvious it hardly merited comment. Yet neither the air companies nor Congress acted to bring positive passenger bag match, the cornerstone in aviation's defense against the saboteur, into the domestic arena.

The domestic airline lobby, successful in keeping positive bag match from the 2001 act, had been at work previously. Ten years earlier, the Federal Aviation Administration had decided to fund research into automating the process for the domestic market. Despite the clear feasibility of an automated procedure, the research and development program was abandoned following heavy airline activity in Washington. Yet the report of the Commission on Aviation Security and Terrorism established by President George Bush had recognized the value of the procedure. This body had been set up following the bombing of Pan Am's flight 103. The commission, under its chairperson, the Honorable Ann McLaughlin, concluded that destruction of the flight could have been prevented if stricter baggage reconciliation procedures had been followed. In Scotland, a coroner's court in the guise of a Fatal Accident Inquiry had reached the same conclusion. The presiding officer, the sheriff principal of South Strathclyde, Dumfries, and Galloway, noted the absence of any reconciliation procedure to ensure that interline (transfer) passengers and their baggage traveled on the same plane. It was an interline bag that contained the bomb. In England, British Airways, one of the largest airlines in the world, had long since designated passenger and baggage reconciliation as "the bedrock of their anti-sabotage program." They applied the procedure to all flights, domestic and international. Around the same time British Airways took their strong position, the Indian High Court inquiring into the 1985 loss of the Air India jumbo recommended to ICAO that "all checked baggage, whether it has been screened by x-ray machine or not, should be personally matched and identified with the passengers boarding an aircraft. Any baggage which is not so identified should be off-loaded." The judge presiding over the inquiry, Mr. Justice B. V. Kirpal, had recognized the shortcomings of x-ray screening in the 1980s. In 1988, the Montreal-based president of ICAO, Dr. Assad Kotaite, had told an FAA-hosted Washington conference "If the airlines throughout the world take effective action to make sure that no piece of luggage is carried on board unless the passenger to whom it belongs has also boarded, the likelihood of sabotage acts would be greatly diminished." Thus positive passenger bag match had a well-founded pedigree long before Congress began its deliberations in the wake of September 11th.

In 1997, the White House Commission on Aviation Safety and Security, chaired by Vice President Al Gore, did decide to recommend the introduction of passenger and baggage matching on U.S. domestic services. The carriers declared their support for the proposal, but behind the scenes they mounted a successful campaign to lessen the strength of the recommendation. The final report to the president recognized that "full baggage match ensures that no unaccompanied bag remains on board a flight and that manual and automatic systems to achieve this have been employed in international aviation for several years." However, it recommended only that "no unaccompanied bag should be transported on a passenger aircraft unless (1) it has been screened by a screening method that meets the FAA standard or (2) it belongs to a passenger who at the time of check in was neither randomly selected for security review nor selected by the profile for further review." This phrasing defeated the whole purpose of positive passenger bag matching. It is to be hoped no one ever suffers from the commissioners' failure to go through with their first thoughts. The commissioners had to know that the Lockerbie bomb bag would have evaded the profile system, since there never was an accompanying passenger to be trapped by this methodology. They would also have known that the x-ray screening process in Frankfurt failed to identify the bomb bag. Little wonder, then, that Victoria Cummock felt obliged to provide a personal addendum to the commission's findings.

Arnold Barnett, a professor at the Massachusetts Institute of Technology who led a study into positive passenger bag match at the time the White House Commission was sitting, believed the jury was still out on the effectiveness of screening checked baggage.

The Aviation and Transportation Security Act was hastily developed to close the latest stable door. Aircraft seizure was uppermost in the mind of Congress. This was hardly surprising, but since new legislation was being developed, it had offered a new opportunity to tighten all U.S. domestic aviation security procedures. Deeper debate would have reinforced the fact that matching passengers with their baggage was an airline concept. It had been made to work highly effectively at international airports (there is none bigger than London's Heathrow) through the cooperation of air carriers and airport managements. International passenger and baggage handling specialists had always held the opinion that automated procedures would operate just as effectively in the United States as in Europe, notwithstanding the traffic volumes and connecting time constraints at major hub airports. The old arguments that domestic civil aviation was not threatened by terrorism should not have been countenanced in 2001. Terrorism of a type even more deadly than that so frequently witnessed in Europe and the Middle East during the 1980s had already arrived in the United States.

Failure to maximize domestic carrier defenses adds to the American public's vulnerability to the saboteur. The al-Qa'eda terrorists selected domestic airliners to hijack for their assault on the Twin Towers and other targets because they had identified the weaknesses in the security procedures applied to these non-international flights. It must be assumed they will identify any weakness in the new act. Hijacking is not the only methodology in their armory, as history has shown. Improvised explosive devices carried in checked baggage have worked for terrorists in the past with dramatic effect. They will not be averse to using such a method again if they deem it a means to hit at their chosen target.

Of course, the new act did not ignore the baggage bomber. However, Congress chose to go down the road of 100 percent baggage screening as the defense against the saboteur. They set December 2002 as the deadline for installation of the necessary machinery at all

U.S. airports. Some aviation managers estimated that up to 3,000 hi-tech machines would be required. At the time the act was signed, only 160 existed. Moreover, only two explosive detection systems (EDSs) had been FAA certified for use at airports. The elapsed time between signing the new act in to law and the installation date was never realistic. The amount of hi-tech equipment needed to put an *effective* screening system into place at every airport never allowed the possibility of meeting the target date. Indeed, FAA administrators were of the opinion it would take manufacturers until the end of 2004 to produce all the machines needed to meet the conditions of the new act.

The Federal Aviation Administration had reason to be cautious. Following the loss of Pan Am flight 103, they had rushed out a directive mandating that U.S. airlines operating from designated high-risk airports incorporate approved explosives detection systems into their baggage-screening processes. In 1988, however, only thermal neutron analysis (TNA) met the administration's EDS criteria and *only six prototypes were available.* In fact, TNA had been the focus of the FAA research and development program throughout much of the preceding decade. The process of detecting explosives required baggage or packages to be bombarded with neutrons. These neutrons reacted with the contents of the bags, causing gamma rays to be generated in varying strengths when nitrogen, a component of almost all known explosives, was present. The TNA process measured the gamma rays, indicating the possible presence of explosive material. However, early tests had shown a range of materials created similar reaction to that of the nitrogen that would be present in an explosive device. Leather and wool, for example, had caused numerous false alarm readings. Technical experts at Science Applications International Corporation (SAIC) in California, who were charged with the FAA research program, developed other measuring parameters such as mass and contiguity to distinguish between inoffensive and potentially dangerous contents of the baggage. Subsequent additions to the initial machines incorporated the use of x-rays, giving a combination of search possibilities, and an automated detection warning was added to overcome the human element problems invariably associated with baggage screening.

The TNA technology had represented a major leap forward in explosive device detection, but at the time of Lockerbie, it was effectively in the research and development stage. The Commission on

Aviation Security and Terrorism criticized the FAA mandate and called for introduction of the TNA program to be deferred until the system had been developed further. They were aware that in its then-existing specification, TNA would not have detected the small quantity (300 grams) of Semtex contained in the Lockerbie bomb. The commission recommended that the Federal Aviation Administration launch a top priority research and development program aimed at producing new techniques. Twelve years later, as reported above, only two explosive detection systems had been certified.

A danger arises from setting unrealistic goals. Knowing targets cannot be met, those for whom the deadlines have been determined have no motivation to act. From the beginning, the prospects of achieving effective baggage screening across the United States by December 2002 were of mythical proportions. Worse still, if ineffective systems were to be put in place just to meet the deadline, the U.S. traveling public would have cosmetic, not realistic, security. Pan Am had tried such a subterfuge prior to Lockerbie. The airline gave security guards at Kennedy Airport fake firearms and had parade dogs hired from a local kennel, passing them off as sniffer canines. The purpose was to mislead the public and help justify a new security levy of $5 per flight that Pan Am had introduced. The money was never used for security purposes. It was instead placed into a central pool to help the carrier's precarious financial position. The truth came to light when two former executives of Pan Am, Fred C. Ford and Tom Plaskett, gave testimony during a consolidated liability trial held in New York in 1991.

Congress may have been influenced in their decision to screen all hold baggage by developments in Europe. There, driven by the British, most major airports had moved to full baggage screening. At London's Heathrow and Gatwick airports and elsewhere, however, baggage screening is conducted in conjunction with passenger and baggage reconciliation. They have both! The Consumers Union in Washington favors this multilayered security approach. The organization believes that the two systems, positive bag match and screening, are necessary. Clearly the Consumers Union has an ally in the European Civil Aviation Conference. In 2001, the conference called for the multilayered model to be introduced at airports throughout its region. It was to be incorporated into European law.

The system of baggage screening used at British airports operates on a three-tier system. This system required massive capital investment by the British Airport Authority. At Heathrow alone, the initial investment was in excess of U.S. $150 million. Following the report of the White House Commission on Aviation Safety and Security, the 1997 federal budget set aside $144.2 million to cover the provision of baggage screening throughout the whole of the United States. Little wonder that Senator Ron Wyden of Oregon, a member of the Senate Committee on Science, Technology, and Transportation, demanded to know "why . . . the city of Manchester, England, purchased more state-of-the-art explosive device detectors than the entire United States." Transportation Secretary Federico Peña's reply is not recorded. Provisions in the Aviation and Transportation Security Act suggest the legislators have moved to address the earlier financial shortcomings. Time will tell if their good intentions are fulfilled. The expense of carrying out the full proposals of the act will be significant, and the cost, which is intended to fall on the government, may prove to be a deterrent to implementation of an effective federal aviation security program.

It is worth considering the evolution of baggage security in Europe. The initial drive for 100 percent baggage screening in Europe had come from the United Kingdom's Department of Transport (DoT), but for less than noble reasons. The sheriff principal at the Scottish Fatal Accident Inquiry probing into the loss of Pan Am flight 103 included in his report that in 1988 "the limitations of x-ray screening as a means of detecting plastic explosives contained in electronic equipment were generally recognized." He noted that Pan Am had not been operating passenger baggage reconciliation procedures at Frankfurt or London and that the unaccompanied suitcase containing the fatal device would have been found if this simple operation had been in force. Yet ICAO had first called for the procedure to be used for international flights in 1986. In the summer of that year, the Federal Aviation Administration demanded its use by all U.S.-registered carriers operating from European cities. The rule was not enforced by the Department of Transport nor effectively monitored by the Federal Aviation Administration. Indeed, DoT officials waited until 1994 before they felt sufficiently removed from the sheriff principal's implied criticism to incorporate full passenger and baggage matching into a new package of rules governing the carriage of hold baggage.

The Department of Transport had always been reluctant to intervene on behalf of British airlines when matters affecting aviation security arose in overseas countries. The department insisted that security at airports in a foreign country was the responsibility of that country's government—an insistence that was quite correct but hardly practicable, given the remote airports to which British carriers operated. But on that basis, the Department of Transport was responsible for ensuring airlines foreign to the United Kingdom, and this included Pan Am, met the ICAO mandates when operating from British airports. Clearly DoT officials had not followed through on their own policy at London. They had relied on the Federal Aviation Administration to police U.S. carriers. Lockerbie had highlighted weaknesses in the DoT performance, and the department came under pressure from a variety of sources. To divert the focus of public attention away from their shortcomings in enforcing the passenger baggage–matching rule, they began to promote 100 percent screening of checked baggage.

In 1991, the British administration took its proposals for full screening of checked baggage to Europe. There, at the Paris headquarters of the European Civil Aviation Conference (ECAC), technical experts declared, "There currently existed no equipment capable in itself of achieving such an objective [discovery of explosive devices] with 100 percent effectiveness." This reinforced the sheriff principal's report on the Lockerbie bombing. He had gone on to say in his report that Pan Am's "reliance on x-ray screening alone in relation to interline baggage at Heathrow and Frankfurt was a defect in a system of working which contributed to the deaths." By this time, Interpol, too, had questioned the effectiveness of x-ray units in detecting explosive or incendiary devices concealed in checked baggage.

So at the time the Department of Transport was developing its own 100 percent screening security policy, using basic x-ray machines to meet a full baggage-screening requirement was a deception providing nothing other than a subterfuge to give the passenger a false sense of security. At some locations around the world, woefully outdated machines and systems were being used to screen bags. Such technology, better suited to a science museum than an airport, was inappropriate as a means to discover terrorists' bombs. The ECAC declined to make the procedure mandatory within their region and suggested that it would take ten years to reach such a point. They set 100 percent screening as a strategic objective to be achieved by 2001 but encouraged member states to work toward its implementation. Individual members did this. More important, so too did a number of airport authorities acting independently of governments.

One such group was the British Airports Authority (BAA). By summer 1998, all bags passing through London's Heathrow Airport were being screened, but not by the machinery of a decade before. They were using "smart" systems developed in America. The Belgians were doing the same at the National Airport in Brussels. Meanwhile, the Belgians were keen to move on. They sought to obtain harmonization of technical standards so that baggage screened in one location could be accepted by the authorities in another. This is an essential part of a "one-stop" security concept favored by the airlines. One-stop security calls for bags and persons screened at one airport to bypass all other security controls along the route of a passenger's itinerary. The intent is to facilitate the movement of passengers and their baggage and reduce airline and airport costs. This would have great validity in the U.S. domestic scene, where hub-and-spoke operations are predominant. Here is a challenge for the Federal Aviation Authority.

The BAA action at Heathrow and its other airports rescued the Department of Transport from its own machinations. 100 percent screening had become a reality. But screening was no longer a matter of simply passing a bag through a basic x-ray procedure. When they began their new programs, both the British and the Belgian authorities recognized that the validity of screening was still highly questionable. They accepted the ECAC position that no single device existed upon which airlines and airports could reasonably rely. They needed something better. They began a research program to identify manufacturers of hi-tech machines that could detect the small quantities of plastic explosive known to be sufficient to destroy an aircraft. The explosives detection industry provided an answer. "Smart" dual-energy x-ray and computer tomography were developed in America. The BAA decided to harness this technology to a three-level approach to baggage screening. They set aside Glasgow's Abbotsinch Airport for an extended series of innovative trials.

The British Airports Authority's motivation to act was their anticipation of a DoT directive mandating the screening of all checked baggage scheduled to be carried on commercial aircraft. The BAA officials wanted to be ahead of the game. They also wanted to steal a march on their competitive airports in Europe. They knew technology had not reached a point where sufficient reliance could be placed on screening techniques in general use at the time they began their experiment. They also knew that ICAO had mandated matching bags with passengers and that any new system would need to dovetail into the reconciliation rule. Although the Department of Transport had chosen not to direct airlines operating from British airports to adopt full reconciliation procedures, the airport authority was aware this would have to change.

It was against this background that, in 1993, the BAA began to experiment at Abbotsinch. In addition to the need to recognize the requirement for passenger baggage reconciliation, the test program had to meet certain requirements of the carriers. It had to allow the baggage to flow through the system with minimum interference to carrier operations. The commercial nature of civil air services had to be recognized and any new security procedures designed to accommodate the operational and facilitation needs of the airlines and their passengers. Punctuality and customer service requirements are important even with added emphasis placed on a safer environment for passengers and crews. Any new system had to minimize the use of human input to the system. The airlines had always seen the involvement of screening staff, often at the lower end of the pay scale, as a potentially weak link in their defenses against air terrorism. Finally, both the airport authority and the airlines wanted to minimize the number of items that had to be searched manually. It was a tough order.

The British Airports Authority sought to gather some of the very latest screening equipment at Abbotsinch. To do so meant resourcing the experiment from America. Vivid Technologies and Thermedics Detection, both based in Massachusetts, were contacted, so was AS & E. InVision of California became involved. Together they formed an impressive testbed operation. Recognizing the reluctance of any carrier to rely on a single technology, the BAA decided to use the machines in a layered approach incorporating two screening devices and one vapor detector to each baggage movement system.

The screening machines were mounted over the existing conveyor belts that moved bags to the baggage makeup area, where aircraft loads were prepared. The task of the first machine, operating in an automated mode, was to seek to identify any bag that contained substances meeting specific parameters built into the machine's memory bank. These parameters included the mass, contiguity, and atomic weights of the objects being screened. Any bag with contents meeting these criteria had to be automatically removed from the normal baggage flow and redirected to a second screening device. Here, an operator acted as the decision maker. He or she monitored a visual display unit utilizing color enhancement to identify the target. The operator could reduce the color content of the image to allow a more detailed examination of the target and its surroundings and, as necessary, magnify the image of any item. During the trials, highly qualified staff were used at the second stage. A similar level of expertise was planned for the system's introduction into operation at airports. This would be possible because the routine first examination had been automated, leaving more funds available to procure the right level of personnel for the detailed examination stage.

The trials enabled the British Airports Authority to experiment with various calibration settings. Calibration was dictated by the Department of Transport. Level-two screening sent up to 1 percent of all bags for a third check, where conventional vapor detection technology was used to test the selected bags for explosive contamination. The bags were "sniffed." Sniffing required the presence of a second operator. A computer linked to a Thermedics EGIS machine was used to identify the substance responsible for the contamination. The airport authority anticipated that only one bag in a thousand would require further examination, whereas the DoT had originally suggested 10 percent of all screened bags had to be manually searched—a process that would have halted operations at any major airport.

The various inspection stages were expected to clear the majority of all bags passing through the system; but for the few that failed to satisfy the specialist monitors at the second and third levels or that had set the alarm bells ringing at the first, other prompt action had to be taken. The question staff representatives wanted answered was, "Prompt action by whom?" Suspect bags could contain an explosive device. Handling potential bomb bags called for the involvement of explosive ordnance specialists. All doubtful bags were to be destroyed by these personnel using controlled explosive techniques developed through years of experience in the streets of British cities attacked by the IRA.

The British Airports Authority spent U.S. $10 million on the trials. The results encouraged the authority to introduce the program as a permanent feature at Abbotsinch. The rest is history. It cost U.S. $150 million to put the system into Heathrow, and this was followed up with similar installations at Gatwick. The Manchester Corporation, which own Manchester Airport, decided to go down the same route. Who paid? Ultimately, the airline passenger. Airports charge airlines fees; airlines charge passengers fares. Given the peace of mind the new security procedures provided when linked to passenger baggage matching, incorporating the higher fees into passenger tickets raised no customer complaints. Many air carriers using Heathrow had been concerned about the idea of funding, or asking their passengers to fund, a security program that had not been mandated by ICAO. With a labor force required at stages 2 and 3, and possible at a fourth stage, airlines considered their long-term objective of minimizing the use of human input in baggage security procedures had not been met fully, leaving the program fallible. However, taking staff responsibility out of the first decision-making process was considered a major advance.

No reports have surfaced of improvised explosive devices having been found by the new systems, but given the infrequency of bombs being secreted in hold baggage, none would normally be expected. The satisfaction for the airlines and their passengers comes from knowing that any attempt by terrorists to infiltrate bombs into the baggage systems is now most likely to fail.

The new three-tier screening system saw the British Airports Authority providing the technical infrastructure for the new screening process, leaving the carriers to manage the operation either directly or through their handling agencies. Ever suspicious, some airlines saw this as distancing the airport authority and the Department of Transport from any litigation should a bombing incident take place, despite the latter having both brokered the scheme. The damages laid at Pan Am's door following Lockerbie were well to the fore in the carriers' minds. Regardless of these concerns, the BAA officials moved ahead with their program. In the years since the airport authority first experimented with 100 percent baggage screening, the hi-tech manufacturing companies have developed their machines further and the authority has been able to refine its operation. Other airport managements that decided to go down the tiered screening route have stayed abreast of the improvements, and thus today, passengers flying out of such airports do so with the satisfaction of knowing the best systems in the world have been used to maximize their safety. Where airports have combined such screening with passenger and baggage matching, the skies are as safe as current technology and practice can make them. If the U.S. domestic flyer is to be given the same protection as his or her European counterpart, similar screening and matching systems, operating to the same high standards as those in Europe, must be put in place at all airports in the United States. Anything less, and the efforts of Congress in developing the Aviation and Transportation Security Act will have been in vain.

It is worth returning to the subject of matching passengers and their bags. The purpose of the procedure is very simple: It is intended to prevent terrorists infiltrating airline baggage systems. It achieves this by stopping unaccompanied, unidentified bags being placed on board an aircraft. Just such bags were used to bomb Pan Am over Lockerbie and Air India over the Atlantic.

Unaccompanied bags with improvised explosive devices hidden among their contents would have destroyed other aircraft but for the implementation of passenger and baggage reconciliation systems. In December 1983, an early attempt to use the airlines' interline baggage system to infiltrate a bomb bag on to a Pan Am B-747 was foiled at Istanbul, Turkey. A passenger had checked in with Alitalia for a flight to Rome, where he was to transfer to the American carrier. He did not board the Alitalia flight and his luggage, tagged for transfer at Rome, was offloaded. When examined, it was found to contain an improvised explosive device set to detonate on board the Pan Am service. Eight months later, in August 1984, passenger baggage match identified two unaccompanied bags at Madras airport in India. A passenger had checked the bags in for a flight to Colombo in Sri Lanka, but he never boarded the flight. The bags were removed from the flight; but instead of being isolated, they were taken into the arrivals hall at the airport, where one of the bags exploded, killing 40 people. Had the detonation been in flight, a great many more lives would have been lost. Passenger baggage matching works. It does save lives. Had the correct procedures been taken at Madras by the ground handling staff, no one would have died.

The ICAO developed regulations covering the reconciliation of passengers and their baggage in 1985. The organization based its rules on the airlines' recommendations put together within IATA. The rules became mandatory worldwide for international air services. For a country to opt out of the rule, its government has to notify ICAO of a "difference." Notification of a difference would normally be accompanied by an explanation advising why a particular rule cannot be met. Having generated the drive for the procedure, IATA went further than its governmental counterpart. The group developed working procedures for use with the new requirement that were later adopted by the UN agency. In doing so, they had to cover the needs of small airlines from undeveloped countries and meet the requirements of the giant carriers operating out of the world's major airports. Different systems were necessary, but they had to be compatible. A bag checked in at a central African airport could well pass through Paris or London en route to a final destination. The system had to be capable of implementation in all operating conditions at all airports in the world. It had to operate where manual procedures were in use and work equally well with full automation in place. A small British company, BRaLS, which had a wealth of ticketing and baggage-labeling experience behind it, took the IATA procedures and packaged them into just such an operating system.

BRaLS combined the standard airline baggage tag containing alphanumeric flight and destination information with a ten-digit bar code. This allowed baggage tags to be read by porters where no automated systems existed and by laser readers at airports that had gone hi-tech. At fully automated airports, the bar code on the baggage tag could be used to drive baggage-handling systems allowing bags to be directed along delivery belts to the appropriate makeup area for an aircraft's departure. By encrypting the same bar code data onto passenger boarding cards, the system umbilically linked passengers and their baggage. By positioning bar code readers at a departure gate, the system sounded alarms when a passenger failed to board an aircraft for which he or she had checked in (had become a no-show). It allowed those responsible for loading the aircraft to identify the now-unaccompanied bag and remove it from the loading process. The package became available in summer 1988, but the British aviation authorities had not yet directed carriers to fully reconcile bags and passengers. Then came Lockerbie, the very tragedy the procedure had been designed to prevent. The aftermath of Lockerbie saw the beginning of DoT efforts to deflect attention away from positive passenger bag match. Eventually, without a government directive to carriers, BRaLS was to fall on the DoT sword. BraLS's work did not fade with the company. It was taken up by the airport authority at Frankfurt, the FAG.

The FAG handles the majority of the scheduled airlines flying into and out of Germany's principal international airport. The airport had always claimed to be Europe's principal transfer airport. To maintain this claim, FAG officials had established a minimum connecting time of 45 minutes. That meant that anyone making a connection at Frankfurt needed only to allow 45 minutes between the scheduled arrival of one service and the departure of another. Transfer of checked baggage was guaranteed. Frankfurt had a pattern of operations very similar to that at an American hub airport. The FAG decided that if the mandatory ICAO security standards were to be met without adversely affecting the airport's operation, Frankfurt needed an airport- rather an airline-based program to match passengers with their baggage. As the FAG began its work, various methods of reconciliation were in force at Frankfurt, all of which were seen as labor, space, and thus cost intensive. Working with computer software specialists, the airport authority developed a program to eradicate the deficiencies of the existing procedures yet meet in full the international standards set by ICAO and the policies of IATA.

The FAG worked in an environment that had seen few of the principal civil aviation powers introduce national regulations calling for full implementation of the passenger and baggage reconciliation rule. Yet these same countries had collaborated with ICAO in the development of the policy. In the United Kingdom, the government's attitude to full passenger baggage reconciliation was hostile. On November 14, 1991, Lord Brabazon of Tara, then the U.K. Minister of Aviation, wrote to a British newspaper, the *Sunday Telegraph,* stating that "positive reconciliation of all transfer baggage on all flights out of Heathrow using existing methods would virtually bring operations to a standstill." But the BRaLS system was an "existing" method. Doubtless the minister's brief had come from the Department of Transport, and he was speaking after the Pan Am bombing. The improvised explosive device that destroyed that aircraft had been in an unaccompanied, transfer suitcase. So too the bomb that exploded on board the Air India aircraft three years before. Lord Brabazon's words were hardly reassuring for the traveling public. The FAG in Frankfurt was able to give a very practical demonstration to the U.K. minister that he was wrong. Once again, a European commercial entity was ahead of British government officialdom.

The Frankfurt airport management won local airline managers over to their new system by making all the necessary financial investments themselves. No carrier had to find money up front. This appealed to the air carriers. Like the British Airports Authority in the United Kingdom, the Frankfurt airport management company knew it would be able to recoup its investment through airport charges. Again as in London and Manchester, no government investment was necessary. Here is a major lesson for Congress as it seeks to make the skies safer over America. The air companies, airlines and airports alike, are capable of funding security investment themselves. Reconciliation is neither difficult nor expensive to achieve, but it does require commitment. Congress should also note for the next occasion they debate positive passenger bag match the major factors working in favor of the automated procedure—namely, the cost benefits and customer advantages that can accrue. It automatically reduces the number of bags that go astray in the normal course of baggage handling. Thus, airlines will spend less money on tracing, returning, and compensating their customers for lost and mishandled baggage. At the time of the Air India bombing, ICAO estimated compensation payments for mishandled baggage stood at U.S. $400 million per annum. Today no one dares suggest a figure. Customers benefit directly from the system by having their bags arrive at the same airports they reach and on the same flight they take.

There are other direct and readily identifiable cost savings that can accrue to the airlines from matching passengers with their bags. In the event a passenger has checked in but fails to board the aircraft, the system obviates the need to deplane all the passengers and their bags to search for any unaccompanied bags that may already have been loaded. These are the bags that pose the most threat to the safety of the aircraft. Both the Lockerbie and Air India bags were unaccompanied. Such bags must be found and deplaned. The reconciliation system, whether automated or manual, can pinpoint the position of a suitcase inside an aircraft's hold, making for easier location and retrieval. Thus improved departure performance times can be added to the other benefits. It is difficult to see why there could ever be air carrier opposition to such a program.

The German airport's investment in hi-tech responses to the need to reconcile bags with their owners has helped achieve, in part at least, the ICAO goal of airlines taking effective action to make sure that no piece of luggage is carried on board an aircraft unless the passenger to whom it belongs has also boarded. The success of the Frankfurt venture led to export opportunities for the management company. Among the first companies to buy the German package were British airlines.

Other companies now offer passenger and baggage matching programs. SITA (the Société Internationale de Telecommunications Aeronautiques) is an airline-owned organization headquartered in Geneva, Switzerland, with offices worldwide. It offers a Bag Manager program that can be linked to a system for tracing lost and misdirected bags. Computer-based baggage-tracing systems were originally pioneered by Eastern Airlines in Charlotte, North Carolina. Ferranti Air Systems in the United Kingdom, part of the Ultra Electronics group, are also global players in the provision of information technology (IT) solutions to the aviation industry. Their Ultra Trak Baggage Reconciliation System has been installed in the international terminal at San Francisco. Here the airport authority has complemented the basic program by adding another Ferranti service, radio frequency (RF) tagging for selectee bags. This module guides the movement of such bags through the baggage sortation system, directing them to a high-level screening station. The program provides a barrier against selectee bags being loaded without undergoing this additional layer of scrutiny.

At New York's Kennedy Airport, Ferranti has created a baggage reconciliation center capable of serving the whole of the United States. By using a combination of local RF and wide area networks, any carrier at any airport can connect to the system. Accessing the JFK facility enables a carrier to conduct automated passenger bag matching at its own location just as if the installation was within the local airport. Already Virgin Atlantic and British Airways are customers of the JFK service, connecting to it from a number of U.S. airports. However, America remains a difficult market in which to sell systems designed to meet security procedures the domestic carriers still look on with disfavor.

Lord Brabazon continued to hold his civil servants' line after his first letter to the press. On January 20, 1992, he wrote to a different newspaper, this time the *Guardian.* His letter stated that "no other nation has achieved this [identification of unaccompanied baggage] for airports with any substantial volume of traffic." He was wrong. At the time the minister wrote his letter, Swissair had introduced a reconciliation system at Zurich Airport. Opposition members in the British Parliament were quick to challenge the minister. The Labour Party spokesman on aviation matters, John Prescott, told him that "it is staggering to say that the technology is not ready." Another MP, David Bevan, added, "If they've got it, we should have it." Shades of Senator Wyden!

Lord Brabazon had failed to create a new myth in respect of passenger and baggage reconciliation but earlier fantasies had come from Whitehall, the seat of Britain's administration. They came after Washington's insistence that a telephone call to the U.S. embassy in Helsinki warning of an impending attack on a Pan Am flight from Frankfurt to New York had been a hoax. The telephone call was received two weeks before the bombing of flight 103. The detail of the warning had been very precise, but the U.S. intelligence services had not classified the message before the disaster. Afterward they very quickly decided the message had been a false one. The U.S. assessment found support in London, where the British had also received details of the warning and failed to act on it. The American line was echoed. In 1996, the private secretary to John Major, then the British prime minister, was still denying the Helsinki warning had any relevance to the bombing of Pan Am flight 103. He was in a small minority.

The obfuscation by British government ministers continued in 1997. Sir George Young, who held a transport portfolio, wrote to a fellow member of the British Parliament, Andrew Smith. He claimed, "It is our view that the United Kingdom has complied with both the intention and the wording of the ICAO provisions for reconciliation since their introduction. The U.K. procedures in 1988 provided for the bags of a no-show passenger to be removed from an aircraft, but not for the removal of a 'rogue bag' which had been introduced into the system without a passenger. This corresponded with the ICAO standard at that time." He was very wrong. The minister had not been present at any of the earlier ICAO debates but representatives of the Department of Transport had participated at all levels within the organization's structure. They had been very well aware of the intent of the proponents of passenger and baggage reconciliation, Transport Canada and IATA, that no unidentified, unaccompanied bag was to be allowed carriage on commercial aircraft. The "rogue bag" had to be identified.

Sir George Young should have known that from 1986, the Federal Aviation Authority had required full reconciliation of bags with passengers at all airports they had designated "extra-ordinary risk" locations. These included London's Heathrow. The administration's delinquency had been a failure to monitor Pan Am's application of their regulations. But for the Department of Transport to suggest through their minister that infiltrated, rogue bags, the very bags that had destroyed the Air India and Pan Am jumbos, did not have to be found and removed was unbelievable and unforgivable. They had overlooked, or had chosen to ignore, their own security advice circular sent to airlines on November 20, 1985. The principal aviation security advisor, Jim Jack, warned the air carriers that "'Interline' . . . baggage represented a possible means to place explosive devices on board aircraft." Jack went on to tell airlines, "When 'Interline' baggage is to be conveyed on board their aircraft, a check should be made to ensure the passenger to whom it belongs subsequently boards the aircraft. Discrepancies should be resolved to the satisfaction of the captain before the aircraft takes off."

The 1991 indictments against Abdelbaset Ali Mohmad Al Megrahi and Al Amin Khalifa Fhimah, accused the two Libyans of having placed or having caused to be placed a suitcase containing an improvised explosive device on board Air Malta flight 180 to Frankfurt am Main Airport in the Federal Republic of Germany. The charges alleged the suitcase was labeled with an interline tag so that it would be carried on from Frankfurt to New York via London, Heathrow Airport. The suitcase containing the bomb became an "Interline" bag the moment it left Malta. Since there was no accompanying passenger in London, according to the transport department's circular, the captain had to be told of the unaccompanied bag's existence. He then had to decide whether or not further action was needed. The DoT officials had shifted the onus to the pilot-in-command and had washed their hands of any responsibility, despite the intent of ICAO.

Whatever transpired on December 21, 1988, had the DoT circular *demanded* that such bags, "rogue" bags, not be loaded, Pan Am flight 103 would not have been destroyed. This assumes Pan Am compliance with DoT instructions. They had not applied the FAA-mandated regulations. In any event, the existence of the circular, with its recommendation rather than a direction, helps explain the nervousness and obfuscation of ministry officials whenever the subject of passenger and baggage reconciliation arises. They had recommended action knowing interline bags were potentially dangerous but had not mandated it. Just as the 1985 circular gave the lie to Sir George Young's position, so too did it destroy the arguments of Lord Brabazon in 1991. His department had actually recommended the very practice the noble lord claimed would bring Heathrow to a standstill.

Eighteen months after Sir George Young had written to his parliamentary colleague, the Department of Transport once again tried to cover up its own earlier shortcomings. Department officials arranged for an article to be published in the December 1998 edition of the ICAO *Journal*. It claimed that passenger and baggage reconciliation was irrelevant to the loss of Pan Am 103. The statement beggared belief. It flew in the face of the report of the President's Commission on Aviation Security and Terrorism and of the findings of the Scottish Fatal Accident Inquiry. The department's perseverence in attempting to perpetuate the myth that they were innocent of any shortcomings in respect of the Lockerbie bombing has shown no bounds.

Of course, this was the same department that had, at the height of bomb threats against civil aviation, instructed airlines to have passengers with laptop computers and radio cassette players demonstrate that the instruments worked before they were to be allowed as hand baggage. If a passenger declined to operate his laptop or radio, the items had to be placed in the hold as checked baggage. Given that the department had previously warned the carriers that improvised explosive devices could be hidden in such instruments, this was hardly the most intelligent advice. It is worth noting that the device that had been used to destroy the Pan Am flight, a radio cassette recorder, would have operated perfectly well. Individual airlines recognized the danger in following the DoT instructions and refused to carry any electrical item they deemed suspicious.

Perhaps the most noteworthy example of security staff discovering an improvised explosive device during a carry-on baggage inspection occurred at London's Heathrow Airport. Screeners found a pocket calculator modified to contain a small explosive. When detonated, it would have ignited a bigger charge of sheet explosive hidden in the lining of an overnight bag. The intending bomber was sentenced to 42 years' imprisonment.

Airlines operating from U.K. airports had followed the recommendations of their own trade association, IATA, throughout the period of the DoT fabrication. The carriers had made the skies safer over Britain. The battle now has to be against complacency. Many years have passed since commercial air services departing from the United Kingdom have been hit by an act of unlawful interference, but terrorism directed against civil aviation will not go away. The emotional attractiveness of such a soft, newsworthy target appeals to those who commit acts of unlawful interference. Terrorists will seek out the weakest link in a carrier's operation. Airline and airport managements, as well as governments, must recognize this fact.

Throughout the time the British administration was holding to its line on passenger and baggage matching, a different mythology was being perpetuated in the United States. Here a key player was the

CIA. Responsibility for the Lockerbie bombing had been placed at the door of Colonel Gaddafi's Libya, and every effort was to be made to bring to justice those responsible for the atrocity. Ten years after the bombing, many Americans had begun to question whether this was still the government's position. The mystery that had developed also shrouded the existence of a double agent who, it was widely believed, had provided the link between the police investigation into the Lockerbie bombing and the indictments naming the two Libyan nationals as the culprits.

Two Lockerbie trials have been held. The first was a civil action in New York in 1991. It considered a consolidated liability lawsuit brought by the families of the victims. The second was a criminal trial held in The Hague, Holland's capital city, ten years later. Investigations by the attorneys acting for the families at the first trial had been impeded by the refusal of the authorities to divulge the evidence that had enabled the indictments to be issued. The New York jury had to reach its conclusions without having access to this information. Disclosure, it was told, could affect any future criminal prosecution. When the "future criminal prosecution" arrived and the indicted men were brought before the Scottish Court, the CIA still sought to withhold much of the evidence. The question was why?

The police investigation into the bombing had identified Malta as the point of origin of the unaccompanied suitcase that, it was believed, had carried the bomb destined to destroy flight 103. Further inquiries had shown that on December 21, 1988, the day of the Lockerbie bombing, passengers departing Malta on a Libyan Arab Airlines flight for Tripoli had been checked in alongside those traveling on Air Malta flight 180 to Frankfurt. Evidence gained from the baggage-handling records at Frankfurt pointed to the suitcase suspected of being the bomb bag having been transferred at the airport from the incoming Air Malta flight into the Pan Am baggage system. Ultimately, this belief was reflected in the language of the indictments: "Such suitcase was thus carried to Frankfurt am Main aforesaid and there placed on board an aircraft of Pan American World Airways, flight PA103A and carried to London, Heathrow Airport aforesaid and there, in turn, placed on board an aircraft of Pan American World Airways flight PA103 to New York, John F. Kennedy aforesaid."

Given the enmity that existed between Libya and the United States at the time, the potential for a Libyan Arab Airlines employee at Luqa Airport to have been involved in the conspiracy to bomb Pan Am had to be high on the any list of probability. Fhimah, the airline's station manager, understandably became a suspect, but the inclusion of Megrahi, who was based in Libya, required a leap of imagination. To justify such a jump, from possibility to indictment, someone in the West had to have had an undisclosed source of information. A "third man" scenario had to exist.

The "third man" story, clouded in mystery, simmered on throughout the 1990s. He was the CIA's secret asset held, it was assumed, to ensure conviction of the indicted men when and if they were ever brought to trial. But during this period, there had been little evidence to suggest such a trial would ever take place, and the third man's existence and identity remained hidden to the world at large. In 1998, however, Secretary of State Madeleine K. Albright and Britain's foreign secretary, Robin Cook, announced a change in their policy over the years'-long standoff with Libya about where to hold the trial of the men the West believed guilty of the bombing. Albright and Cook had decided that a trial could be held in a neutral country but before a Scottish court, with Scottish judges applying Scottish law. In April 1999, following the intervention of UN Secretary General Kofi Annan and Nelson Mandela, a Scottish court was established in The Hague. Libya agreed to the two men surrendering themselves for trial. Something dramatic had happened behind the scenes, but this too was to fall under the cloak of secrecy despite major efforts by U.S. families of the victims and by congressional representatives and senators in Washington, all exerting their considerable pressure on the administration.

The families of the victims asked if a deal had been done to bring Megrahi and Fhimah to trial and wondered whether any such arrangement would affect the outcome of the proceedings. Rosemary Wolfe, whose stepdaughter had died on board the Pan Am aircraft, expressed her concern during an interview with CNN News on the eleventh anniversary of the bombing. She wanted to know "how far the Scottish prosecutors are going to go to bring out the rest of the evidence about who was involved in the Libyan government, from Gaddafi to the rest of his political and military leaders." Correspondence, thought to be relevant to these concerns, was believed at that time to be in the possession of Madeleine Albright but had not been made public. These "classified" documents were said to have outlined an arrangement between the UN leader and Gaddafi granting the latter immunity from any prosecution that might result from a trial of the indicted men. The colonel would have wanted, and needed, more than that. Libyans would have had to be convinced that no punitive action would be taken against them. George Williams, president of the Victims of Pan Am Flight 103 Inc, pressed for release of the UN letter. Cliff Kincaid, an American journalist, requested the documents from the United Nations. He thought the texts had had the approval of the administration in Washington and of the British government of Tony Blair. Kincaid believed the letter affirmed that the trial would not undermine the Libyan regime.

Rep. Benjamin Gilman, chairman of the House of Representatives International Relations Committee, wrote to Madeleine Albright in August and September 1999. He asked for "any and all information that the State Department had or was aware of on purported assurances or other guarantees from the UN to the ruling Libyan regime on the Pan Am 103 terrorist bombing." He wondered about "possible limits on the Pan Am 103 prosecution in pursuing high-ups and other culpable individuals besides the two Libyan agents now awaiting trial in The Hague." The congressman wanted "to have this matter aired and debated long before the trial begins in The Hague." In the Senate, Edward Kennedy of Massachusetts and Robert Torricelli and Frank Lautenburg, both of New Jersey, all sought copies of the Annan documents. The text of a letter UN Secretary General Kofi Annan had sent to Colonel Gaddafi during his negotiations to bring the men to trial was released in August 2000. It showed that the Libyan leader had been assured that neither the United States nor the British authorities would use the trial to undermine the Libyan government.

The trial had opened on May 3, 2000, but several months were to pass before the unidentified double agent was finally named. He was Abdul Majid Giaka, a former assistant to Fhimah at Luqa Airport. Giaka, supposedly once a member of the Libyan Intelligence Service, had become a double agent for the United States four months before the bombing. His testimony was expected to explain the precise nature of the indictments' language, in particular that Megrahi and Fhimah did "conspire together and with others to further the purposes of the Libyan Intelligence Services by criminal means, namely the commission of acts of terrorism directed against nationals and the interests of other countries and in particular the destruction of a civil passenger aircraft and the murder of its occupants." The aircraft in question was flight 103.

Giaka arrived at the court in The Hague in late August, but his actual appearance on the witness stand was to be delayed by counsel argument. When seeking to establish Giaka's credentials as a witness, the CIA had submitted to the court redacted messages that were said to have been exchanged with Giaka. The prosecution had been allowed to see the unabridged versions, but the full text was denied to defense counsel. The editing was said to be necessary to protect U.S. national security and because the redacted portions were not pertinent to the case. The CIA was deciding what was and what was not relevant to the criminal trial. Citing both Scottish law and the European Convention on Human Rights, William Taylor and Richard Keen, attorneys acting for the defendants, demanded full access. They were supported by the chief judge, Lord Sutherland, who urged the chief prosecutor, the Lord Advocate Colin Boyd, "to use his best endeavors to ensure that all material in these cables be disclosed." New versions of the cables were proffered but still with evidence of editing. The defense attorneys claimed that the latest versions of the messages suggested there were yet more cables that had not been seen by the court. More than ten years after Giaka had turned double agent and the smokescreen had been put in place, the CIA were still intent on maintaining its cloaking power. Observers wondered whether the agency's behavior was linked in any way to the change in the West's policy.

America, Scotland, and the world had waited for more than a decade to see the indicted men brought to trial. Now the agency appeared to be prevaricating. They did tell the court they would scour their archives for more secret material relating to Giaka, but it was hardly possible that during the time the man had been under U.S. protection, the agency had not collected all the data on him that could possible have existed. Could it be that full disclosure of Giaka's story would reveal some failing on the part of the agency either before, during, or after the bombing of the Pan Am aircraft? Similar questions about the performance of the agency and of the FBI were to arise again in early summer 2002. By then, it had become clear that evidence in the hands of subordinate members of both agencies before the al-Qa'eda onslaught of September 11th might have provided a means to have prevented the attacks. Did the same apply to Pan Am flight 103?

When Giaka eventually took the stand, he was questioned by the prosecution for just half a day. His testimony proved to be anticlimactic. He did not claim to have seen the indicted men place a bomb in a suitcase. Nor did he testify that either Megrahi or Fhimah had told him anything about the plan to blow up Pan Am flight 103. Without such testimony, it was difficult for the prosecution to press home the charges against the men. Given the paucity of Giaka's testimony before the court, there was little to explain why had he been kept under wraps for so long by the U.S. intelligence agencies. Had his story been different at one stage? The language of the indictments suggests it had.

Giaka was said to have told the CIA nothing about the bombing, nor, it was alleged, had he been questioned about the tragedy until September 1989, nine months after Lockerbie. Yet the double agent had been on the CIA's payroll in December 1988. Furthermore, from evidence already in the hands of the German police and from reports circulating in the media, the agency had known within weeks of the bombing that the suitcase suspected of having concealed the Lockerbie bomb was believed to have arrived at Frankfurt on an Air Malta flight. Luqa Airport in Malta had become the focal point of the investigation. It is inconceivable that the CIA would not have immediately questioned their man on the inside of the Libyan Arab Airlines operation at the Maltese airport. However, this was the agency's stance. If true, it suggested a level of incompetence difficult to comprehend, at least until the disclosures following September 11th. It might explain why the double agent and his testimony had been kept away from public exposure. Release of such information would have been most embarrassing to the agency.

The timing of Giaka's alleged disclosure is significant. A CIA message dispatched in September 1989 was read into the records of the Scottish court by the defense counsel, William Taylor. It stated, "If P1 [Giaka's code reference] is not able to demonstrate his value or ability to give information by January 1, 1990, we will stop his salary." It was at this time Giaka allegedly pointed to Megrahi and Fhimah. The attorney considered Gaika's whole story "an invention that comes along late in the day." It was an invention instigated because, the cable suggested, someone within the CIA had begun to express doubts about his value as a spy for America. It was even being wondered if he had ever penetrated Libya's intelligence services or been a member of them.

There is another possible scenario. Giaka had been questioned early in 1989 but had said nothing. In this case, his value as a double agent must surely have been in doubt. At the very least his revelations when his livelihood was being threatened should have raised serious doubts about the veracity of his testimony. Certainly years later his value as a prosecution witness should have been questioned, and not just by the CIA.

Giaka was alleged to have claimed seeing Megrahi and Fhimah at Luqa Airport in possession of a brown Samsonite suitcase before the bombing. He was also supposed to have seen a cache of explosives hidden in Fhimah's office desk. Fhimah was said to have required him to prepare a study showing how a suitcase could be infiltrated into the baggage system at Malta. All of this supported the substance of the indictments against Megrahi and Fhimah. But because he was on the CIA payroll when this was happening, he would surely have been expected to have passed this information on to his handler without delay. If he had done so and the agency had known of a possible conspiracy to commit an airborne attack before the bombing of Pan Am but had not acted, this could have initiated a "least said, soonest mended" policy as a form of self-protection from questions that must otherwise have followed the tragedy. There is a darker possibility. Could Giaka have linked the conspiracy directly to a planned Pan Am attack? The indictments point this way, yet the attack went ahead. If any government agency had been in possession of such information and nothing had been done, surely not even the densest fog could have hidden the facts from Washington.

Whatever the truth behind the story of the third man, from the moment the indictments against Abdelbaset Ali Mohmad Al Megrahi and Al Amin Khalifa Fhimah were issued, the United States turned its wrath on Libya and its bête noir, Gaddafi. America sought and gained from the United Nations the imposition of sanctions on Libya. Disturbingly, ten years later a Scottish court was unable to convict Fhimah on the evidence submitted to it. Many professors specializing in Scottish criminal law even found it surprising that the charges against Megrahi had held up. Had the court been presented with the same evidence that had spawned the indictments?

What the double agent said to whom and when, and why he seemingly made an about-turn, is never likely to be known outside the inner sanctums of government. Whether any deal was made with Libya, other than the promise in the Annan letter, is another imponderable. What is clear, however, is that the Lockerbie tragedy did not bring out the best in the administrations on either side of the Atlantic.

If questions can still be asked of the CIA about their role in the

Lockerbie story, what of the FBI and September 11th? In May 2002, eight months after the al-Qa'eda outrages, stories circulating in the media were alleging that FBI field agents had warned their headquarters of possible threats from bin Laden's followers weeks before the attacks took place. The *New York Times* and the *Washington Post* published details from a leaked memorandum written by Coleen Rowley, an FBI agent and counsel in Minneapolis. She claimed that requests for a search warrant allowing them to pursue an inquiry into Zacarias Moussaoui, indicted after September 11th as the twentieth hijacker, had been rejected by FBI Headquarters. Moussaoui, a French citizen with roots in Morocco, had been arrested in August 2001 for infringing immigration regulations. The agents were disturbed by his attendance at a flight-training school, where he was interested only in flying aircraft once they were airborne. Armed with information provided by the French Intelligence Services, they had wanted access to Moussaoui's personal computer. After September 11th, the go-ahead to move against the Frenchman was given—a classic case of shutting the stable door after the horse has bolted.

Even before the Minneapolis request for a search warrant, agents from the FBI's Phoenix office had reported its concern that terrorists linked to bin Laden might be seeking flight training in American flying schools. Thus, in the month preceding the suicide attacks, the FBI had a possibility of linking intelligence in the hands of their agents with information that had been in their possession ever since the arrest of Ramzi Ahmed Yousef. He was alleged to have talked of plans to use an aircraft as a missile to attack ground-based targets. Should the combined intelligence available to the FBI have directed the bureau to the potential for an attack where an aircraft is employed as a weapon of mass destruction? It is for the congressional hearings, already underway by summer 2002, to identify just what the FBI had known before September 11th and what action they might reasonably have been taken.

Given that several of the September 11th terrorists appear to have freely entered the United States (some with the knowledge of the CIA, who had been monitoring their movements overseas) and once in the country, to have moved about at will, one thing would seem certain: Any myth of invincibility still cloaking the FBI from their foundation days under J. Edgar Hoover is likely to have dissipated by the time the congressional hearings have been concluded.

INTERNATIONAL CONVENTIONS

Three international conventions have been established to deal with acts of unlawful interference. They are known as the Tokyo, The Hague, and Montreal Conventions. They are the framework around which national responses to acts of air terrorism are built. The conventions are named after the cities in which they were enacted. Briefly, the Tokyo Convention[6] covers all acts that "may or do jeopardize good order and discipline on board" whether or not they are offenses. The Hague Convention[7] was enacted in 1970. It reflected a changing international scene that had witnessed an alarming growth in the number of aircraft hijackings. It preceded the Dawson's Field spectacle mentioned in the preceding chapter when three of four jet aircraft, seized within days of each other, were destroyed in front of the world's media. This act is generally accepted as the birth of international terrorism as we know it today. Its similarities with events on September 11th are most noteworthy. Four aircraft hijacked from different airports and used to create a major event. Their seizure took place exactly 31 years before the traumatic events conducted by the al-Qa'eda terrorists.

The Hague Convention specified the action that had to be taken by states when an aircraft was seized unlawfully. It took into account the deterrent effect punishment could have on offenders and called on all ICAO contracting states to make the offense "punishable by severe penalties." An offender was defined as any person on board a flight who "unlawfully, by force or threat thereof or by any other form of intimidation, seizes or exercises control of, that aircraft, or attempts to perform any such act." Any accomplice of a person who performs or attempts to perform any such act was also deemed to be an offender.

Offenders had to be extradited to answer for their crimes in the country claiming jurisdiction or be brought before the competent authorities in the country in which they were apprehended for the purpose of prosecution. They were not to walk away from their acts unscathed. This language, if enacted fully by the contracting states of ICAO, would have ended all politically based acts of aircraft seizure of the type experienced in the middle and late 1900s. If there had been no havens to which hijackers could escape after committing their acts of terror, much of their motivation would have disappeared. The language of the Hague Convention reflected the times. To be relevant to the third millennium following the events of September 11th, governments and aviation managements will have to work to ensure the al-Qa'eda attacks are never repeated.

The importance of preventing the repetition of hijacking incidents, a prospect promulgated by the existence of safe havens, was made very clear early on in the evolution of air terrorism. In 1969, Leila Khaled, a member of the Popular Front for the Liberation of Palestine (PFLP), led a group of hijackers who seized a TWA Boeing 707 operating a scheduled service from Rome to Tel Aviv. She directed the pilot to make a pass over Tel Aviv before setting course for Damascus. Once the aircraft was on the ground, she freed the passengers, but her plan for the aircraft to be destroyed failed when the fuse failed to ignite the explosive charge. Subsequently, the Syrians traded the aircraft and two of the passengers who had been detained by the authorities for a number of prisoners held in Israel. Khaled was allowed to go free. Syria had provided her with a safe haven from which she was able to emerge and strike again, this time with the benefit of experience from the earlier seizure.

In September 1970, Leila Khaled made news once more. Her group was responsible for the Dawson's Field spectacle. Khaled's colleagues successfully seized their targeted Swissair and TWA aircraft, but her attempted hijacking of an El Al Boeing 707 failed. She was supposed to have led a team of four PFLP members, two of whom, she herself and a Nicaraguan, Patrick Arguello (there were close links between the Palestinians and Nicaragua) began their journey in Germany and transferred to El Al in Amsterdam. The transfer went smoothly, but the remaining two were beginning their journey in the Dutch city. They failed to board. Because the airline had overbooked the aircraft, the two could not travel on the El Al aircraft. Instead they boarded a Pan Am 747, which they promptly hijacked instead. They forced the captain to fly to Cairo, where they destroyed the aircraft. Meanwhile, Khaled and her remaining team member went ahead with their plans to seize the El Al aircraft but were stopped by in-flight sky marshals. Arguello was shot and killed and Khaled captured. The aircraft diverted to London, where Leila Khaled was taken to a police station near Heathrow. Her presence in the United Kingdom led to a major political crisis.

The importance of Khaled to the Palestinian cause was made clear very quickly. The PLFP hijacked a British Airways VC-10 and flew it with its human payload to Dawson's Field, where they had now accumulated more than 300 hostages drawn from a variety of countries, including America. They demanded that Khaled and certain other PLFP members being held in Europe be freed. Release of secret U.K. government documents under the 30-year rule (in the United Kingdom, cabinet papers are released after such a period unless state security demands their further retention) highlighted the dilemma facing Prime Minister Edward Heath. Consideration was given to a military intervention but was discarded as unfeasible. Negotiation with terrorists was abhorrent to the British, but exchanges were begun through intermediaries. This brought the release of many of the women and children being held. To put further pressure on the West, the PLFP hijackers blew up the three aircraft at Dawson's Field. This underlined the strength of their bargaining position and put added pressure on the delicate position of King Hussein's government in Jordan. With Syria already backing the king's domestic opposition in what had degenerated into a civil war and with the king turning on the Palestinians, the area was fast becoming a tinderbox. Israel and the United States became involved in the debate, which already included the Swiss, Germans, and Jordanians. Ultimately, Edward Heath agreed to release Khaled. Six other Palestinians held in Switzerland and Germany were also freed.

In 1973 Leila Khaled published an autobiography, *My People Shall Live: The Autobiography of a Revolutionary*. She is still active politically. In June 2002 she spoke at a pro-Palestinian conference in Teheran, Iran.

The inclusion of provisions for extradition in the Hague Convention was significant. It allowed a state to extradite offenders regardless of the existence of bilateral arrangements between involved parties. The Hague Convention provided a truly international piece of legislation. It did not preclude extradition treaties. Indeed, it called on ICAO's members to incorporate appropriate language when developing bilateral agreements, but it showed that the absence of such need not stand in the way of bringing hijackers to justice.

The text of the convention also laid down instructions for handling seized aircraft, its passengers and crew, as well as its load. Governments of countries in which seized aircraft landed had to "take all appropriate measures to restore control of the aircraft to its lawful commander or to preserve his control of the aircraft." The authorities were also required to "facilitate the continuation of the journey of the passengers and crew as soon as practicable" and "without delay return the aircraft and its cargo to the persons lawfully entitled to it."

In August 1990 a British Airways aircraft became an early victim of Iraq's invasion of Kuwait. It had landed in the oil sheikhdom just as Saddam Hussein's forces rolled into the country. The aircraft was seized and the 367 passengers, including 60 Americans, were held hostage for five months while Saddam Hussein used them for propaganda purposes. He did not meet the terms of the Hague Convention.

The third treaty, the Montreal Convention,[8] was aimed at attacks on aircraft, whether in flight or on the ground. Its scope was widened in 1988 to cover attacks on airports. The original text had three key definitions. The first defined a person who commits an offense as "one who performs an act of violence against a person on board an aircraft in flight if that act is likely to endanger the safety of that aircraft." The second described an offender as "one who destroys an aircraft in service or causes damage to such aircraft which renders it incapable of flight or which is likely to endanger its safety in flight." The third definition covered a person who "places or causes to be placed on an aircraft in service, by any means whatsoever, a device or substance which is likely to destroy that aircraft or cause damage to it which renders it incapable of flight."

The three conventions provided a framework within which governments could work to eradicate air terrorism. The problem was that some governments failed to uphold the agreed principles. They played politics and provided safe havens for terrorists. Western governments attempted to overcome this predicament. In July 1978 they developed the Bonn Declaration. A summit meeting of the seven Western industrial powers was held in Bonn, then the capital of what was West Germany. The participating countries were Canada, the Federal Republic of Germany, France, Japan, Italy, the United Kingdom, and the United States. Each country was represented by its prime minister or president. They agreed to suspend air services with any country that failed to honor the international conventions. Their declaration read:

> The Heads of State and Government concerned over terrorism and hostage taking declare their governments will intensify their common undertakings to fight international terrorism.
>
> In cases where a country refuses extradition or prosecution of those who

> have hijacked an aircraft and/or do not return such aircraft, the Heads of State and Government are jointly resolved that their Governments should take immediate action to cease all flights to that country. At the same time their Governments will initiate action to halt all incoming flights from that country or from any country by the airline of the country concerned.

The declaration was clear and precise. Missing were the details of how their intentions would be implemented. These were left to legal and technical experts who met subsequent to the summit. The complexities of the legal questions requiring answers precluded finalization of any procedures during the time the heads of government were meeting. They agreed to consult with each other on a case-by-case basis. The intent of the leaders may have been honest. We must assume it was, but aircraft attacks continued, and it is a matter of record that in the years following the Bonn Declaration, the terms were invoked only once—against Afghanistan. The Seven considered that country fell short of its obligations in respect of the seizure of a Pakistan International Airlines flight in 1981. At a meeting of the Seven held in Montebello in July of that year, participants reaffirmed their commitment to the Bonn Declaration and declared:

> The Heads of State and Government are convinced that, in the case of the hijacking of a Pakistan International Airlines aircraft in March, the conduct of the Babrak Karmal regime of Afghanistan, both during the incident and subsequently in giving refuge to the hijackers, was and is in flagrant breach of its international obligations under the Hague Convention to which Afghanistan is a party, and constitutes a serious threat to air safety. Consequently, the Heads of State and government propose to suspend all flights to and from Afghanistan in implementation of the Bonn declaration unless Afghanistan immediately takes steps to comply with its obligations. Furthermore, they call upon all states which share their concern for air safety to take appropriate action to persuade Afghanistan to honour its obligations.

This action was exactly what the seven leaders had promised but had not previously enacted. It is perhaps cynical to note that there were virtually no international airline operations to Kabul at the time and very little commerce. The Bonn terms have not been invoked since (sanctions against Libya were established through the United Nations). The failure to apply them and the too frequent nonapplication of the Hague Convention over the years sent a very clear message to terrorists: They could get away with their acts of aggression.

It told states that failed in their international obligations that they too could go unpunished. The Bonn Declaration appears to have been a government bluff.

Glaring examples of noncompliance with the Hague Convention since the Bonn Declaration was delivered have been provided by Algeria. The TWA saga in 1985 included visits to Algiers. The Kuwait hijacking in 1988 ended there and the terrorists went free. Following the last episode, Canada's *Montreal Gazette* (the oldest English-language newspaper in North America), published the following on the front page of their April 21 edition:

> In Montreal, Mr. Rodney Wallis, the Head of Security for the International Air Traffic [Transport] Association said the reported promise of safe conduct out of Algeria for the hijackers was a victory for international terrorism.
>
> In Helsinki, U.S. State Secretary George Shulz said yesterday it was wrong to allow the hijackers to get away. They are not only hijackers but murderers, Shulz said during a stopover on a trip to Moscow for pre–summit talks.
>
> In London, Prime Minister Margaret Thatcher said the hijackers should not go unpunished. She said she would bring the issue before the European Community.

Thatcher may have done what she said she would, but there was no public evidence of any action. The Iron Lady, along with the other members of the G7 industrial powers, would have done well to remember the words of Thomas Hobbes[9] written more than three centuries earlier: "Covenants without swords are but words."

Regardless of the failure of some governments to uphold the strictures of the three international conventions, in September 2001 ICAO reaffirmed its belief in them. At the Thirty-third Assembly of the ICAO, members adopted a resolution calling on those states that had not become parties to the Tokyo, The Hague, and Montreal Conventions to do so. Tokyo was enacted in 1963. Some states move slowly.

CHAPTER 4

Practical Airport Security

The events of September 11th questioned, as no other event ever could, the adequacy of airport security in North America. Two Presidential Commissions[10] had failed to raise security standards at U.S. airports. Throughout the tail-end years of the twentieth century, domestic aviation security performance in America was on a par with that of the poorest states in the developing world. During this period, the print and television media periodically investigated the level of U.S. airport security. In doing so, they were mirroring the actions of their counterparts in other countries. In the United Kingdom, the popular press and even the British Broadcasting Corporation (BBC), took it upon themselves to highlight weaknesses in airport defenses against terrorists. As 2001 came to an end, a British tabloid newspaper, the *Sunday People,* once again showed it was possible to carry weapons, albeit small, ingeniously designed ones, onboard aircraft at two of England's premier airports. Their conduct came in for criticism from the administration and certainly their motives had to be questioned. Were they acting in the best interests of the traveling public by highlighting security failures, or were they simply playing to form, sensationalizing a situation to sell more copies? Were they experiencing a quiet news day that had to be enlivened?

Newspaper exposés such as those revealing security weaknesses can work against the public interest. The journalists could be doing future terrorists' research for them, pointing out where to infiltrate the system. The editors would doubtless claim their intention was to put pressure on the governments and airport managements to put things right. But this could be done by limiting their reporting to a note to the government of the day or to the appropriate airport management. However, experience may have shown the newspaper reporters that "quiet words" seldom work in the corridors of power when the words imply criticisms of a system set up and maintained by the mandarins. They had doubtless decided a headline was so much more effective and it would sell more newspapers. In the United States, the Columbia Broadcasting System (CBS) television program *60 Minutes* was among those documenting domestic airport weaknesses.

Europe has had to maintain tight security programs. Acts of terrorism had been experienced widely in Britain and on the Continent. The Irish Republican Army (IRA) was always a threat, and in Spain, the ever constant problem with the Basques threatened peaceful operations in many areas of life, including air transportation. Other groups with national vendettas existed elsewhere. The problem facing the Europeans was the close affinity of the good and the bad. They lived side by side. The enemy were also Europeans. In contrast, in the United States, until 1993 no one perceived a threat from terrorism on the mainland. Those who harbored grudges against America were all believed to live far away. They had their homes in North Africa and in the Middle East and perhaps points even farther afield. Security was perceived by most Americans only to have relevance to them when they went abroad. American aircraft became possible targets only when they operated overseas. With this perception, weaknesses identified by the media or by outspoken critics within the aviation industry, were allowed to go unanswered. Poor security defenses were accepted for the same reasons security shortcomings at many third world countries' airports were tolerated—the low level of perceived risk from terrorist activity.

In the United States, such thinking should have changed when the first attempt was made to bomb the World Trade Center towers in New York. Again in 1995, the car bomb that destroyed the Federal Building in Oklahoma City, killing 120 men, women, and children, should have triggered a change. Even the pipe bomb detonated during the Atlanta Olympic Games was indicative of the fact that terrorism was no longer something that happened "over there." Terrorism of the type experienced by Europeans was now a U.S. phenomenon. Canada had known since summer 1985 when the Air India jumbo jet was bombed with a device originating in Vancouver that international terrorism was not confined to a single continent. Transport Canada developed security programs and policies designed to protect their airports and airlines from internal attack. But the lessons learned in Ottawa did not percolate south of the border.

Despite evidence directing attention to the existence of terrorism on the North American continent, U.S. airport managements and the domestic airline companies failed to raise standards. Their administrations still believed themselves to be immune. They certainly could see no justification for investing capital in systems that they believed had no relevance to them. Was this the lack of *"sincerity and willingness"* identified by Commissioner Cummock? Or was it simply a naive, insular thought process at work?

The earlier beliefs of the U.S. domestic aviation industry in a "Fortress America" could be justified to a point. Historically, for the United States the threat from terrorism had been directed against U.S. owned and operated land-based installations and civil aviation operations at overseas locations. The most notable aviation examples had been the attacks on TWA in the mid-1980s and the tragic destruction of Pan Am flight 103 in 1988. Terrorist groups considered most threatening toward the United States struck at targets within easy reach of their home bases or within reach of a "friendly" nation. This method of operating required short lines of communication. Consequently, U.S. carriers operating nationally considered their sphere of operation to be a long way from the terrorists' safe havens. Additionally, controls put in place by the customs and the immigration services were thought to have a sufficient deterrent effect to prevent infiltration by a potential terrorist. How wrong this was proved to be in 2001. Should the Federal Aviation Administration and the airline and airport companies have anticipated this situation? The answer has to be yes. The first World Trade Center attack told the United States and the world that times had changed. Ramzi Ahmed Yousef's links to Osama bin Laden were already known. All the signs were there.

Combating Air Terrorism, an airline security textbook published in 1993, had sounded a warning. "Should the attitude of terrorists bent on harming the United States change with groups of 'disposable' or 'suicidal' young people emerging among the terrorists who see that country as their enemy, isolationism would no longer provide the protection the United States has relied upon in the past and domestic air transport targets would become vulnerable." These words were written following the outbreak of hostilities between the U.S.-led UN forces and Iraq over the latter's hostile military invasion of its tiny neighbor, Kuwait. The book went on to warn that "the 1980s level of performance in much of the security field would have to improve." *Lockerbie: The Story and the Lessons*, published in January 2001, referred to the outbreaks of terrorism within the United States and suggested that attention may now "focus on domestic airline vulnerability to the saboteur." Until September 2001, the focus always fell elsewhere.

Between the publication of the two books, the White House Commission on Aviation Safety and Security sent their report to President Bill Clinton. It noted:

> The Federal Bureau of Investigation, the Central Intelligence Agency, and other intelligence sources have been warning that the threat of terrorism is changing in two important ways. First it is no longer just an overseas threat from foreign terrorists. People and places in the United States have joined the list of targets, and Americans have joined the ranks of terrorists. The bombings of the World Trade Center in New York [1993] and the Federal Building in Oklahoma City are clear examples of the shift, as is the conviction of Ramzi Yousef for attempting to bomb twelve American airliners out of the sky over the Pacific Ocean. The second change is that in addition to well-known, established terrorist groups, it is becoming more common to find terrorists working alone or in ad-hoc groups, some of whom are not afraid to die in carrying out their designs.

There was ample intelligence available to warn of potential future catastrophes, but it was not acted upon. The traveling public in America was left unguarded. The Aviation and Transportation Security Act acknowledged the vulnerability of American airports. The new legislation called for significant changes. Were they the right ones and will they work? Would practical airport security come at last to domestic operations in the United States? To answer these questions, it is worth studying what happens elsewhere.

Throughout much of the world, airport security is based on the Standards and Recommended Practices developed and published by ICAO (the International Civil Aviation Organization).[11] The organization is part of the United Nations. For more than 50 years, it has been the supreme law-making body relative to international civil aviation. It is a political organization, as any agency of the United Nations must be. This does mean that the results of its debates and the language developed for international usage are inevitably compromises. Smaller member states are often reluctant to adopt what they see as expensive measures. They either do not have the money for them or lack the necessary technical skills to maintain hi-tech machinery. In most instances they do not perceive a threat to their national carriers. Because of this, they block recommendations seen as important to the developed world. Thus ICAO rules—the standards—are always the minimum acceptable. They are set at the level of the lowest common denominator. Countries with major aviation infrastructures have to make additions to the recommendations to ensure threats applicable to operations in their jurisdiction are fully covered. Some airlines operating to the less well protected airports have to overlay additional procedures of their own on to those provided by the local airport management.

Knut Hammarskjold, the Swedish director general of IATA (the International Air Transport Association), sought to cover this problem. He laid the foundations for the airlines' development of defenses against airborne terrorism. His negotiations with Fidel Castro are credited with the successful closing down of Cuba as a venue for the first wave of U.S. domestic hijackers. In 1967, he established within IATA a specialist security committee. For 20 years the Security Advisory Committee (SAC), with a membership comprising the security chiefs of major airlines and led by the association's own director of security, studied attacks on airlines. The committee sought to identify the lessons to be learned and developed collective policies for preempting acts of aviation terrorism. The SAC members recognized that their companies' exposure to terrorists varied from airport to airport. Standards of implementation of the internationally agreed security procedures differed wildly. Although the ICAO had established security rules and published them in Annex 17 to the Chicago Convention, the rules had not been adopted by all governments. The SAC learned from the early terrorist incidents and noted the ICAO's inability to obtain international implementation of its own provisions. They developed an airline response, the IATA Intensified Aviation Security Program, an airport survey activity that coupled inspection with a security advisory service. The inspection activity centered on the provisions of Annex 17, the ICAO Security Manual, and a list of eight easy-to-understand rules developed by the airlines. Over the years the eight rules have been amended to reflect the existing environment, but at the height of the terrorist campaigns of the 1980s they called for these specific conditions:

A sterile area to be established for the boarding of all flights. Passengers and their hand baggage to be screened prior to entering this area. All other persons and items entering the area to be authorized to do so and be subjected to security control measures.

Direct and discreet communication systems to link the passenger screening points and other access points to an airport control center capable and designated to respond quickly in cases of unlawful action.

Duly authorized law enforcement officers, armed and equipped with mobile communications, to conduct patrols within airports and be readily available to assist in cases of suspected or actual unlawful interference with civil aviation operations and for an airport security crisis management program to exist.

Areas of restricted access to be adequately enclosed, clearly marked with signs and admission controls, applying to all persons and vehicles, established to prevent unauthorized entry to the airside of the airport.

Positive airport identification to be visibly worn by all persons authorized to be airside at an airport and for this identification to be checked at control points before entry to the airside.

Physical barriers to be installed separating public areas from all baggage, mail and cargo after its acceptance for carriage and for facilities to exist to enable such items to be x-rayed or otherwise security screened when required.

Aircraft parking areas to be adequately controlled, protected and well lighted.

All public observation view points overlooking the airside to be adequately protected to safeguard security.

The last point was considered necessary to preempt any possible terrorist attacks against targets from within a terminal. Gunmen were not to be given advantage points from where they could direct fire onto the public. (Sterile areas [lounges], armed response capability, and access control are touched upon elsewhere in this book.) Implementation of these elements of the airlines' eight rules can be seen in operation today at most international airports around the world. They are as relevant to the air transport industry's defenses against terrorism in the current millennium as they were in the last. Control of the operational areas of an airport, especially the ramp, is perhaps even more relevant today. With aircraft becoming ever bigger and requiring more and more vehicles, equipment, and personnel to service them, the difficulty of maintaining tight security control around them while they are on the ground is increasing.

The IATA 8-points, as the airline program became known, were aimed at airport security. They became the basis of a survey team's checklist for use when inspecting an airport's security operation. The group's airport surveys did much to help raise the level of aviation security around the world. Airports selected for review ranged from heavily utilized but primarily holiday destinations to major business centers. Western European airports were surveyed, as were many in Africa, Asia, Australasia, and Central and South America. The same criteria were used in the assessments, but local conditions, political environments, and fiscal possibilities all helped to shape the recommendations that resulted from the surveys.

Selection criteria for airports to be surveyed varied. Some airports were nominated by airlines concerned with what they perceived to be poor standards. Sometimes an airport authority would approach IATA asking for a survey. Singapore, one of the world's premier airports, did this when the local airport authorities wanted an outside, objective assessment of their security operation. Whichever method led to an airport's being placed on the list of those places to be visited, the study was undertaken with the full agreement of the authority concerned and at no cost to that body. This was not an altruistic action by the airlines. It was simply a very cost effective way of ensuring that airlines serving a particular airport were afforded the maximum protection against terrorist attacks.

Teams participating in the survey were international in their flavor. Members were drawn from experienced, senior security managers of airlines serving the airport or that had an interest in the region. Individual carriers bore all the costs of their representative's participation. This was acceptable to the airlines because of their vested interest in ensuring that the airport being visited was secure for their operation. The mix of nationalities on the teams had many advantages, not least the avoidance of a national bias in the study and subsequent recommendations. Careful selection of the members ensured that the teams were recognized to be working in the interest of civil aviation in general. The commercial motives of the airlines and the need to safeguard their passengers and crews were obvious. Their interest in the operation of an airport's security procedures was understood by the airport administration whose facilities were under review. Clearly, there was no hidden political motivation. Thus IATA was given greater freedom to inspect a facility than a carrier would have been afforded if working alone. The fact that IATA worked with the civil aviation administration or airport management subsequent to a survey to eradicate any security weakness identified, and at no cost to the authority, was an additional benefit.

The status of the IATA Intensified Aviation Security Program was underlined by the Council of Europe in a review of aviation security. The council referred to the IATA activity as the "only objective survey program available to the industry and to governments." A 1989 ministerial-level meeting convened by ICAO also made reference to the airlines' survey activities. The ministers recommended that the UN agency should provide an international security survey program under the organization's auspices to states—*on request.* ICAO was not to initiate moves. Even with this limitation (the airlines did not have to contend with such restrictions), such a service from ICAO to its members could have been of value. However, the political nature of the UN agency made implementation difficult to achieve. In 2001, thirteen years after the idea was first mooted within ICAO, the Thirty-third Assembly of the ICAO reached the same conclusion as the earlier meeting of ministers. Delegates to the Assembly resolved that the UN agency should conduct "regular, mandatory, systematic and harmonized aviation security audits to evaluate security in place in all Contracting States at national level and, on a sample basis, at airport level for each State, under the ICAO Aviation Security Mechanism." Another high-level ministerial aviation security conference resulted from the Assembly's conclusion. It convened in February 2002 and recommended that a multigovernment-sponsored survey program, the Aviation Security Plan of Action, be established. It was proposed the plan should be implemented in June of that same year. On past performance, it may be some years before air travelers see any benefit from the regurgitation of the old proposal. This assumes the plan gets off the ground this time around. In 1989 the idea of an ICAO survey program proved to be little more than a political soundbite.

ICAO will still have to contend with difficulties of national sovereignty. This was a barrier the first time a survey program was mooted. Carriers doubtless had an easier time working with individual government agencies than teams comprising representatives of "foreign authorities" would have done. Some administrations contended the latter could have had ulterior motives in examining another country's airport defense system. Events in the new millennium may have made things easier for ICAO. For the sake of improved aviation security around the world, it is to be hoped this is the case. If ICAO can achieve even a percentage of the success of the earlier IATA survey program, the UN agency's efforts will have been well merited. The skies will be safer.

One difference between any ICAO program and that of IATA might be in the experience of the teams chosen to undertake the monitoring task. The airline teams were all practicing security professionals with line responsibilities within their own airlines. They had to maximize protection for their companies and its customers. There is a danger the ICAO teams will comprise civil servants, volunteered for the task by individual countries, but who have had no direct, practical aviation security experience at airports or within airlines. With its new responsibility for screening at more than 400 airports on the mainland, the Federal Aviation Administration may, in the short term, find it difficult to develop sufficient inspectors to monitor its own operation. The authority does, however, already have a commitment to inspect overseas airports served by U.S. airlines. Some link to the ICAO project—where politics allow, for the United States will not be acceptable everywhere—could be developed to the advantage of world aviation. Outside such collaboration, the possibility of U.S. participation at any meaningful level must be considered small. In the United Kingdom, the Department of Transport only ever had a short-lived commitment to overseas airport inspection. Budget cuts brought the department's program to a quick end. Thus the department will have no experts to lend to ICAO. Although DoT staff may be available, if audits are to be conducted with any meaning, provision of personnel just to make up numbers will be of little use. Continental governments that with their national air carriers have regularly participated in monitoring security standards around the world may be able to provide a nucleus around which ICAO can build. Canada, Australia, Singapore, and Japan may also make valid input. A combination of personnel from such governments plus aviation industry professionals, who have more than a passing interest in the standard of security at international airports, could be the way ahead. In any event, ICAO officials will have to bite on one unpalatable bullet: They must accept that most of their contracting states will not have the expertise to participate as team players in any audit program. Such states will instead need to be recipients of the service.

The ICAO ministerial-level conference was given an indication of the cost of the oversight program when ICAO estimated it would need U.S. $17 million to put the plan into position for the period commencing June 14, 2002, to 2004. Fifteen of the 17 million would have to be new contributions from member states. As this book was being finalized, there was no indication as to whether such a sum had been forthcoming.

Dr. Assad Kotaite, the ICAO president, said of the decision of the ministerial meeting, "This is a historic moment in the evolution of civil aviation. I am extremely proud of the work we have achieved at this Conference and I am convinced that it will contribute greatly to protecting lives, restoring public confidence in air travel, and promoting the health of air transport." Let everyone hope that the good doctor's statement does not turn out to be, to quote Eliza Doolittle from *My Fair Lady*, just "Words, words, words."

Auditing an independent state's security implementation is something for the ICAO's future; wheels turn slowly within the UN agency. Meanwhile, only national governments can compel enforcement within their territories, and even they frequently forget that rules are only as good as the means that exist to enforce them. It follows that international rules and recommendations are varied in their application around the world. Western European compliance with international standards is, by and large, very good, as it is in the major countries of Asia and Australasia.

Some airport security performances can be seen and measured by travelers as they pass through terminal buildings. Consider, for example, the requirement for passengers and their hand baggage to be screened. The purpose of screening is to prevent any weapons being carried on to an aircraft. ICAO recommends that screening points should comprise an x-ray unit, for hand carried items, positioned alongside a walk-through metal detector (a magnetometer) for passenger screening. The UN agency calls for this equipment configuration to be manned by teams of five screeners, the team members rotating their functions on a 20-minute cycle. This is achieved by separating the five with one directing the flow of hand baggage while another monitors the video display unit (VDU). This shows images of the items being x-rayed. A third team member hand searches any items selected during the x-ray process for further examination. The fourth screener controls the movement of passengers through the magnetometer while the fifth person is there to manually frisk those who trigger its alarm. The fifth person will sometimes be seen using a handheld metal wand as a frisking aid. The purpose of rotating staff is to minimize the boredom associated with routine security tasks and in particular to prevent the person monitoring the video display unit from becoming ineffective. Twenty minutes is considered the maximum time a screener can view a screen effectively. Rotation adds variety to the team members' tasks and ensures an all-round understanding of the total function.

The above description of a five-person team at work describes the optimum. Around the world variations on this theme will be seen. At some locations the magnetometer is dispensed with, screeners using a handheld wand to search all passengers. At some airports, screeners physically hand search all passengers. A passenger passing through an airport security check point can see at a glance whether the ICAO-recommended screening unit is in place. Travelers can judge for themselves the effectiveness of other systems. In Europe the ICAO configuration, with teams of five screeners, is in widespread use. In the United States it was seldom seen before September 2001. At most domestic airports two-person units were the standard, and their performance always left much to be desired, as did the quality of their management. This situation appears to be changing as this book is being written—but why should it have been this way before?

Poor security performance was not simply attributable to a lack of perception of the threat facing U.S. civil aviation targets. It had more to do with cost saving. In the United States, responsibility for passenger and hand baggage screening had been delegated to the airlines. (Their attitude to the threat of terrorism has already been discussed.) The air companies had to comply with FAA directives to implement screening, but it was never a priority issue with them. To minimize costs, the carriers hired agencies to undertake the task on their behalf. To win the screening contracts, these agencies entered into a bidding situation where the lowest figure was almost certainly going to be the winner. A natural outcome of such a bid was a low wage for the staff. Frequently their emoluments were set at the minimum allowable level authorized by the government. This was often lower than that paid to a counter assistant at an airport fast food outlet. Inevitably the caliber of personnel hired correlated to the wage structure, and standards fell far short of what was needed for the job to be performed adequately. The Federal Aviation Administration's own monitoring program set up to assess screening efficiency identified widespread shortcomings in performance.

For years the efficiency of the passenger screening process at U.S. airports had been measured by the number of weapons identified and confiscated. Constantly ignored was the obvious—it is the weapon which is not found which is the danger! In 1987, the Federal Aviation Administration began testing screening performance at a number of airports in the United States by concealing mock and real weapons in hand baggage passed through the security checkpoints. Screeners failed to identify the test items on 20 percent of occasions. The results identified the weaknesses in previously applied test criteria. Administration officials decided to crack down on the inefficiency they had uncovered and in 1988 imposed heavy fines on airlines for breaches in passenger screening. The immediate result saw 32 carriers fined a total sum exceeding $1 million. A second round of penalties saw another $1 million added to the carriers' bill. The carriers' response was an improvement in the discovery rate from 80 percent to 85 percent. But screening efficiency never reached the levels achieved in other major aviation countries. This may not have mattered too much in America in the 1980s, but following the al-Qa'eda outrages in late summer 2001, the U.S. Congress recognized it was no longer acceptable. They demanded change. As in so many areas of aviation security, it had taken a major act of violence to bring significant action.

The changes came not before time. In March 2002 *USA Today* reported that weapons were still getting past security checks at passenger screening points. Indeed, the discovery rate had deteriorated. In an article headed "Weapons Slip Past Airport Security," the newspaper used data from a confidential memorandum to the transportation secretary, Norman Mineta. Inspections conducted between November 2001 and February 2002, the period just prior to the Federal Aviation Administration's assuming responsibility for screening activities at all U.S. airports, had shown that staff at passenger and hand baggage checkpoints failed to identify guns in hand-carried items on 30 percent of the occasions airport security was tested. Knives in hand baggage escaped discovery on seven out of every ten attempts made to pass them through screening points. Simulated explosives went undetected 60 percent of the time.

Nor was access control any better. Federal inspectors had been able to board aircraft secretly or gain illegal access to the tarmac on 48 percent of the occasions they attempted to do so. The ramp, which forms part of the tarmac, is the soft underbelly of an airport. It is the operational area immediately adjacent to the terminal building and where most aircraft are parked while on the ground. At airports that lack air bridges linking the terminal building to the aircraft, passengers have to cross the ramp when leaving or joining a flight. When aircraft arrive or are preparing for departure, the ramp is a hive of activity. The larger the aircraft, the more airport workers and service vehicles need access to the area. All have to be security screened and supervised. The aircraft has to be guarded against unauthorized entry. Terrorists will seek to infiltrate the area. They may try to position weapons, explosive devices, or even drugs on unprotected aircraft. The two under-seat bombs used to attack Pan Am in 1982 were believed to have been taken on board in this way. The investigations into the Lockerbie bombing showed that in 1988 the Pan Am aircraft that ferried passengers to join flight 103 in London had been left unprotected while on the ramp at Frankfurt. This lack of protection for the aircraft was to be a plank used in the defense of Abdelbaset Ali Mohmad Al Megrahi and Al Amin Khalifa Fhimah in summer 2000 when they stood trial for the bombing. The ramp has to be protected at all times.

The Aviation and Transportation Security Act mandated the Federal Aviation Administration to assume responsibility for all passenger and baggage screening at U.S. airports. Screening staff members were to become government employees. A newly appointed under secretary of transportation for security[12] had to "develop standards for the hiring and retention of security screening personnel." He was also to be responsible for their training. The under secretary has to be aware that once staff have been engaged and deployed on the screening task, their management becomes a key ingredient in the security process. The actual function of checking passengers and their hand baggage is a highly routine and therefore potentially boring job. As ICAO recognized, with boredom comes inefficiency, and this has to be guarded against. Acts of unlawful interference are not everyday occurrences, and the likelihood that a screener will actually be in a position to prevent a tragedy is extremely remote. Indeed, a person may work as a screener for years and never be able to claim a "strike" against terrorism. Boredom and complacency have to be met with effective human resources management routines. These same supervisory techniques have to offset the proven inability of people to monitor VDU screens for periods in excess of 20 minutes without becoming blind to the objects of their search.

Staff performances at the interface between security personnel and the traveling public can, to an extent, be judged by passengers themselves. The general attitude of the screeners is easy to see. Personal presentation of the staff—that is, their appearance—is readily observable. Staff attentiveness is equally visible. Their technical ability is a covert asset or shortcoming, and this is something the new under secretary would do well to take on board. He must also note that not all people can be trained. Some may have inherent weaknesses that would prevent them from functioning properly in the role of a screener. If, for example, use is being made of color-enhanced x-ray machines to identify different types of metal or other material, there is little point engaging a color-blind person for this particular task. It does happen, though. Airlines have employed baggage handlers with an inability to differentiate colors when the baggage-sorting system was dependent upon the use of color-coded baggage tags. The potential efficiency of personnel should be considered at time of recruitment. Education to understand human behavior patterns and human psychology in general would be a valuable additional facet of the training process. These changes would move the Federal Aviation Administration several steps beyond the pre–Aviation and Transportation Security Act approach to recruitment and training. Most critics would say, not before time.

Air passengers on intrastate services within the United States will be able to see for themselves what effect the legislation enacted in 2001 by Congress has on security screening performance. Passenger and hand baggage screening is an overt operation. Evident at a glance will be whether two- or five-person teams are working at the checkpoint. Merely changing the employer without adjusting the system would add very little to travelers' security. To maximize domestic airport security, standards have to be raised to the international level.

One immediate benefit from the FAA assumption of responsibility for screening personnel was expected to be a massive jump in the salaries previously on offer. The anticipated gain for the traveling public was an improvement in the quality of personnel used to provide security screening at airports. But this will take the federal authorities into new territory. In addition to being administrators, they are now line managers—a difficult combination. Had Congress considered what happened in Europe and elsewhere?

In the United Kingdom, the major London airports come under BAA management. Like other airport managements in the United Kingdom, the BAA was charged with providing passenger and hand baggage screening checkpoints. They adopted the full ICAO recommendations. The BAA obtains its income from the airlines that use the airports and from the commercial franchises that operate there. Any outlay on security is ultimately recovered from these companies. The BAA does not go out to tender for the service, nor does it seek the lowest bid. The security service is provided from within the authority's own resources, and the cost is simply recovered from its customers. The BAA can afford to offer the highest standards. The Department of Transport—now named the Department of the Environment, Transport and the Regions—is the administrative body responsible for aviation regulation, including monitoring performance. The British system means that the standard of security is not inhibited by the Treasury Department, since it is not funded by the government.

ICAO recommendations can also be seen in operation at Swiss airports, but at those locations screeners are employed through the police. This is another way of ensuring standards are high.

Other examples of how other countries have achieved high standards of security exist. One such is Malaysia. The Malaysian airport security policy is very relevant to the task Congress has given to the Federal Aviation Administration. The country is a federation of 13 states, of which 11 are on the southern half of the Malaya Peninsular (the independent city-state of Singapore is the southern tip). Two of the states are on the island of Borneo. Malaysia Airlines provides the key communication link among the various parts of the federation and operates both domestic and international flights. The many airports throughout Malaysia's continental land mass and the islands come under the responsibility of the Civil Aviation Authority (CAA). To meet the security task, the CAA created a national force with staff ranks ranging from guards through a gambit of officer grades up to the director. This has provided a career structure for persons entering the security service. When the authority was first created, the salaries of the airport security force exceeded that of normal police officers in similar positions. This made recruitment easy. Some personnel transferred to the airport security force from the national police force itself.

The links to the federal police remained strong. Training was based on police service standards, and many courses were supervised by personnel from the federal force. Leadership training to identify possible candidates for promotion was an early feature of an educational development program created by the CAA. Recruitment was conducted at three levels. Entry into the lower grades required a high school education. For engagement at the rank of sergeant, educational achievements had to be equivalent to university intake standards. The third level of recruitment was from university graduates. The latter join the force as inspectors; their training required them to spend one year at the police academy and a further year on the job before achieving substantive rank. Because the CAA has control of all the country's airports, possible posting to the many locations in the Malaysian system created a wide range of opportunities for those employed in aviation security.

The Malaysian model would adapt well for the United States. Although individual U.S. airports have their own managements, the Federal Aviation Administration now has responsibility for passenger and baggage screening at all of them. A recruitment and training program of the type established by the Malaysia CAA could be implemented in America. (Such a program could also apply to sky marshals). Flexibility of staff movement given the existence of a single employer, the aviation administration, also exists. A centrally managed licensing or certification program, essential if competency standards are to be regulated, is also possible. Promotion should be dependent, in part, upon qualifications gained through a central system of federal examinations. A federal qualification would have validity should an individual wish to move location. In this way performance throughout the country could be standardized.

Whatever system of management is put in place, the Federal Aviation Administration will have to work within the constraints placed on it by Congress. Only U.S. citizens can be employed as screeners. This must not be allowed to lead to a false sense of security. Not all citizens have the interests of their fellow Americans at heart. It would be as well for the agency to remember Timothy McVeigh, the Oklahoma Federal Building bomber, and more recently José Padilla (aka Abdullah al Mujahir) arrested in June 2002. The latter was alleged by Attorney General John Ashcroft to have planned to build and detonate a radioactive "dirty" bomb on the U.S. mainland. A second constraint, which might have protected the system against

Padilla had he sought to become a screener, is a bar on anyone with a criminal record being employed in such a role. The attorney general told a press conference audience that the arrested man had served a prison sentence in the United States in the early 1990s. It would be highly beneficial if FAA officials were to seek screening personnel who speak a second or even third language. Not all air travelers in the United States are English speaking. Unilingual screening teams may need the support of translators to ensure that any questions they put to passengers are understood and that they, in turn, understand the responses. Language proficiency pay might be one way to attract staff with the appropriate qualifications into the service.

Passenger and carry-on baggage screening proved to be an effective procedural countermeasure to the hijacking scourge of the 1980s and 1990s. Its worldwide introduction can be given much of the credit for the reduction in aircraft seizures. During this same timescale, such screening also uncovered a number of explosive devices hidden in checked baggage. Attempts to check in such bags for carriage in the hold were made on numerous airlines, including Lufthansa, MEA (Middle East), Iraqi Airlines, El Al, and Iberia. At Frankfurt, the screening process identified one passenger's passport as false. Subsequent examination of his baggage uncovered liquid explosive contained in liquor bottles. The passenger was Mohammed Ali Hamadei, later to be convicted of the 1985 hijacking of TWA flight 847.

The procedure is not foolproof—no security system can be—but it is very effective when poor performance, for whatever reason, is kept at bay. In the United States, Congress has recognized that inadequate supervision, defective staff selection, and inferior training are unacceptable and has laid down the ground rules for the Federal Aviation Administration. The legislators believe a properly funded and managed security operation will ensure that none of these inadequacies exist. Congress has shown the direction by which the skies can be made safer. The ball is now in the aviation administration's court. FAA officials must not be too proud to tread the path others have taken, successfully, before them. They must guard against failing to apply procedures consistently across the country. Terrorists will seek out any weak links. As suggested previously, officials will also have to guard against the twin dangers of staff boredom and complacency.

The preceding paragraphs have considered the human element in a practical airport security operation. Rightly so because even where machinery is used, it is generally operated by a staff member. But effective and appropriate equipment is a vital part of the security mix. An x-ray is of little value if it cannot do the job for which it is intended. The Lockerbie bomb bag was x-rayed before it began its fateful journey. Its operator was not trained in x-ray use, and by itself the machine could not sound an alarm. Times have changed. Hi-tech machines are providing part of the answer. In Europe, the Far East, and elsewhere heavy capital investment has brought such technology into the security equation. But despite the two Presidential Commissions and other acts before the passing of the Aviation and Transportation Security Act, no appropriate investment was made in the United States. Even congressional directives to the Federal Aviation Administration had failed to move forward the standards of airport security.

The President's Commission on Aviation Security and Terrorism (August 1989) had found that "the U.S. civil aviation security system is seriously flawed." It was still flawed in September 2001. The commission wanted the FAA research and development program to be "significantly intensified to keep pace with the changing terrorist threat." The agency was called upon to "launch a top priority research and development program to produce new techniques and equipment that will detect small amounts of plastic explosives, operationally at airports." Research and development did take place in America in the laboratories of the hi-tech companies. Their results were tested overseas. The British Airports Authority made funds and airports available. They had not shown any "lack of sincerity and willingness to address safety and security on behalf of their customers."[13]

United States aviation can now benefit from the experience gained in the international arena to move beyond the research and development stage. Study must continue, but FAA officials can and must act now with the experience gained by the U.S. manufacturers and the users of their products around the world. Senator Ron Wyden of Oregon should not have to ask again, "Why has the city of Manchester, England, purchased more state-of-the-art explosive device detectors than the entire United States?"

Whereas passenger and hand baggage screening forms part of the overt security found at airports, checked baggage security is frequently covert. It generally happens away from the eyes of the general public. The Glasgow experiment, which successfully sought to combine baggage handling with security screening, was based within the bowels of the airport. It was part of the baggage-handling system. At some airports, hold baggage passes through x-ray machines before it is checked in. This is the procedure followed at many U.S. airports for international departures. In such situations it is an open-to-view process played out in front of the passenger. At some locations, "play" can too often become the operative word.

Most baggage x-ray systems in use around the world offer little more than a cosmetic exercise intended to create a false sense of security among the traveling public. The equipment is often unsuitable for the task. So too are the procedures generally associated with it. For example, at one airport in Asia, a busy international location by any standards, all baggage to be carried in the hold has to be screened and security banded. This occurs before the passengers take their bags to the check-in counter. In the days when every suitcase was hard-sided, security banding was a potentially useful procedure. Today, when the majority of bags are soft-sided and each one has a myriad of external side pockets, there can be no value in a single band around the bag. Frequently, because of the nature of the bag's design, the band becomes dislodged before check-in is reached. In any event, unless there is a tight physical security presence, a device can be slipped into the bag or into one of its pockets between the screening point and the check-in desk. Such a system, even if hi-tech machines are used at the screening point, has no value. Yet international passengers will confirm, it is a system in wide use around the world.

Battery-powered articles were of particular concern following the loss of Pan Am flight 103. Security specialists meeting under the auspices of the ICAO and the European Civil Aviation Conference (ECAC) discussed at great length the problems associated with such items. Some aviation authorities had demanded a complete ban on the carriage of battery-powered items on passenger aircraft, and some airlines were forced to introduce such a prohibition. In Asia, Korean Airlines was one. The airline had lost an aircraft in 1987 to an improvised explosive device hidden in carry-on luggage. The device had used a battery as a power source. In Europe, Lufthansa experimented with a ban, but the federal prohibition was dropped when thousands of battery-powered items were confiscated in a single day, resulting in great chaos at the German airports and for the airline. None of the items taken from passengers was found to pose a threat.

The German ban had shown what the airlines already knew, namely, that normal belongings of the average person going on vacation or traveling on business include many battery-powered items, for example, cameras, traveling clocks, and hair dryers. Laptop computers and electronic notebooks carried by a great many business men and women have batteries as a power source. By the late 1980s most watches and many medical items, such as heart pacemakers, used batteries. So too did many children's toys. Any of these items could be adapted to power an improvised explosive device, but banning such a wide range of goods was impractical. The idea failed to gain international support.

Congress has called on the FAA to assume responsibility for hold baggage screening. The new salary structures will give the administration an opportunity to hire the right people for the job. But the question of equipment and procedures has to be considered. Only the latest hi-tech machines will do. Bags do not become "cleansed" by passing them through an x-ray device, hi-tech or not. Qualified staff will have to monitor and interpret the VDU images. An overt baggage-screening system, in particular, must be policed. The hold baggage-screening area has to be a fully secured sterile zone, limited to passengers only. Barriers must be effective. It must not be possible for weapons to be passed to anyone in the zone from persons outside the area. A passenger-screening system, magnetometer and/or hand wand, has to be employed before individuals are allowed access.

Travelers can facilitate their passage through an airport and minimize delays at security checkpoints. When packing for a trip, they should limit their hand baggage to a single, easily manageable piece and not carry in it or on their person any sharp objects that might be construed as a danger. Scissors, nail files, knitting needles, tools, all fall into this category. So too do containers holding flammable gases and liquids. These can be turned into very dangerous weapons and will not be allowed in the cabin. Carrying such items will lead to possible confrontation with check-in agents or security guards and lead to delays and inconvenience. Electrical items tend to raise concerns with security screeners. These are known to be potential hazards. Radios, cassette recorders, laptop computers and battery-driven toys all fall into this category. They each have a power source that can be used to generate rather more than the manufacturers of the item intended. Passengers must be prepared to have such items examined carefully by screeners. If it is possible to travel without such goods, so much the better, but business people in particular will continue to need their laptops and personal organizers with them in the aircraft cabin. If such items are positioned in a readily accessible part of the carry-on baggage, this will facilitate their scrutiny and save the passenger time.

As a check on the efficiency of the x-ray machines and their operators, a minimum number of bags should be selected at random for hand searching. Random selection has the benefit of preventing observers from identifying search patterns. Some bags will be chosen for physical examination because their owners fit profile specifications developed by the authorities. In any event, a proportion of all bags will have to be opened before a qualified screener can be satisfied that the contents do not pose a threat. This procedure can act as a deterrent to those individuals who think they might be able to beat the x-ray system. They will not be so sure about the physical search process. Such physical searching requires space and, ideally, privacy. Few passengers are terrorists, and they should not be treated as such. They should not be embarrassed during a security procedure.

The Europeans found that a tiered structure of baggage screening maximized security against the baggage bomb. Nothing less should be provided at domestic airports within the United States or indeed anywhere else airlines operate. This is not possible in many parts of the developing world, and in such places the airlines have to supplement whatever process is in force. In the United States, European standards are achievable and should be a must. Congress should require nothing less. Equipment development has continued since the days of the Glasgow experiment. Machines suitable for overt operations are now available. Whether this is a practical way to go, given that provision for checked baggage screening would not have been incorporated into most airports' design, has to be decided on a location-by-location basis.

Other equipment questions demand attention. Passenger screening requires the use of magnetometers or electronic hand wands to identify any metal object carried on the person. Both have to be calibrated. Frequent and even occasional flyers changing planes during their journey will have passed through such devices at one airport without tripping the buzzer only to be halted on the next occasion by an alarm. Passengers need not have anything different on their person. What is acceptable to one machine is not to the next. This is because the machines have been calibrated differently or possibly because they have not been plugged in to an electricity supply. All too frequently, around the world equipment can be seen in position but not powered up. If security is to be standardized, calibration standards have to be set by a central authority. In the United States this will be the Federal Aviation Administration. On normal journeys, air travelers throughout the United States should expect identical standards. When high threat situations occur, procedures will be enhanced to meet the additional risk. Once passengers leave the mainland, standards will vary according to the decisions of national or local authorities overseas.

In his alleged attempt to destroy the American Airlines flight from Paris to Miami, the would-be bomber Richard Reid hid an improvised explosive device in the heel of his athletic shoes. Many magnetometers are calibrated to identify even the smallest amounts of metal. Normally, electronic detonators have metal elements that will trigger the alarms. Where calibration is set to very sensitive levels, passengers can frequently be seen divesting themselves of belts and shoes as the metal elements set off the warning buzzers. Calibration to suit a particular environment is important. Some machines now have the capability of indicating where the metal object is being carried on a person's body. But today, ceramics are frequently being used in the manufacture of detonators. These present a new challenge.

Plastic explosive material (Semtex, CN4) used as the charge in most improvised explosive devices is becoming more detectable, not by magnetometers but with vapor detection and analysis systems. An American manufacturer took an early lead in their development. EGIS trace detection machines built by Thermedics Detection were used in the Glasgow experiment. The machines provided a high-speed chemical analysis process to determine whether chemicals, including explosives, had contaminated the contents of a bag. They can indicate whether an individual has been in recent contact with such material and would certainly have identified the explosive charge in the improvised explosive device secreted in the shoes worn by Richard Reid. Of course, hi-tech detection machinery should not have been necessary in that instance. Staff had identified the man as a possible threat. The inadequacy of the French border police let him go. If these same police officers had been responsible for operating hi-tech equipment, it might be they would still have missed the bomb.

Another element of overt security at airports is the presence of armed guards, often police officers, sometime military personnel, patrolling the terminal building. Congress has called for armed guards to be positioned at each baggage-screening point. In other countries, armed support is generally provided by means of a rapid response team. Even where armed patrols are used, employing rapid response teams capable of reaching any threatened point within two minutes is the preferred approach. It is a highly cost effective way of maximizing security.

Much airport security is conducted away from the public gaze. Perimeter security, access control, and facilities protection are all largely unseen by the public. All are vital to an airport security program and can have a direct impact on passengers. Consider the attempted seizure of a Pan Am jumbo in Pakistan. At Karachi, the terrorists dressed themselves to resemble airport guards. They obtained a vehicle similar to those used by the airport authority and then drove up to a perimeter checkpoint that guarded the entrance to the airside of the airport. Despite instructions requiring identity cards to be examined, no challenge was mounted to the vehicle or to the men. The terrorists were simply waved through. This gave them unimpeded access to the Pan American aircraft that was in the process of boarding. Poor perimeter security had a very direct impact on the passengers: Twenty-two of them died in the attack.

All operational areas of an airport have to be protected against terrorist infiltration. That requires tight perimeter access controls. Consider, then, another international airport on the Indian subcontinent. A security review found the following:

> The airport has, for the most part, an adequate fence with access points controlled by security staff. There is, however, a problem caused by the presence of two villages situated outside the perimeter fence. Access to these villages can only be obtained by the inhabitants entering the airport through the "controlled" pedestrian gates and walking across the airfield near to and sometimes across the runway. Furthermore, the villagers graze their cattle and other livestock on the lush grass inside the perimeter and cut grass and reeds for their personal use.

Not surprisingly, the survey report called for urgent review of both safety and security questions raised by this situation. The inspectors recognized the political and humane considerations involved if the villagers were to be prevented from using the airfield as a means of access to their homes. They also recognized the difficulties that would arise for the villagers if they were unable to graze their livestock within the airport boundaries. Even so, they advised that total prohibition had to be the ultimate goal. In the interim, the inspectors called for mobile patrols to be introduced with the specific task of stopping pedestrians from crossing the runway and taxiway and from approaching aircraft parking areas. The patrols were further charged with preventing livestock from wandering onto these areas, especially in the hours of darkness.

On the African continent, similar situations were found. Over the years, Lagos airport had earned a bad reputation, as indeed had the whole country of Nigeria, for corruption and disorder. The airport perimeter security fence had actually been dismantled when an international inspection team visited the airport. There was no control over access to the operational areas. In the months immediately prior to the inspection visit, a number of aircraft had been accessed while they were on the runway waiting permission to take off. Thefts were made from the cargo and baggage holds. Crews reported seeing individuals approaching their aircraft from the bush while a get-away vehicle waited to whisk the criminals away to safety. Aircraft parked overnight on the ramp had also been illegally accessed, with personal property and instruments removed. Access to the ramp area of Lagos airport was simply a matter of walking or cycling from the neighboring roads. Among the attractions for the local residents were two waste disposal containers positioned at the end of the airport piers. These containers were regularly sifted through at night by the locals who were seeking to salvage the contents.

Another airport on the same west coast of Africa had large swathes of its perimeter fence stolen. The fence was later discovered some miles away forming a brand new cattle enclosure on a local farm.

These incidents might be regarded as amusing interludes, especially since few Americans or Europeans venture to such countries on their annual vacations. But consider the recent experiences of British Airways (BA), whose aircraft serve all the airports in question. In the latter half of the 1990s, on a number of occasions BA aircraft departing from developing world airports carried stowaways in the nose-wheel bay of their vehicles.

In 1998 the English newspaper the *Daily Telegraph* reported airport workers finding the frozen body of a young man in the nose wheel bay after a BA aircraft had landed at Gatwick Airport. The plane had arrived from Baku in the former Soviet republic of Azerbaijan. The newspaper quoted an airline spokesperson, "This raises very serious questions about security at Baku that have to be addressed." A year earlier, newspapers had reported a frozen body of a ten-year-old boy being found in a similar location on an aircraft that had arrived from Nairobi. Doubtless the same spokesperson would have suggested that this too raised very serious questions about security at Nairobi. In March 1999 a young man's body was found in the undercarriage of another BA jet that had arrived from Dar-es-Salaam in Tanzania. Later that same year the frozen body of a stowaway was found hanging from the undercarriage when a BA jet arrived from Cuba. A spokesperson for the airline quoted in the *Daily Telegraph* on August 23, 1999, said, "This type of incident is extremely rare." He had obviously not been reading the British press. Maybe he did read reports in December 2000, when two young boys died after stowing away in the nose-wheel compartment of another BA flight, also from Cuba. They had mistakenly boarded the aircraft thinking it was heading for Miami. One fell from the aircraft when the undercarriage was lowered on its approach to Gatwick Airport. Doubtless for the spokesperson these incidents raised serious questions about the security at Havana and at Dar-es-Salaam. Of course, none of the stowaways had threatened the safety of the aircraft or the passengers on board, but clearly little had been done to close this very real security loophole.

If it is possible for would-be refugees to access an aircraft undetected, what of terrorists who could so easily plant an improvised explosive device in this very vulnerable position? A timing mechanism could be set to detonate a device at any point in the aircraft's flight, including over a major metropolis. British Airways has been fortunate that the United Kingdom's international political agenda has not created enemies among factions whose members resort to revenge attacks on civil aviation targets. The war against terrorism, in which the United Kingdom so openly supports the United States, could change matters. Threat assessment management teams will have to build this factor into their equations in the future.

Standards for the fencing and control of airport perimeters have been developed by ICAO. So too have rules governing the security of aircraft on the ground. These have been endorsed by most of the organization's member states, including the United States and Great Britain, but the latter recognize only their responsibility for airports within the United Kingdom. They do not accept responsibility for the protection of British-registered aircraft at overseas airports. As has been discussed earlier in this book, many locations in third world countries do not apply ICAO rules. In such countries there is no effective airport security. The airlines are on their own. They have to take whatever action is appropriate to protect their operation. Security standards applicable at their home airports will not exist throughout their network. If airlines fail to introduce company security procedures to supplement those provided by the airport managements at deficient locations, their passengers and crews are at genuine risk. Given that some aircraft have been penetrated on the runway itself, their programs might have to be extended to include mobile patrols escorting aircraft before takeoff.

The ramp, as has been noted, is an airport's soft underbelly. It is very vulnerable. For passengers to identify weaknesses may be difficult, but it is a simple matter for efficient airport managements to do so. In America, in Europe, and the highly developed countries of Asia and Australasia, effective ramp security should be a matter of course. But complacency, satisfaction with their product, can lead to weaknesses. It is these weaknesses that have been shown up by investigative journalism. Perhaps it is a pity that these same media activities are not directed at security operations in the less salacious parts of the world.

An aspect of airport security, pioneered by the airlines' trade association, IATA, is the "sterile lounge." Passengers benefit from this innovation at most international airports. It is the result of airline facilitation and security managers working together. Screening stations are placed at an early stage of passengers' movements through an airport. Generally the stations are immediately beyond the check-in desks. Passage to the sterile area is limited to ticketed, processed travelers only. Having passed through the central screening points, passengers find themselves in a sterile zone where they wait until their flights are ready to depart. At international airports, managements have leased much of this area to duty free shopping franchises and other commercial enterprises that offer a wide range of goods and services. Airports such as Sydney and London's Heathrow and Gatwick have veritable shopping malls in the sterile lounge areas. Their commercial success helps the profitability of the airport operation. This activity does not open up opportunities for terrorists to exploit, assuming the responsible authorities ensure that both the employees working in the shops and the goods to be sold there have been security screened. All airport and airline personnel moving from the landside to the airside of the airport have to be similarly security controlled to maintain the efficacy of the lounge.

The central screening–sterile lounge concept has distinct security advantages. It provides a distance barrier between the potential discovery of terrorists and their ultimate target, the aircraft. It allows time for police or other covert forces to respond to an incident before any would-be hijackers can reach their goal. Passenger and hand baggage screening remoted to the departure gate allows the terrorist to approach within paces of their objective before being challenged. In the latter scenario, anyone intent on seizing an aircraft and believing there is a danger that their weapons will be discovered can use them at that point. In a matter of a few steps they are on the aircraft. Delaying security screening until the departure gate area actually simplifies the terrorists' task.

Operational and customer service benefits come from the sterile lounge concept. Any delays to passengers caused by the screening procedure will occur well ahead of the scheduled departure time of the aircraft. This provides an opportunity for the airline to recover the situation and maintain an on-time service. In Europe with its continuing problems of air space congestion, this is especially important. Ten minutes lost on the ground can result in air space slots being forfeited, adding hours rather than minutes to the journey time. This is detrimental to the passengers' peace of mind and highly costly to the airline. A delay on the ground resulting from security screening at the gate is likely to be obvious to the passengers. It is an unnecessary additional worry for the traveling public.

Gate screening requires individual teams of personnel (ICAO recommends a minimum of five workers for each such point) to be present for each aircraft operation. An airport with 20 gate departures in an hour would need 100 people to be on duty. In the early stages of the operation, passengers are likely to arrive in small numbers with sizable time gaps between them, thus underutilizing the staff. Nearer to the aircraft leaving, the numbers increase causing lines. Almost inevitably delays occur. With a central screening system, the same 20 departures could probably be handled with four checkpoints that could be supplemented as necessary but that in any event present major savings in personnel. It has to be remembered that unless a government authority is picking up the cost of security and placing the burden on a central treasury, the airline passenger will eventually pay for any waste of personnel and equipment through the price of the airline ticket.

There is an equipment cost saving in a centralized screening operation. For each of the 20 gates in the above example, twenty x-ray and magnetometer configurations will be needed against the four in the central system. With advances in detection technology inevitably pushing up the cost of such items, the expense factor of the gate system becomes significant.

One aspect of airport security airline passengers should never have to experience is the provision made to receive aircraft that have been hijacked. A holding area for the seized aircraft must be established away from the main ramp. This will allow the normal business of the airport to continue while the hijacked aircraft is being handled. The location of the holding area is selected to allow the security forces to oversee all the activity around the aircraft. Singapore's Changi Airport offers a good example. It is particularly well equipped to deal with such incidents. Its efficiency and capability were tested in 1991 when four young Pakistani men seized control of a Singapore Airlines Airbus flying from Kuala Lumpur to Singapore. Their initial demand had been to fly to Sydney, Australia, but the aircraft had to make a stop in Singapore for fuel. The hijackers called for the release of a number of people held in Pakistani jails, including the husband of Benazir Bhutto, the former prime minister. They were ill prepared for an act of this nature, being armed with firecrackers resembling explosives and with assorted knives. The aircraft was positioned at the previously designated stand. This was adjacent to the command post from which the Changi crisis management team operated. Lengthy negotiations failed to bring about the release of the passengers and crew. Then the terrorists threatened to kill one passenger every ten minutes. The decision was taken to storm the aircraft. All the passengers and the cabin and flight deck crew were freed unharmed. The four hijackers were killed by the assault team.

Changi Airport is a byword for efficiency in all matters of its operation. Most travelers who have passed through the terminals will recall only the excellent standard of customer amenity on offer. It has a magnificent shopping facility and offers day rooms at the airport hotel for long transits and even has a swimming pool among its passenger facilities. Security at Changi is second to none. Opened 20 years ago, the airport made implementation of its security plan top priority. Responsibility for security rested in a single command within the state police. A police division was stationed to one side of the main runway. Support was made available both from a nearby section of the city police force and from a military unit based a few minutes of the airport. Two auxiliary police forces were established to support the commercial activities of the airlines operating at Changi. In emergencies they automatically fell under the command of the state police. Standards for the auxiliary forces and background checks on the employees were set and conducted by the state police, thus a uniform performance was ensured. A "crack" police intervention team based inside the airport was placed on 24-hour call.

From the outset, the physical policing operation was supported by a crisis management plan bringing in the appropriate executives in the event of a security emergency. Each member had to know his or her role, and test exercises were regularly conducted. Overseeing both the airport and other state security activity was the National Security Planning Committee, which met to conduct reviews and to undertake risk analyses. It linked the aviation requirements with state needs. The airport administration had seats on this key body. The manner in which the Changi authorities brought to a successful conclusion the one seizure they have experienced to date underlines the efficiency of the program and the professionalism of those tasked with its implementation.

Virtually since its inauguration Changi has been lauded around the world as the most aesthetically pleasing, customer friendly and efficient international airport. As suggested above, to these plaudits must be added another for its security standards. One example perhaps exemplifies the attention to detail afforded security at the airport. In 1986, planning for a second terminal was well under way. This meant the destruction of part of the perimeter fence—an essential element in the defense of an airport as already discussed. The tender required the contractors bidding for the right to build the new structure to include in the specification a temporary perimeter fence meeting the same standards as the original one. The result was a provisional fence that exceeded the standards found in permanent structures at many airports in the rest of the world.

It is interesting that the airport at Singapore reached its high security standing without central screening. It positioned passenger screening at the departure areas, with individual holding lounges beyond the security check point. This allowed the airport management to overcome what was a shortcoming in the design of the building, namely, incoming and outgoing passengers using the same walkways. ICAO calls for segregation of inbound and outbound passenger flows. Most modern airport designs incorporate this separation. At Changi, the authorities allocated sufficient human resources to ensure security standards were met, accepting the additional cost of the increased staff numbers. A "panic" button that linked all screening stations with the covert response team also locked access to the boarding gate in the event of a terrorist incident, thus affording additional protection to any aircraft parked alongside the terminal building.

There does not have to be, cannot be, one single plan for airport security. ICAO has published guidelines in the shape of a model International Airport Security Program,[14] but they are only guidelines. Airports considered to be at high risk will necessarily have to massage the model program to meet their own needs. Airport design will affect the implementation of any security plan. Geographical locations and physical environments will dictate aspects of any program. Municipal, national, and federal policing arrangements will have an influence on an airport's security defenses. National and international politics will affect the level of threat posed to operations at any given airport or to any given airline. This threat has to be assessed and a program put in place to control the risk. For this reason, an airport management cannot simply take a security proforma and adopt it as its own. It has to be worked upon, preferably in a collaborative effort by the airport management, the airlines using the facility, and the local, national, and federal security services.

CHAPTER 5

Airline Security

Just as ICAO publishes a model security program for international airports, so too does it issue a security framework for airline operators. It is part of a series of such outlines that range from guidelines for a National Civil Aviation Security Program to Certification of Screening Personnel. ICAO recommendations have relevance to any country with a civil aviation operation. They have been developed with input from the major civil aviation authorities from around the world and from the industry's trade associations (airlines, airports, and pilots). But an airline's approach to security, though based on ICAO guidelines, will vary according to the carrier's perception of the threat it faces and the regulations mandated by its own government. The degree of the threat will clearly affect the content of an airline's program. Pakistan International Airlines (PIA) and Air India, for example, operate against a national and regional background of unrest. Militants seeking independence from India have struck at aviation targets in the past. Pakistan is a country beset with agitators, and street murder is rife. As 2002 opened, Pakistan and India were again threatening to go to war against each other. Both have a nuclear arsenal. Security appropriate for Cathy Pacific or Japan Airlines would certainly be inadequate for either PIA or Air India. A U.S. carrier flying in the Middle East will have security requirements very different from those of SAS (Scandinavian Airlines System) flying much of its operation in Europe and over the Atlantic. All should have certain similarities. They will have an objective that seeks to protect the customers, the staff, and the capital items of the carrier. They will each recognize and acknowledge the rules and regulations the ICAO model program is seeking to meet. The principal parameters within which the airline will have to plan are those laid down in their own national legislation. The regulations of the countries to which the airline flies will have to be appended to ensure the airline complies with the requirements of en route and destination airports. There may be special company objectives that need to be blended into the program.

Airline security programs embrace activities both on the ground and in the air, in their countries of registry and abroad. Airport programs, whether established by a governmental authority or through an airport administration, provide the basis for controls to defend the physical facilities at a fixed site. At some locations, these controls may include guarding of aircraft. One example of where they do not is the United Kingdom. At British airports, aircraft guarding is the responsibility of the airlines. Airline programs have to supplement any gaps in an airport's security plan.

Can the air traveler identify an airline's security operation? In some instances, yes. Passengers are exposed to an airline's security at check-in. "Is this your bag?" "Did you pack it yourself?" "Has it been out of your sight since it was packed?" "Are you carrying anything for someone else?" These, or similar questions are asked of all passengers by the check-in agent. They are part of an airline's activity to identify a possible unwitting accomplice to a bomber. The most startling examples of an unwitting accomplice, a dupe, scenario involve individuals who are prepared to send "loved ones" to their deaths along with hundreds of others by packing a time bomb into the luggage. One such attempted incident was uncovered at London's Heathrow Airport. A young, pregnant Irish girl was planning to travel to Tel Aviv on an El Al service. She was flying to Israel to marry her Jordanian boyfriend. He was also in London but had persuaded her to go ahead while he attended to certain matters before leaving England. He gave her a calculator to carry for him (a scientific one that she couldn't operate). He also provided her with an overnight bag to take into the cabin with her. The bag was lined with plastic explosive, and the calculator carried an improvised explosive device that when detonated, would have exploded the main charge hidden in the lining of the bag. The items were found by El Al security guards. Their discovery prevented a major disaster from happening. The pregnant girl was a most fortunate survivor, along with the rest of the passengers and crew. Nezar Hindawi, the Jordanian "boyfriend," was arrested and charged with attempting to destroy the El Al jet. He was sentenced to 42 years' imprisonment,

Close to the time of the El Al incident, American Airlines operating on a domestic sector in the United States did have a bomb explode in flight. Fortunately, there were no fatalities. On this occasion, the saboteur was a man who was trying to rid himself of his family. He placed an explosive device into his wife's luggage. Despite his military background, he bungled the job. His incompetence with explosives saved everyone's lives.

Procedures have to be in place to ensure passengers do not unwittingly take explosive devices on board aircraft. This is down to the airline, hence the security questions asked at check-in. Subsequent to the September 11th aircraft seizures, passengers are being asked at check-in whether they are carrying any "sharp" items in their hand baggage. The agents warn passengers that any items such as scissors, penknives, knitting needles, even nail clippers carried in their cabin baggage will be confiscated at the security checkpoint. Passengers are given the opportunity of transferring such items to their hold baggage before they leave the check-in counter.

The next key element of an airline's security program is generally covert, conducted in the inner workings of the carrier's computer and within the bowels of the baggage hall. It applies only in those countries that have adopted the ICAO recommendation to match all bags with their owners. The techniques used by airlines will vary according to the passenger and baggage control systems they have in use. At small airports without automation, reconciliation is very open to passenger inspection, for it can be as simple as lining up alongside the aircraft all the baggage to be carried on a flight. Passengers are asked to identify their bags and only those suitcases pointed out by their owners are loaded onto the aircraft. An example of how effective such a simple system can be was demonstrated at Yesilkoy Airport in Turkey.

In 1983, physical identification of baggage was in force at the Turkish airport. On December 29, an Alitalia flight was scheduled to depart for Rome. The baggage check revealed one bag that could not be linked to a passenger on the aircraft. The baggage handlers isolated the bag, and a subsequent search found a bomb secreted inside. The bag had been labeled with an interline tag to take it to Rome, where it was scheduled to connect with a Pan Am flight heading for the United States. Had the bomb not been discovered by the procedures in place at Istanbul, an earlier "Lockerbie" would have overtaken Pan Am. As discussed earlier, in 1986 the Federal Aviation Administration mandated that all U.S. airlines match passengers and their baggage at airports designated to be at "extra-ordinary" risk.

Air Lanka, the national airline of Sri Lanka, also required physical matching of bags by passengers. The procedure saved one of their aircraft from destruction by a bomb. The procedure had been recommended to the Sri Lankan authorities some years after the Yesilkoy incident by a former director of security for Air Canada, Ed Johnson. The matching process caused a bag, labeled to be carried on an Air Lanka flight departing from Madras in southern India, to be identified as unaccompanied. Johnson's recommendation had called for such bags to be taken to an isolated area, but at Madras, the baggage-handling agency staff wrongly and tragically returned the bag to the terminal building, where it exploded. The aircraft and its passengers were saved, but considerable damage was caused to the terminal building and, more significant, 40 lives were lost. To this day, at some airports with an automated process for reconciling passengers with their bags, some airlines will additionally intersperse their routine program with physical reconciliation.

Whether manual, automated, or semi-automated systems are used, passenger and baggage reconciliation is an airline responsibility. A handling agent can perform the task for or in conjunction with a carrier, but the airline remains accountable. Such a program has been described earlier in this book.

After check-in, the next time a passenger can expect to encounter an airline's security program is at the departure gate. By this time, air travelers will have passed through a passenger and hand baggage security checkpoint. With the Federal Aviation Administration now charged with conducting such procedures within the United States, primary screening is almost universally conducted by an authority rather than by the airlines. But at the gate, where a secondary inspection may take place, air carrier personnel generally perform the screening. They conduct their own check because they doubt the efficiency of the first inspection. Indeed, U.S. carriers were among the first to introduce what they call "redundant" screening. It had an early introduction at Paris.

Today, however, many airline departure checks are not to supplement central screening but to identify potential illegal asylum seekers, individuals who might be refused entry at their destination airport and be declared "inadmissible." Some will be traveling on false or forged travel documents. Others may have disposed of their passports and any other identification before reaching the boarding gate. This needs some explanation.

Recent decades have seen an enormous growth in the illegal movement of people from economically poor countries to the richer, developed world. By the end of the 1980s this movement had reached almost mass migration levels. It continued to grow throughout the 1990s. Illegal attempts to migrate across land borders between Mexico and the United States, for example, and from Eastern Europe and the Balkan states to Western Europe were widely reported in the media. Mass migrations in Africa and Asia often went unremarked or were paid little attention by citizens of the developed West—that is, until elements among the criminal fraternity in the source countries decided to "manage" illegal migration for profit.

For the most part, the motivation fueling the growth in illegal movement was economic rather than political. The intending immigrants were seeking better opportunities for themselves and their families than they could get in their homeland. Very frequently, they came from simple backgrounds and often had spent their life savings to purchase tickets and travel documents. Many had their own funds subsidized by family collections and money raised from mortgaged farms. They became easy victims of criminals who promised them passage and entry into their dreamland. The criminal gangs took money in advance from the intending migrants. Fellow citizens preying on their less well educated countrymen, the criminal gangs arranged for their victims to travel as tourists on "normal" visitor documents, thus making them acceptable to airline check-in staff in the country of departure. This spawned a subsidiary industry of document and ticket falsification and forgery, adding to the organizers' income. For their arrival in the selected country, the migrants were briefed on claiming political refugee status. In the beginning those who were educated might have had expected that the countries who were signatories to the 1951 Vienna Convention on refugees would grant them asylum. But very few qualified as political refugees. Even so, a number of states did allow the claimants entry while their cases were reviewed.

In Western Europe and in North America many of the early intending émigrés arrived by air. Later land and sea travel, often under horrendous conditions, were added to the travel methods organized by the criminal gangs. In an attempt to involve the airline carriers' security forces in policing the illegal movement of aliens, the U.S. Immigration and Naturalization Service (INS) imposed fines on airlines that brought incorrectly documented passengers to the United States. The fines were set at $1,000 per passenger. The Canadians, who were suffering from an identical influx, imposed similar fiscal penalties on airlines. The United Kingdom followed suit, setting the penalty at £1,000. Soon other European countries followed suit as the migration grew. The airlines had to meet not only the fines but in many instances all the associated costs of an applicant's stay while his or her appeal was being heard. Not untypical of such cases was one in Canada: A woman had claimed asylum on arriving in Toronto. She was granted leave to stay in Canada while her case was reviewed. During her stay she gave birth. The Canadian authorities sought to recover from the airline that had brought her to the country all the costs incurred by her detention *and* those arising from her medical treatment and hospitalization for the baby's birth.

The profits made from their involvement in the illegal movement of people failed to satiate the gangs' greed. Some gangs began to send couriers with the migrants in order to retrieve travel documents so they could be used again by some other misdirected soul. Before airlines put security checks in place at airports, the retrieval process would take place after travelers passed through outbound immigration controls or at transfer airports. Once the checks were introduced, couriers began traveling on the aircraft with the migrants. The documents were then collected during the flight. The migrants had no more use for them. When claiming asylum on arrival, the fewer documents, the more difficult it became for liberal Western countries to refuse entry.

Soon IATA took on a dual role of negotiating with states to protect the airlines against the growing fiscal penalties and preempting the illegal travel in the first instance. The latter took the form of collaboration with government agencies to teach customer contact staff in source countries the techniques used by the criminal organizers. As discussed previously, among the various methods employed by the immigrants was the use of forged or counterfeit passports, often coupled with the use of similarly fraudulent tickets. Staff at airline check-in counters had to be trained to identify forged and counterfeit documents. The intent of the airlines' departure checks was and remains to preempt illegal travel in the first instance. This, it was hoped, would avoid the human trauma and misery inevitably associated with a refused entry. At the same time, the carriers anticipated that successful identification of bogus asylum seekers at the point of departure would avoid the heavy penalties imposed by the receiving states. The airlines never accepted the idea that it was their responsibility to act as surrogate immigration officers, but they needed to protect their revenues.

The growth in the illegal movement added to the threat of aircraft seizure. Some persons refused entry at their intended destination, have seized the aircraft returning them to their point of departure in a last desperate attempt to avoid being sent to their home country. The most notable incident occurred in the Middle East, where one carrier decided to return on a single aircraft 123 people who had been refused entry or were being deported. The airline provided only four guards! Not surprisingly, the aircraft did not reach its intended destination.

Inadmissible passengers, individuals who have been refused entry on arrival at their planned destination, do not normally pose a threat. Should they be deemed to do so, the airline will insist on their being escorted. A deportee, in contrast, is a person who has been admitted to a country but once there has fallen foul of the law and been ordered to leave. Airlines do require deportees to have escorts. As a general rule, carriers insist on there being never less than one escort for every four deportees and no more than eight deportees on any one flight. This was a far cry from 123.

Other passengers may be on board an aircraft against their will. On rare occasions, prisoners are moved on commercial air services. When prisoners are carried, most airlines demand two escorts for each prisoner and no more than two prisoners on any one flight. The type of escort and the procedures they have to follow are strictly maintained. Outside of America, escorts are not usually allowed to carry any weapons, for the reasons explained in chapter 6, In-Flight Security. Very occasionally, passengers may see inadmissible passengers and deportees and even prisoners on an aircraft, but their carriage is normally handled discreetly so that few fellow travelers will be aware of their presence. Each airline has its own rules for carrying such individuals, who are generally boarded first and deplaned last.

Much of an airline's security program is implemented out of the public gaze. Security training is one such element. Occasionally passengers will witness the results of classroom instruction, a recent example being the disarming and detention of the would-be shoe bomber on the American Airlines flight from Paris to Miami. The cabin crew had first to subdue him, with help from other passengers. Then they had to deal with the improvised explosive device hidden in the heel of his shoes. Similar scenarios are enacted in the classroom. Each aircraft type has a predesignated safety zone where suspect objects can be placed. The crews secure the items with blast-resistant blankets. The classroom training was immaculately followed in the real-life emergency on board American Airlines.

Security training given by airlines to their ground staff and flight crews is extensive. Much of the curriculum is dictated by the national or federal civil aviation authority. In the United States, the aviation authorities spell out their requirements in federal aviation rules; for airlines, these include the requirement for each carrier to have a standard security program. This program must be detailed in printed form and submitted for FAA approval. Individual airlines will add to the program any company policy dictates. These will reflect security and marketing requirements the company considers appropriate for the routes they operate. Inevitably, given the current flying environment, training for cabin crew covers handling drunk, unruly, and otherwise obnoxious passengers guilty of "air rage." Air rage incidents have become frequent in the past few years. Some have been sufficiently threatening for the captain to divert his aircraft to offload the offending passenger. Training will also have prepared flying crew to deal with bomb threats made while the aircraft is in fight. Using role-playing techniques, all conceivable situations are enacted during classroom sessions so that when tested by real-life situations, crew response is automatic.

A point of weakness in an aircraft's operation arises when it makes a transit or transfer stop in its journey. Passengers deplane, often leaving belongings behind them. These belongings can pose a threat. Consider two incidents. The first has already been described in Chapter 2: A female passenger alighted from a TWA aircraft at Athens leaving an improvised explosive device behind. She had secreted it under her seat. The bomb detonated in mid-flight after the aircraft had put down at Rome and was on its return to Athens. The second incident cost the lives of 115 passengers and crew. En route from Baghdad to Seoul in South Korea, Korean Air flight 858 was destroyed by a cabin bomb in November 1987 while flying over the Andaman Sea. Two passengers posing as Japanese tourists had taken an improvised explosive device on board as hand baggage. It was detonated using a simple timing device some hours after the terrorists had left the aircraft when they transferred to another service at Abu Dhabi.

South Korean authorities moved very quickly following the destruction of the aircraft. They studied a print-out from the airline's computer based departure control system and the flight coupons pulled from the tickets prior to the aircraft's earlier departure from Baghdad for Abu Dhabi. Two persons were very quickly designated as suspicious: Shinichi Hachiya and Mayumi Hachiya, a couple traveling as father and daughter. The couple had given their nationality as Japanese and had presented genuine travel documents. These were later shown not to belong to them. Their itinerary was scheduled to take them to Bahrain after their transfer at Abu Dhabi. The flight coupons showed they had no checked baggage, and the Korean investigators noted a similarity to the TWA bombing.

Within hours of the aircraft's destruction, the pair were confronted at Bahrain International Airport. Shinichi Hachiya committed suicide by swallowing a cyanide pill. His compatriot's suicide attempt failed. South Korean authorities later identified Hachiya as Kim Sung-il. He was, the authorities alleged, an agent of the North Korean Workers Party. His bogus daughter's real name was Kim Hyon-hui. Much later, during her confession, Kim Hyon-hui described how the pair had taken liquid explosives on board the aircraft disguised as alcohol. They had used a radio to hide the detonator. They placed the armed device in an overhead rack and simply left it there when they disembarked.

The report of the subsequent investigations carried out by the South Korean investigators[15] was aided by the woman's confession. It showed that the pair had traveled from Sunan near to the North Korean capital of P'yongyang on November 12, 1987 and had flown over a circuitous routing to Moscow, Budapest, Vienna, and Belgrade, where the explosives had been obtained.

One outcome of this and the earlier disasters were new recommendations covering the control of passengers at transit and transfer airports. Today passengers experience those changes when they travel on aircraft making more than one stop or change planes en route to the final destination. Each major incident in the 1980s led to tighter security controls. By 1990, the international rules and regulations had been sufficiently refined to take civil aviation security procedures well into the new millennium. Indeed, no substantive change in the rules has appeared since. Vast improvements have occurred in security equipment, but the rules themselves have stood the test of time. As always, universal implementation remains a challenge.

The Korean Air disaster demonstrated once more that neutral airports and countries are used to springboard attacks on civil aviation targets. There is little value in building a fortresslike facility at an airline's home airport if locations along its network are left unguarded. Terrorists research their target. They will always seek out the weakest link in an airline's armor.

Just as an airline's security training is conducted away from the view of passengers, so too are many other facets of its program designed to protect its customers. Passengers will take them for granted. The meals served on board flights have to be prepared. They must be put together in an area that is sterile, not just from a health aspect but from a security one as well. It must not be possible to smuggle weapons on to an aircraft via a catering trolley. Similarly, engineering bases have to be protected against illegal entry. Security controls have to be in place to ensure that engineers and mechanics working on aircraft, whether at a maintenance base or on the ramp, pose no risk. Cabin-cleaning staff have to be subjected to strict security controls. Airlines have experienced all three work areas being used as a conduit to get weapons and explosive devices on board aircraft. One tragic example of this occurred at Colombo Airport in Sri Lanka. Militants hid a bomb among engineering spares that were then loaded onto an Air Lanka Lockheed 1011. The boarding process had just begun when the device detonated. Twenty passengers were killed.

Special security handling processes are applied to cargo and mail carried on commercial flights. Historically, airlines operating to and from Central and South America have been more concerned at the prospect of drug syndicates making illegal use of cargo shipments to smuggle illicit narcotics than of attacks by terrorists. The IATA secretariat and U.S. Customs recognized as early as 1984 the potential destructive power of those engaged in drug trafficking. Their joint staffs developed guidelines to support each other's efforts aimed at preventing civil aircraft being used to transport illicit narcotics. In September 1985, in an address to an assembly of security chiefs of the international airlines, the commissioner of U.S. Customs, William von Raab, said:

> On the thirtieth day of July of this year, Customs and IATA took a bold step against a common and dangerous enemy. On that day, Dick Shaw,[16] Rodney Wallis and I announced that our two organizations had agreed to an extensive and historic four-part protocol to combat international narcotics smuggling.
>
> This action put narcotics smuggling squarely at the top of the international agenda, where in my opinion it belongs. In fact, Rodney Wallis and I have spoken on numerous occasions about the threat narcotics smuggling poses not only for the health of all our nations but also the very safety of the planes that carry drugs unsuspectingly from one country to another.

The protocol specified a series of steps airlines would take to protect their aircraft from illegal infiltration by the drug traffickers. In return, the U.S. Customs committed themselves to providing intelligence input and training assistance to support the airline activity. The techniques that the airlines were required to implement at identified high-risk, drug vulnerable airports were, in fact, similar to those needed when high-alert terrorism situations arose along their networks. The defenses needed against the traffickers and terrorists have many parallels. The U.S.–IATA protocol went on to become the basis of a Memorandum of Understanding between the airlines and the world body for customs matters, the Customs Cooperation Council (CCC).

The initial motivation for the airlines to cooperate with U.S. Customs was a financial one. Just as fines were being imposed on carriers that brought inadmissible passengers into the United States, so too were fiscal penalties levied when drugs were discovered to have been flown in illicitly. In the case of illegal passengers, the fines placed on an individual airline reached into millions of dollars per annum. When narcotics were involved, the penalties could total in the millions for a single incident. In the United States, the Anti Drug Abuse Act of 1986 established the level of penalties at $1,000 per ounce of heroin or cocaine and $500 per ounce of marijuana. In addition, the aircraft on which the illicit narcotics were carried could be confiscated. The financial impact of a Boeing 747 being held out of service while impounded by Customs would, in many instances, exceed the fine. The motivation to avoid such draconian punishment was very clear.

Despite the harsh treatment (from a carrier's viewpoint) and even with the guidelines being adhered to by many of the airlines, the inflow of narcotics on commercial aircraft continued. So too did IATA and U.S. Customs collaboration. In January 1988, the commissioner was again able to announce that a joint agreement had been reached to "step up high-tech detection methods to fight international drug smuggling on planes." The Swiss *Journal of Commerce*, carrying news of the accord, reported:

> The plan involves the use of x-ray machines, closed circuit television and electronic scales linked by satellite to other countries. Other possibilities include new x-ray equipment that can penetrate fully loaded containers and vehicles and equipment that pinpoints drugs by analyzing vapors from baggage and packages.

The fight against narco-terrorism and airborne terrorism was progressing hand in hand.

The need to use satellite links to protect aircraft shipments arose because very real threats to life existed in the major source countries when airline personnel identified and reported illegal shipments of cocaine. Staff members were regularly being warned to "look the other way, or else!" A security manager of Colombia's national carrier, Avianca, was murdered for opposing local drug barons while performing his airline duties.

Cocaine from Colombia, the principal source country in South America, was generally carried in boxes of cut flowers. Trade in flowers had reached amazing proportions by the mid-1980s, and a number of airlines did nothing other than ferry such produce from Bogota and other cities in that country to markets in the United States. The traffickers used this mass movement to cover their own exportation of cocaine. In some instances, illegal shipments of cocaine exceeded a ton. Because of the homogeneous nature of the boxes containing the flowers, x-ray scanning proved to be an ideal method to uncover packages of cocaine surreptitiously placed in the cartons. However, the fear factor remained. Thus the control of x-rays and the use of electronic scales and surveillance cameras had to be removed from the local scene to a safer operating location. This was to prove a highly successful practice. Even so, some carriers opted to move away from the cargo scene altogether, and in July 1988, Avianca withdrew from the northbound freight market and put its Boeing 747 freighter up for sale.

Illegal narcotics were also arriving in the United States on small private aircraft. In 1989 the commissioner proposed shooting down aircraft that failed to respond to challenges by the control authorities. This proposal was supported on the floor of the Senate. The final bill containing the proposal was defeated, however, though only by the narrow margin of 52 to 48. IATA's director general, Gunter Eser, had objected to the Secretary of Transportation Samuel Skinner over the potential use of force against aircraft. The airlines feared a commercial aircraft might be mistakenly shot down. After September 11th, the United States took the decision to scramble fighter aircraft with the purpose of destroying any commercial aircraft should its flight pattern became erratic and it appeared to pose a threat to land-based targets. In January 2002, jet fighters took to the air when a young boy stole a light aircraft and flew it into the Bank of America building in Tampa, Florida.

Airline defenses against narco-terrorism in the 1980s have many similarities to those put in place to prevent acts of unlawful interference with commercial airliners today. The proposals to use satellite communications in the fight against the drug barons could have great relevance in future airline security programs. Already underway at the start of the millennium were moves to harness iris recognition, image identification, and finger print and other biometric recognition techniques to aviation security needs. Also developed was a new lie detector process that focused on the change in the blood flow around the eyes when a person lies in response to security questions. Whether any of these techniques will offer practical value in the passenger contact field only time will tell, but they will doubtless have roles to play in other aspects of airline and airport security operations. If, however, data gathered at check-in, by whatever method, could be transmitted real-time and analyzed in a mainframe computer databank deep inside an intelligence agency's headquarters, then a Star Trek addition to airline security may not be too far away.

Recruitment of staff for any aspect of airline and airport security work should incorporate background security checks of the individuals. The same should be done with employees who work in a restricted area. Each airline and airport should have a security manual, and this will normally specify the nature of the checks. The U.S. Aviation and Transportation Security Act requires that "an individual to be hired as a security screener undergo an employment investigation (including a criminal record check)." The better international airlines and airports have had "Codes of Practice" for the recruitment of security staff in place for many years. Transport Canada established criteria for recruitment and testing staff as far back as the late 1980s.

Airline "Codes of Practice" set out procedures to be followed in the decision-making process before any person is engaged in security operations. The recruiting parameters include a full education, employment, aptitude, and criminal check. They require recruitment interviews to be conducted by a personnel or security officer trained for the task and all appointments to be endorsed by a senior-level manager. The best airlines take recruitment very seriously but frequently omit a restriction included in the new U.S. legislation. They do not necessarily limit staff to the nationality of the carrier. The new American act requires persons hired for a security screener's role to be citizens of the United States. Congress would be wise to remember Oklahoma City. The enemy can come from within.

An airline's security manual deals with all security matters within the company. It identifies the chain of command and those people to whom any authority is delegated. The regulations it promulgates will have worldwide applicability but may have to be adjusted to suit different environments and to reflect variations in operating conditions. They will all have been designed to protect passengers, staff, aircraft, property, and equipment. The regulations should incorporate standard operating procedures and those procedures necessary when threat levels rise or when an emergency occurs. One section of the manual will define those areas where coordination with other agencies is necessary. These agencies will include the local police, air force, and airport security force as well as the customs and immigration services, medical organizations, and the airport operators committee. The manual will include an outline to assist security managers in assessing the degree of risk to the airline from unauthorized or illegal acts. It will include pro-forma checklists to cover the various incidents that may occur during a company's operation; for example, when the need arises for aircraft to be searched or when telephone bomb threats are received.

Airlines receive many bomb threats. Some are specific, nominating a particular service or route; others are general in their content.

Threats may be received by telephone or in writing. The airline manual will spell out how each category should be handled. In some countries, local laws may require a carrier receiving a threat to report it immediately to the local police, who may then take over. Major airlines normally prefer to assess the threat for themselves, with the help of specialist input, and decide on any action to be taken. Such carriers will have established a special team to do this.

Threats made to airlines are seldom published. Publication of bomb threats would simply encourage those wretched, maladjusted people who make the many hundreds of hoax bomb calls to airlines every year. Fire and ambulance emergency services suffer from this same syndrome.

Study of bomb threats made to airlines in the United States prior to the creation of the Commission on Aviation Security and Terrorism had shown that whenever such calls were made, they were almost invariably false. Only when linked to extortion attempts did any of the warnings have validity. The commission noted that some 600–700 anonymous aircraft threats had been received annually during the decade prior to their sitting. None had resulted in the discovery of a bomb. This knowledge may well have influenced the different interpretations of the Helsinki warning. Even so, the commission suggested, "Public notification of threats to civil aviation should be made under certain circumstances." They also believed that "on balance passengers are entitled to be notified of credible aviation threat information where the information is specific enough to assist the traveler in avoiding or minimizing exposure to the potential risk, and where there is no assurance that the threat can be nullified." This conclusion suggested that airlines should pass on to the traveling public the responsibility for assessing terrorist threats. The better airlines employ personnel designated to undertake threat analysis. If they are unable to give an assurance that the threat can be nullified, should the responsibility be delegated to the public? Did the commission intend that a carrier may opt to fly even if it has not been able to nullify the threat, providing the intending travelers have been told of the situation?

An airline has to ensure that any warning has been expertly analyzed. Should analysis or the application of any additional procedures deemed necessary by the threat satisfy the airline or any involved authority that the service is not at risk, the aircraft should be free to operate. The threat would no longer exist and the need to broadcast it would have passed. If, however, the analysis and any precautionary measures taken by the airline, or by another appropriate authority involved, fail to satisfy the airline that the service is safe to operate, *the flight should be canceled.* The primary objective must be the safety of the passengers and the operating crew.

Apart from the copycat morons, there is one other group of people who would gain from any publicity given to bomb threats if, as the "to tell" protagonists believe, passengers would move away from a targeted airline. They are the terrorists. They would only have to make a telephone call to disrupt a carrier's operation.

An area of an airline's operation that can impact on passengers is cargo handling. Wide-bodied aircraft have huge amounts of hold space available for the carriage of commercial goods. Cargo is generally loaded before passengers' baggage, but as they wait to board, air travelers will often see last-minute items being placed in the hold. Security controls will have been applied to these shipments just as they would have been to passengers' baggage. The very nature of cargo does, of course, require a different approach.

Air cargo shipments, like freight at seaports, have always presented a temptation to the less honest employees of companies handling the import and export of goods. Pilferage at docks was at one time endemic. Workers saw theft not as crime but more as a "perk" of the job. With the growth of air cargo, this idea transferred to airports. On one or two occasions, the theft of bullion shipments and precious stones and currency had lifted the thefts from petty larceny and onto the front pages of the newspapers. In February and March 2002, banknote robberies at London's Heathrow Airport were to do so again. Shipments totalling U.S. $9 million were stolen. (These audacious thefts are described in more detail in Chapter 8, The Lessons.)

Long before terrorism became a scourge, many airline security departments came into being to fight cargo and baggage crimes. Former police officers were hired to protect air shipments. The general theft problem appeared to abate, and in those parts of the world given to the illegal export of narcotics, policing began to concentrate on the dangers of putting things into cargo shipments rather than taking items out. At the same time, terrorists were changing. They were becoming more threatening, and they were turning to the bomb as an alternative to hijacking as a favored way of attacking civil aviation targets. The drug traffickers had demonstrated the ease with which items could be infiltrated in cargo shipments. Airline security managers recognized the same approach could be used to infiltrate improvised explosive devices.

Air carriers had been sheltered from the threat of cargo being used for sabotage purposes by a series of inbuilt deterrents. The export and import of goods required detailed documentation in order to clear customs and health controls. Such documentation, quite apart from the physical examination of shipments by the authorities, could well lead to pre-incident discovery. The trail of paper that went with a shipment of goods by air would also have facilitated post-incident investigation leading to a greater possibility of identifying those who had carried out any attack. Many of these deterrents remain even though computer databanks have replaced much of the paperwork. A further barrier had been the uncertainty surrounding the actual aircraft that would carry the goods.

Cargo had been seen by most airlines as a second-class commodity—a potentially profitable one, but nevertheless one of secondary importance. It filled space not wanted for passengers' baggage. An anticipated heavy passenger load or even adverse operating conditions requiring the aircraft to lighten its load could cause cargo to be left behind at the shipping point. Cargo could also be switched from one airline to another, making it difficult for anyone contemplating an attack on a particular airline.

Much of this has changed. Cargo volumes have grown, so much so that the occasional all-freight carrier of 25 years ago has become a myriad of giant air companies concentrating entirely on the movement of goods and mail. Some of these carriers are bigger than their passenger counterparts. Despite the growth of the all-freight air carriers, the volume of cargo now carried on passenger aircraft makes pre-flight inspection at an airport very difficult. Airline marketing departments sell cargo hold capacity on specific flights. Consignees know on which service their goods will travel. Express parcel and courier traffic has added to the goods carried on board aircraft that bypass traditional controls. Much courier traffic remains undocumented. All this has added up to a growing vulnerability of air transportation operations from cargo shipments. With such growth, security has had to be put in place to preempt the use of cargo for terrorism purposes. Neither governments nor airlines could wait for an incident to occur before taking effective defensive measures. Cargo was thus to become the one area where preventative programs did not wait for the horse to bolt before the stable door was shut. The licensing of known shippers to whom responsibility for security clearing goods could be delegated became a major plank in the cargo security program. This moved the first link in the security chain away from the airport.

Hi-tech screening devices have been developed and positioned in airlines' cargo warehouses. Mass-spectrometry and other vapor analysis systems able to handle bulk shipments have proved their potential. Pressure and simulation chambers of the type built at some airports in the early days of terrorist attacks never achieved a practical level of use, however. Terrorists became too sophisticated in their bomb-making skills to use simple barometric devices whose mechanisms could be tripped inside such chambers. The cargo market became too big for each item to be carried on an aircraft to be tested in this way. Similarly, time delays that were frequently imposed on certain shipments 20 or more years ago were no longer considered appropriate in many parts of the world. Cargo security has moved with, and in some cases ahead of, the times. Hi-tech defenses have been harnessed to take air cargo security into the twenty-first century.

One other commodity carried on aircraft for which security is necessary is mail. Mail is a traditional item for airlines and on many routes was carried before passengers. Air transport companies cannot, of course, interfere in any way with the mail. Postal authorities apply security measures, but airlines assume responsibility for security-cleared shipments of mail once they are delivered into their care. The airlines protect the shipments from pilferage, but learning lessons from the drug barons, reverse pilferage, putting things in rather than taking things out, has greater security priority. Individual items of mail may have little value for the terrorist because of the vagaries of routing, but mail sacks are a different proposition. They may be directly identified with a specific flight after acceptance by airlines, and thus their protection from interference is vital. Procedures to ensure such protection have proved very successful. In recent years, no major terrorist incident has been put down to interference with cargo or mail shipments.

CHAPTER 6

In-Flight Security

Should aircraft flight deck doors be kept locked during flight? Should they be made bullet proof? Should every flight carry an armed sky marshal? Could any or all of the forgoing have prevented the tragedies of September 11th? The questions were asked around the world as civil aviation authorities debated what had to be done to prevent a repetition of the World Trade Center attack. Yet these were not new questions. They had been debated many times during the previous three decades.

Many governments hold relaxed views on whether or not to lock cockpit doors. Most of their air carriers are happy to have selected passengers go on to the flight deck, especially on long flights. It is good for customer relations. Flight crews are generally pleased to explain the intricacies of modern flight to the passengers, especially to children. An argument against open door policies is the ease with which they allow anyone wishing to reach the flight deck and seize control of the aircraft to do so. Carriers decide on their individual policy after assessing the level of threat posed to their services. They, of course, have to meet any regulation dictated by their governments. In America where domestic carriers have had a history of aircraft being seized by Cubans wishing to return to their Caribbean base, policy has always favored the locked door philosophy mandated by the Federal Aviation Administration. The Aviation and Transportation Act strengthened U.S. legislation on locked doors. A prohibition has been placed on accessing the flight deck of aircraft engaged in passenger transportation. Flight deck doors and locks have had to be strengthened. Flight deck doors have to be kept locked while aircraft are in flight. Keys to the doors may be held only by flight crew assigned to the flight deck.

The U.S. policy was picked up during the ICAO high-level ministerial conference on aviation security held in Montreal in 2002. Among the endorsements of that gathering was one requiring Annex 17 provisions to be strengthened to include protection of the flight deck. Interestingly, at a security conference held in London just a few days after the ICAO meeting, delegates suggested priority should be given to improving security on the ground. They believed terrorists had to be prevented from boarding in the first place and that focusing on the cockpit door was putting the cart before the horse.

Congress also directed the Federal Aviation Administration to develop and implement systems that made use of video cameras and monitors to enable the aircraft captain to see what is happening in the cabin without opening the flight deck door. In addition, the agency was mandated to develop a system of "panic" buttons that cabin crew can use to alert the pilot of any untoward incidents arising in the passenger cabin.

Within their own trade associations and in international forums (ICAO, IATA), pilots have debated the subject of locked doors. They have considered their probable reactions if would-be terrorists found their way to the flight deck barred by a locked door, seized a flight attendant as hostage, and threatened them with injury or even death unless the door were opened. The majority were in little doubt they would open the door to protect their crew. None offered the opinion that they would keep the door locked at all costs. Happily few crew members, if any, are likely to be put in a position to make such a decision. Nonetheless, the debate has validity on both sides. A locked door would buy time for the pilot to warn the nearest air traffic control that his aircraft is under attack. But such a warning would require only the touch of a button, an action that can be measured in fractions of a second. A counter argument is the advantage gained by terrorists if they successfully forced a pilot to open the door giving them entry to the cockpit. Pilots see the initiative passing to the hijackers in such a scenario. They believe regaining authority would be a difficult task.

Countries hold differing opinions about whether to require flight deck doors to be kept locked. There is nothing wrong for the aviation security policies of one power to differ from those of another. Indeed, in some instances there should be differences. Geographic locations and political environments will dictate policies appropriate to the region. A government's politics, especially its relationship with foreign governments, can make its airlines a target for international terrorism. Such an administration must insist on its airlines' having security procedures in place to reflect any increased danger. These will necessarily differ from programs demanded by states faced with little external threat. Aircraft of different nationalities flying the same routes can face very different levels of threat. El Al operating from Frankfurt to Tel Aviv must have a more extensive security program than Lufthansa flying the same route. El Al is at greater risk and its security program must reflect this. If the threat posed to an airline changes, carriers must have the ability to respond, but to impose routine standards that neither the government, the airline, nor its passengers recognize as necessary is not in anyone's interest.

Not surprisingly, the Israeli carrier draws a veil over much of its security operation, although its customers can identify obvious differences, such as the requirement for them to check in well ahead of the reporting times demanded by other airlines. Passengers will recognize too, the much deeper questioning by screeners, part of El Al's profiling program, and the more detailed searching of carry-on items. The latter is generally part of a secondary screening process. It was just such searching that uncovered the improvised explosive device carried by the woman duped by Nezar Hindawi into being an unwitting accomplice.

Different requirements existed for European carriers and their U.S. competitors throughout the 1980s and 1990s. In the new millennium, variations in carriers' security programs may become even more marked. In the past, whenever the Federal Aviation Administration has attempted to tighten security requirements for carriers coming under their jurisdiction, U.S. airlines have demanded the same changed standards be imposed extra-territorially on European and other airlines. The demand was driven, not by the desire to raise the levels of security on the foreign flag carriers—in some instances they would have been higher in any event—but merely by the intent to "level the playing field." American carriers simply did not want to incur costs they believed were not borne by their rivals. Congress identified in its new act a need for sky marshals on U.S. services. They have imposed their use on U.S. carriers deemed to be at high risk. Governments around the world, and their airlines, will have noted the U.S. action and reviewed their own positions. If they have identified a different level of threat, then their risk assessment will call for a different response. For the U.S. airlines to demand that armed guards be carried on their competitors' services would be inappropriate, for in some countries their employment would be against the law. The imposition of sky marshals was designed by the Congress to meet an identified threat posed to American services. By their action, Congress has leveled the playing field. It will be for the traveling public to elect with whom they will travel.

Assessing national threat levels is a primary role of governments. Danger for the traveling public arises if an administration's assessment is wrong. A government's policies may create enemies overseas. If for whatever reason a government declines to understand or accept the fact, then most probably its direction to its airlines will be wrong. In such circumstances, the carriers' mandated defenses will be inadequate. They would not have been designed to preempt attacks by people who believe they have a quarrel with the state. This is a scenario many non-Americans believe U.S. air carriers have found themselves in over the years.

The Western world gathered round the U.S. in consolidated support following the vicious attacks of September 11th. Governments proclaimed the strikes were made against the entire free world. The people of much of the developed world stood side by side with Americans in their sorrow and anger. But the truth seems to be that the al-Qa'eda attacks were directed in this instance against a very specially selected country. Reports have shown that the terrorists who attacked the World Trade Center and the Pentagon entered the United States many months, in some instances many years, before the attacks took place. They became sleepers, awaiting orders to emerge for their mission. Some learned to fly aircraft sufficiently to turn their chosen flight into an airborne missile. Their anger was directed against America. There can be little doubt that the targets were selected to damage the United States, a country seen by Osama bin Laden's followers as hostile to the Palestinian people, among others. Airports and domestic carriers in the United States have to develop their security programs against this background.

Terrorism cannot, must not, be seen to change any government's policy. Yet much of the Arab world perceives U.S. policy to be biased against it. Thus until U.S. diplomacy is seen by Muslims everywhere to reach equilibrium, terrorism, which fell to new levels of depravity in 2001, will remain as a threat to American carriers' operations. Danger from the action of militants exists on the American mainland and wherever U.S. airlines operate. That this is recognized is important. It is a precursor to the development of an effective domestic and international aviation security policy. Such a policy will be different, at least in degree, from that of, say, Switzerland or Sweden. For different, read "tighter." Tighter security has allowed El Al to operate safely despite the constant threat posed against it. United States carriers are equally able to counter the threat, but doing so successfully will take "the sincerity and willingness to address safety and security" matters that Commissioner Cummock told President Clinton were missing. The new act developed by Congress is intended to raise the level of security on U.S. air services at home and abroad. Unless this is achieved, U.S. travelers will be at higher risk when they board an aircraft registered in the United States than when flying on an aircraft of a foreign airline.

FAA policy on locking cockpit doors is an example of a regional differentiation. In order to meet a recognized threat, the rules have been made more rigid than those applicable in much of the rest of the world. But not all rules export well. FAA ideas in other areas of flight deck security have highlighted this. They share the view of most Western civil aviation authorities that the best place for a seized aircraft is on the ground. Once there, it has to be kept grounded. Differences begin at this point. With their experiences of domestic aircraft seizure, FAA officials saw the evacuation of the air crew as a highly effective way of immobilizing an aircraft. They incorporated the recommendation into their training programs. It was an effective response to the lone hijacker of the Cuban period, but it did not translate well into the international arena.

The crew evacuation policy backfired in September 1986 when the Pan Am Boeing 747 was attacked on the tarmac at Karachi. When the first shots were fired, the captain and his flight deck crew used the emergency escape rope to evacuate the flight deck. In taking this action, the crew was simply following FAA recommendations developed much earlier and for a different operating environment. The evacuation by the pilots left the cabin crew and the passengers on board. Review of the incident suggested that the absence of the pilot led to an increase in the tension among the terrorists. The gunmen, already in a high state of anxiety, were left without a recognized figure of authority on the aircraft. There was no one with whom they could deal. They had no capability of establishing communication between themselves and the authorities on the ground. As technical problems began to arise with the aircraft, there was no one to whom the hijackers could or would listen. There was no one able to advise them of the imminent failure of the aircraft's power source. When the cabin lights failed and at the same time the airport lights were turned off, the anxiety that had been growing throughout the incident exploded into carnage that was to cost the lives of many of the passengers. Criticism was aimed at the aircraft captain, but this reproach was wrong. He had behaved correctly according to his training. Yet the American media made great play with headlines such as "Air Crew Flee Hijacked Aircraft." This reflected public opinion. What would the newspapers and television presenters have to say if a captain remained behind locked doors while his stewardesses were maimed or murdered?

Procedures developed for the United States or any domestic scene and applied worldwide have to be questioned. Leaving passengers at the mercy of any terrorists will surely always lead to at least some being killed if only to strengthen the bargaining power of the hijackers. The captain of a seized aircraft is a key player. At the time of the attempted seizure of Pan Am in Karachi, IFALPA (the International Federation of Airline Pilots Associations) training recommendations covering aircraft seizure were all based on the assumption that the captain remained on board the aircraft. Captain Testrake's actions during the TWA seizure in 1985 and those of the captain of the Kuwait 747 hijacked in 1988 emphasized the value of the aircraft commander's continued presence.

Beyond North America, the FAA recommendations for aircraft evacuation by the flight deck crew found few takers. With their aviation law based on maritime rules and regulations, some countries pointed out that if a commander were to abandon his vessel and passengers in the face of danger, this would be a criminal offense. This would have relevance in many non-U.S. territories to a rigid locked door policy that led to crew members being killed. Should an aircraft be seized or an attempt made to seize it, the captain should not be hamstrung by rules dictated from the safety of a legislative office in some faraway capital. Governments, with the advice of experts, should develop policy. The civil aviation authorities must establish guidelines. Real-time decision making inside an aircraft must be down to the pilot-in-command.

Arguments can be made in favor of a locked cockpit door. Had a former staff member of U.S. Air had his access to the flight deck barred, the lives of 43 passengers and crew on board Pacific Southwest Airlines (PSA) flight 1771 might not have been lost in December 1987. A recently dismissed employee boarded the aircraft carrying a loaded gun. He had tracked his former supervisor, the man the gunman held responsible for his dismissal, onto the aircraft. Once in flight, the former employee shot his supervisor and then went to the flight deck and killed the pilot. The aircraft went into a fatal dive. It will never be known if a locked door would have seen a different result. More obvious was that domestic airport security had been so poor that the gunman had been able to bypass the passenger and baggage checks while carrying a lethal weapon. *In-flight security must begin on the ground.*

Another valid argument for keeping flight deck doors locked can be made in relation to the growing number of air rage incidents being reported by airlines. An irate passenger, perhaps under the influence of drink or drugs, trying to reach the cockpit might be restrained by a locked door. Airlines and aviation authorities have to give this growing phenomenon deep thought. It could be the strongest argument for keeping flight deck doors closed.

Should flight deck doors be made bullet proof? There is no evidence of terrorists shooting their way onto the flight deck of an aircraft. Bullet-proofing doors would, therefore, seem excessive. It certainly presumes enforcement of a strict locked cockpit door policy. Where would this leave the passengers? Certainly on the wrong side of the safety door. This proposal is likely to be the subject of long discussions raising again all the earlier issues.

The debate on the carriage of sky marshals is another highly charged one. Armed in-flight guards, sky marshals, contributed to the total destruction of an Iraqi Airways flight in December 1986 with the loss of 71 lives. The Iraqi tragedy, which happened on Christmas Day, underlined a danger always present when armed guards are used on aircraft. A mid-air gun battle was fought between security officers and terrorists when the latter attempted to seize the aircraft. The hijackers used grenades as well as guns, and the firefight was waged over the heads of the passengers. The use of grenades has featured with some frequency in Middle East hijacks. The British passengers on board the Kuwait Airways aircraft seized on the flight from Bangkok to the oil-rich sheikdom told of their experiences with such weaponry. One technique used by hijackers has been to take the pin from a grenade, thus arming it. The grenade is then held harmless by placing a thumb over the firing mechanism. If, however, the terrorist is attacked—or in the case of the Iraqi incident, shot—the already armed grenade will fall and explode. Any attack on a hijacker in such circumstances must lead to the deaths of many on board and possibly, as in this case, to the total destruction of the aircraft. The incident led one airline chief executive, a former military commander, to comment: "An armed sky marshal in a hijack situation has either to act the coward and do nothing, or act the fool and bring about the deaths of passengers by using the weapons with which he has been provided. This is no choice for a man."

Use of firearms by Egyptian armed, on-board guards is believed to have initiated the gun battle that resulted in the killing of 56 people just one year earlier. An Egyptair Boeing 727 had been en route from Athens to Cairo when three terrorists took control shortly after it had taken off from the Greek capital. Witnesses who survived the ordeal suggested that subsequent to the seizure, shots were fired by sky marshals. The guards' fire was returned by the terrorists, with at least one bullet fracturing the outer skin of the aircraft and causing some decompression. The aircraft put down in Malta. Shortly after landing, some female passengers were released, but at the same time, the hijackers began shooting some of their captives. The pattern of killing suggested that passengers with Israeli or Jewish identities were identified, followed by passengers with U.S. citizenship. Egypt, using treaty rights they had with Malta, sent troops to Valetta. Some ten hours after the last shooting was reported, they stormed the aircraft. The decision to storm the aircraft has been criticized. Certainly the use of troops insufficiently prepared for such a task had to have had a major bearing on what followed. Survivors alleged there was indiscriminate shooting by the commandos, but grenades were certainly responsible for many deaths within the cabin. Others died on the tarmac. The majority of those who died during the incident did so as the result of the rescue attempt.

Among the major lessons that should have been learned from this incident was that use of armed sky marshals on board aircraft can endanger the very passengers the agents are traveling to protect. If the marshals had not reacted to the aircraft seizures detailed above, the incidents might have become "normal" hijackings with the possibility of passengers and crew being talked free. A second lesson has to be that only highly skilled troops from a truly elitist squad can hope to retake an aircraft from terrorists by force if the loss of life among the passengers is to be minimized. Few countries have such troops. Indeed, until the island state of Singapore successfully stormed a seized airbus in 1991, no country outside of Europe and Israel had a proven ability to undertake such a task. The United States doubtless has the potential through its special forces, but they have not had to prove themselves in a real life aircraft hijacking.

The four aircraft seized from the East Coast airports in 2001 saw multiples of terrorists take control, but they had no firearms. The mere presence of an armed sky marshal may well have been a sufficient deterrent to have thwarted the criminals' efforts. If so, the guards would have prevented a great loss of life. We will never know. The terrorists may have overcome a single guard. They would then have had a gun. The weapons actually carried by the hijackers were items that should have been detected by alert, properly trained security staff on the ground. The use of sky marshals should not have become a debating point, but in the event, it led the U.S. Congress to make provision for deployment of federal air marshals on every U.S. registered passenger flight. Congress ordered their deployment on any flight the aviation administration determined to be at high risk.

As has been said previously in this chapter, *in-flight security begins on the ground.* A Muslim radical's attempt to bomb American Airlines in December 2001 is another example of this same premise. He should never have been able to get past French airport security. The AA check-in staff had referred the man to the police. The airline agents had become suspicious partly because of the man's appearance and partly because he had no checked luggage and had bought his ticket with cash. The man had no fixed address and was vague about his travel plans. He fit a profile.

Passenger security at French airports had always been poor. At the height of terrorists attacks on aviation targets in the mid-1980s, ICAO's recommendation for five-person rotating crews at security screening checkpoints were never implemented at Paris's Charles de Gaulle Airport. Then still among the giants of international air travel companies, TWA introduced a secondary security check of its own.

This was positioned after the official border police controls. The carrier introduced the procedure to raise the level of security offered to its passengers.

It was noteworthy that following the bungled American Airlines bombing, newspapers carried reports that the French border police had disclaimed any responsibility for the lone bomber's clearance to board the American Airlines aircraft. British difficulties with lax, even deliberately poor French border police controls have not been limited to air transportation. Ever since the Channel Tunnel was built between England and the French port of Calais, many thousands of would-be asylum seekers, some of them Afghans and Iraqi nationals, have attempted to use the facility to enter England illegally. They have tried to walk through, hitch rides underneath the train carriages operating between the two countries, and traveled concealed in freight wagons. Al-Qa'eda followers are thought to have been among them. Facilitating rather than preempting the attempts, the French authorities actually established a collection camp for such people at Sangatte, just a short walk from the entrance to the tunnel. Despite British requests, for a long time the French government refused to close the camp. On Christmas Day 2001, some 550 persons from the camp attempted to storm the tunnel. Of that number, 130 individuals penetrated seven miles inside before security forces caught them. They had chosen Christmas Day to make their move because fewer trains were operating over the holiday period.

A key factor to emerge from the attempt to bomb the American Airlines aircraft was that the man, traveling alone, was overcome by a combination of cabin crew and passengers. There was not any need for sky marshal intervention. Media reports suggested the bomber was tied up with passengers' belts. Most carriers have special retaining straps on board for use in emergency situations. The crews are trained in their use.

One of the four aircraft seized on September 11th was diverted from its intended target by passengers who fought with the terrorists on board. Their heroic actions doubtless saved the lives of many others who would otherwise have come within the orbit of the terrorists' objective. They have caused executives with civil aviation security roles to reconsider policies developed to deal with airborne hostage situations prior to the al-Qa'eda attacks.

When asked what a passenger should do if faced with an aircraft seizure situation, the response of aviation security specialists has been, "Do nothing. Stay calm. Do not draw attention to yourself." Airline policy has been to get the aircraft onto the ground, where it can be isolated and appropriate containment and rescue procedures put in place. Passenger intervention, they believed, was less than helpful. But this policy was developed before the advent of the suicidal airborne terrorist. It presumed an aircraft hijacking would be by individuals or by trained, armed terrorists working in multiples but who wanted to survive the hijacking. Kuwait Airways, in the example discussed earlier in this book, had been seized by as many as nine men. They had been armed with handguns and grenades. Passenger intervention in that situation could have led to the loss of the aircraft in flight. Three or four men with minimal weaponry attempting to take control of an aircraft was a different scenario altogether. The aircraft that crashed in Pennsylvania might well have been saved by the action of the passengers. Sadly, it was not. But the passengers' brave attempts to thwart the terrorists meant the latter were stopped from reaching their intended target, generally believed to have been the White House. Just as the captain of the aircraft or a sky marshal may have to make decisions based on the environment in which he finds himself, so too the passengers. In most situations matters will still be best left to the crew, professionals who have or should have been trained to deal with in-flight terrorist situations. Just occasionally, though, passenger intervention might be the right thing.

The foregoing should figure in any debate on the use of armed sky marshals. It is important that the possible consequences of their use be understood. If this is done and a system of armed guards is used, whether in America or elsewhere, the debate should have identified strategies to be implemented in the various scenarios that might arise. The first response need not necessarily be the discharging of an officer's gun. Indeed, the situation might call for a passive reaction such as a "do nothing" response. As with the opening of the flight deck door when the captain has to make the decision, situations will arise when only the sky marshal can make the call. The depth of training given to such officers has to enable such persons to make the right decision. A vital factor will be the coordination necessary with the pilot-in-command. This might be best achieved by placing the guard in the cockpit.

Clearly, the al-Qa'eda terrorists' method of seizing control of the four domestic aircraft on September 11th gave advocacy to Congress's decision to expand the U.S. Sky Marshal Program. The American public can expect to see a growth in their use on domestic and international services. Congress called for appropriate training, supervision, and equipment to be provided to sky marshals. The training program must be broad based, incorporating psychological and political awareness. An understanding of the history and nature of terrorism and terrorists is also important. It cannot be simply coincidence that the intending bomber of American Airways made his first attempt to board the aircraft on December 21. This was the anniversary date of Lockerbie. The seizure of the four aircraft by al-Qa'eda coincided with the thirty-first anniversary of the Dawson's Field episode when three hijacked jet aircraft were bombed at the remote airstrip in the Jordanian desert and a fourth was firebombed in Cairo. Middle East terrorists have a penchant for anniversaries, even, in one instance, forming a new terror organization—Black September—to mark one. Black September was, so named to recall the time when Jordan expelled Palestinian forces from its territory. This group was later responsible for the attack on Israeli athletes at the 1972 Munich Olympic Games. Eleven of the Olympians were killed.

Knowledge of the international political scene will help sky marshals and security managers to understand and appraise situations in the field. At all costs, sky marshals must not be insular in their outlook. Traveling guards must soundly understand the political environment of the countries to which they will be flying. Airline security managers must have similar knowledge of any country in which their company operates. One North American company with major assets overseas appointed as its "international" security chief a former city police officer who had never previously left the U.S. mainland. It was an appointment some believe played a role in the deaths of colleagues. They died through the failure to implement a security policy designed for the overseas territories in which the men had to work. Exposure to cultures alien to the United States will broaden the understanding of U.S. sky marshals and thus improve their ability to do their job. An understanding of the geographic variations and the routes operated by U.S. flag carriers is another must. Training for sky marshals of any nationality should be designed to broaden their knowledge and understanding of the world, especially where it poses a threat to the well-being of their fellow citizens. Taking a psychological approach to a hostage situation may be preferable to catering to those who might simply demand, "Shoot the bastard!"

Indeed, becoming involved in an exchange of fire because "that is my job" is a temptation to be resisted.

An armed sky marshal has to be a very special individual. His or her job, once in the air, may be highly boring with an entire career going by without the need for heroic action. But equally, on day 1 or on day 1,001, a sky marshal may be required to act. Boredom, the bugbear of the security manager, may have—indeed, almost certainly will have—set in over the months and years. It could affect the sky marshal's ability to act. Thus training and operational duties have to be designed to overcome the inertia resulting from such boredom. As in other forms of security, some form of rotation of duty is a must.

Sky marshals or traveling security guards can support an airline's ground staff by performing security duties at check-in or at a secondary screening point where the carrier employs double-jeopardy systems. Many airlines already use their own, unarmed security staff for such duties. Based at their home airport, these traveling security guards are positioned on outgoing services to conduct security checks of passengers and baggage for the return flight. An additional benefit arising from this policy is the early opportunity it gives to the security guards to eye the passengers boarding the aircraft. Anyone arousing suspicion can be interviewed, and searched if necessary, before boarding. Such passengers could be refused boarding or directed to a specially designated seat from which they can be monitored by the guards during the journey. Since the security guards fly on the same aircraft as the passengers they screen, they have double motivation to do a good job.

A policy of providing traveling security officers could be followed whenever a carrier believes it needs additional screening at an airport to which it operates and where the security provided by the local authority is deemed inadequate. By using home-based staff for this function, the carrier minimizes costs yet has in place a level of security checks it can trust. Using a carrier's own staff in a foreign airport requires the approval of that location's administration, of course, and of the local government. For U.S. registered airlines to operate in this fashion, the State Department would have to work with the Department of Transportation to clear the way. Adoption of such a policy would broaden the job description of sky marshals and add to their job satisfaction. It would lead to greater confidence among passengers and crews.

The U.S. administration should explore the possibility of using federal sky marshals in such a dual role, which would undoubtedly help improve performance standards and go a long way to achieving the result Congress is seeking—safer skies. Airlines could be required to meet some, if not all, of the cost of employing the federal guards.

Other questions remain in respect of sky marshals. Should they operate singly or in multiple units? Given the techniques used by past international terrorists, a single sky marshal operating on a flight may have little value. One man or woman would have little opportunity to act in the seizures scenarios of the 1980s. A sky marshal operating as a single unit could not have been expected to overpower the eight or nine armed and determined young men working as a team on Kuwait Air flight 422. Although a single guard would probably have been unable to overcome the several terrorists who seized TWA flight 847 following its departure from Athens, that single individual might have been able to identify the terrorists as a potential threat prior to take off had his or her duties included pre-boarding inspection. Preemptive action is always the better policy.

Just days after the September 11th tragedies, the British transport minister, Stephen Byers, proposed using sky marshals on British flights. By January the idea had been dropped. Fierce resistance to it had been mounted by the airlines, which had no appetite for armed guards. They raised their concerns at the prospect of terrorists seizing the guards' weapons and using them on passengers and crew members who resisted attempts to hijack an aircraft. The carriers believed that it would be easy to identify sky marshals operating in plain clothes or even disguised as crew members. The *Sunday Telegraph,* which carried news of the minister's about-turn, carried a quotation from one airline executive: "A determined hijacker would only have to hit him [the sky marshal] on the head from behind and suddenly you are dealing with a terrorist who has a gun—and that's more dangerous than a terrorist with a knife." Passenger groups in the United Kingdom supported the airlines' position. The chief executive officer (CEO) of the Air Transport Users Council considered sky marshals impracticable. Interestingly, he raised the question of cost: "There are 460,000 flights from Heathrow alone each year. Where would the guards come from? And who would pay?"

It must be repeated that the safest place for a seized aircraft is on the ground. Once there, a successful in-cabin policing action might be possible, perhaps undertaken in conjunction with activity initiated outside the aircraft. Even here danger is present. Special forces storming an aircraft may have insufficient time or be unable to differentiate between good and bad guys holding the gun. Anyone holding a firearm will inevitably be killed—all successful recovery actions have shown this to be so. The action in Singapore when the island state's police resolved an aircraft seizure situation, saw all four hijackers killed without loss or damage to the passengers. The hijackers were armed only with small knives. Special forces simply do not have time to ask questions.

The decision to use sky marshals will inevitably be political. It will be a judgment call. When their use is mandated, however, the right men and women must be selected for the job; their training must be broadly based and detailed, and their management must be of the highest quality. Used intelligently and not simply to ride shotgun, mimicking the days of Wells Fargo stagecoach travel, they can play a vital role. Ideally, they should be viewed, not as an add-on to in-flight security, but as a component in the overall security mix.

Any chapter on in-flight security must consider the carriage of guns inside an aircraft cabin. International policy developed within ICAO is opposed to allowing any weapon onto a passenger aircraft. Several ICAO standards (rules) are aimed at preventing their carriage, yet many people want to carry weapons aboard. Escorts of VIPs, government dignitaries, and the like, often want to bring guns into the cabin of aircraft. In the United States, an incredibly large number of people are entitled to carry guns at all times. Many of these people want to keep their weapons with them in flight. Regardless of practice or of claims that the Constitution gives citizens the right to bear arms, taking weapons onto an aircraft is against the interests of everyone on board. Airline security is all about maximizing the safety of passengers and crews. Introducing any gun into the cabin of an aircraft—and this includes stun guns—is unlikely to facilitate this goal. If September 11th sets a pattern, al-Qa'eda hijackers operate in multiples; more than one operative will be on board. A single sky marshal with a stun gun or perhaps the captain with a stun gun—if, as some suggest, pilots are provided with such weapons—is unlikely to be able to mount an effective response. Furthermore, any attempt to use the stun device will bring a response from the terrorists. Armed hijackers are likely to reply to the sight of anything that resembles a gun by shooting the person wielding it. At such a time, all on board would be at risk. A case might be made for using such weapons in "loner" situations, but the pros and cons need to be evaluated. It is worth noting that all major hijackings in the past three decades have been by groups of terrorists rather than by individuals.

An area of in-flight security to which a growing focus of attention is being paid in some quarters is the possible bomb-proofing of whole aircraft. For some years, research has been conducted into manufacturing baggage containers that can withstand the blast effects when bombs explode inside them. The goal is a container able to restrict the effects of high explosives being detonated when an aircraft is in flight. In 1994, Royal Ordnance, a British defense contractor, demonstrated a prototype version. The airline industry was not overenthusiastic, however. Industry representatives saw unacceptable bottom-line costs arising from retro-fitting whole fleets of aircraft with new, expensive containers. The carriers also anticipated weight penalties with the new containers, which would add to the operating costs. They argued that even if all existing containers were put to one side in favor of bomb-proof models, a high percentage of baggage and cargo would still be carried on pallets (trays) or loose-loaded into aircraft holds. Aircraft would still be vulnerable. To be valid for commercial operations, bomb-proofing programs have to cover all the goods carried in the holds of aircraft.

Given that improvised explosive devices carried in hand baggage have proved to be equally as devastating as a bomb carried in checked baggage, the whole physical structure of an aircraft needs to be protected. This requires revisions in aircraft design and construction. The timescale for such changes has to be measured in years. ICAO could prioritize discussions on the desirability of all new commercial aircraft designs incorporating some form of bomb-proofing. Such debates would help accelerate the evolution of the necessary technology.

Progress is already being made. In 1998, four years after the first bomb-proof containers were produced, television newsreels and the print media showed footage and published pictures demonstrating the advances already achieved. A test-bed aircraft, variously protected along the length of its fuselage, was "attacked," with the simultaneous detonation of devices placed throughout the vehicle. The trials, conducted by the Defence Evaluation and Research Agency on behalf of the British Civil Aviation Authority and its U.S. counterparts, were evaluating bomb-proof cargo holds. The detonations made good viewing, but the scientists needed a more flexible tool, for once an aircraft has been destroyed, it is finished for laboratory experiments. Work switched to computer modeling, which will allow economic evaluation of bomb-proofing techniques. Scientists and security specialists can now experiment freely with a wide variation of potentially hazardous situations: bombs or other devices, including biological weapons, carried in hand baggage or in checked (hold) baggage, both in containers or loose-loaded onto aircraft. They will be able to examine containerized and palletized cargo scenarios. Experiments, all using computer models, will doubtless include sabotage scenarios where bombs are planted inside an aircraft, perhaps alongside the central fuel tank or in the nose-wheel compartment. Even so, it may take an upsurge in terrorist activity to bring about changes in the airlines' attitude to bomb-proofing developments. As history has shown, security improvements generally follow a tragedy rather than precede it. Meanwhile, the need to balance the cost and operational penalties of bomb-proofing aircraft against the security gains from such a process may remain a deterrent to early practical progress in this area of airline security. If so, then for some time to come, the security of air travelers will depend on effective passenger security controls and on today's defenses against saboteurs and bombers—positive bag match and hi-tech baggage screening.

CHAPTER 7

Unexplained Crashes: Accidents or Terrorism?

"How safe are our skies?" When this question is asked, events like the al-Qa'eda attacks and the bombing of a Pan Am flight over Lockerbie are uppermost in the thoughts of most English-speaking people. Deeper consideration gives rise to thoughts of other air disasters that have not, so far as has been proved, involved terrorists.

Some areas of the world are more prone to air accidents than others. This may simply reflect the heavier movement of commercial airliners in such regions. But does it explain the frequency of incidents involving aircraft departing from New York's Kennedy Airport? Consider four major crashes: TW 800, Swissair 111, Egyptair 990, and AA 587.

TWA FLIGHT 800

On July 17, 1996, a Trans World Airways Boeing 747, flight 800, took off from New York's Kennedy Airport and headed for Paris. It was an hour behind schedule. The aircraft was above the waters off the coast of Long Island when, at 8:48 P.M. local time, its image disappeared from the air traffic control radar screens. What had been flight 800 fell into the ocean. All 228 people on board, 210 passengers and 18 crew members, died. Many of the bodies recovered from the water were badly burned. None were wearing life jackets indicating that the demise of the aircraft had been sudden, without any warning. All early speculation was of a bomb having been detonated on board. Similarities with the Pan Am disaster over Lockerbie were sought, but there were differences.

The stories told by the many eyewitnesses varied in detail. Witness accounts always have variations regardless of the nature of the disaster. People see or hear things differently. In this instance, some claimed to have seen a streak of light rising from the ground in the direction of the aircraft before flight 800 was destroyed. Some talked of more than one explosion; others of two or three. All talked of a fireball. A pilot flying a private aircraft described a great ball of flame that had lit up the whole area. He saw bits dropping from the aircraft. The crew of an Air National Guard C-130, a transport plane, also witnessed the explosion. From that aircraft, Colonel William Statemeier "saw two large orange fireballs—they looked liked comets—coming straight down."

Talk of a missile strike on the aircraft gained much ground during the early days of the investigation. Pierre Salinger, a former press aide to President John F. Kennedy, claimed that TWA flight 800 had been struck by a surface-to-air missile fired during a naval training exercise, something the U.S. Navy hotly denied. They claimed their nearest vessel was 180 miles away. James Kallstrom, who led the FBI investigation, accused Salinger of basing his claims on erroneous chatter on the Internet. Pierre Salinger was later to appear in Holland as a witness during the trial of two Libyans charged with the Lockerbie bombing. He claimed the men, Abdelbaset Ali Mohmad Al Megrahi and Al Amin Khalifa Fhimah, had not committed the crime. He had interviewed the men, with the permission of the Libyan government, shortly after they were indicted. He insisted he knew who really was responsible for the attack on the Pan Am aircraft and why the bombing was carried out. Lord Sutherland, who chaired the panel of Scottish judges hearing the case in The Hague, Holland, warned him not to name names in court. Neither the defense nor the prosecuting lawyers asked Salinger to elaborate on his theories.

If the TWA scenario suggested by Salinger had been true, it would not have been the first or last time a naval vessel had destroyed an aircraft operating in a recognized air corridor.

In July 1988, a warship, the USS *Vincennes,* opened fire on an aircraft with surface-to-air missiles. The inexperienced young gunners thought the plane was an attack fighter bearing down on them. It was, in fact, a commercial airliner operating to a published timetable, climbing, not descending, and following an internationally recognized flight pattern. The mistake left 290 passengers and crew dead. The destruction of the Iranian airbus in the Gulf had been a tragic accident with terrible consequences

In October 2001 a surface-to-air missile fired by a Ukrainian naval vessel accidentally shot down a chartered Tupolev 154 aircraft of Siberian Airlines, operating from Tel Aviv to Novosibirsk in Siberia with 76 people on board. The warship had been taking part in a war games exercise in the Black Sea when a live projectile went astray and hit the airliner, which was 160 miles away.

Perhaps one reason for doubting the veracity of Salinger's theory was the absence of any leak from crew members of the ship that had allegedly fired the missile. In times when newspapers pay handsomely for salacious stories, someone would have talked. No one did.

In war zones, there have been a number of occasions when surface-to-air missiles have been used to shoot down civil aircraft. Twice in the 1970s during the conflict in Rhodesia, now Zimbabwe, dissidents used SAM-7 shoulder-launched rockets to bring down Viscount aircraft of Air Rhodesia. In 1986 in the Sudan, rebels also using SAM-7s claimed 60 lives when they successfully destroyed an aircraft in flight. In the 1980s, rockets were used in Afghanistan during the Soviet occupation to attack commercial and military aircraft. Heat-seeking Stingers had been provided to the mujahideen by America. If there were any truth in a surface-to-air missile strike on the aging Boeing, terrorists with contacts in Afghanistan would certainly have been able to lay their hands on the necessary ordnance. How they had smuggled the weapons into the United States would have remained a matter of conjecture.

Mitigating against the missile theory, whether the projectiles were land launched or fired from a vessel, was the absence of any evidence from among the wreckage of the Boeing. The debris had been salvaged from the sea and taken to a former hanger at Grumman Airfield in Calverton for forensic examination. According to the investigators, nothing showed signs of having been struck by a rocket. Neither was any confirmed evidence uncovered of a bomb exploding in the aircraft, despite several reports of traces of Penta-erythritol tetranitrate (PETN), a constituent of plastic explosive, having been found on pieces of wreckage. These traces had been identified by investigators using vapor detection machines manufactured by Thermedics Inc. of Woburn, Mass., the same machines as those used by the British Airports Authority in their baggage screening trials in Scotland. However, the positive findings of the Thermedics machine were not repeated when the items were subjected to secondary examination in the FBI's laboratory in Washington. No one was able to say if the failure in the FBI laboratory to match the findings of the initial tests meant the machine's diagnosis had been erroneous or merely that the results had not repeated themselves when put through a second examination. There was additional talk of traces of nitroglycerine having been found. Sabotage could not be ruled out. Terrorists capable of placing an improvised explosive device on an aircraft certainly existed in New York at the time the TWA Boeing was lost. At the trial of Ramzi Ahmed Yousef, it had been shown how easy it was to smuggle such weapons past airport security. But if it was a bomb, the device had to be considerably more powerful than the one used to destroy Pan Am flight 103 or one more strategically placed. That device had detonated in the cargo hold at 30,000 ft. Decompression had ripped the aircraft apart once the skin was ruptured. TWA flight 800 had not reached anything like this height when it was destroyed. A baggage bomb would not have had the same effect.

The FBI leaned to the theory that a bomb had destroyed the aircraft. Their difficulty was the failure of the initial investigation to identify the usual signs a bomb leaves on an aircraft and its structure whenever high explosives are detonated. Bomb signatures are created by the tremendous temperature and pressure generated by an explosion. The National Transportation Safety Board (NTSB) urged caution from the outset and looked for mechanical or structural failings as reasons for the disaster. The two agencies were to stay miles apart in their beliefs. Meanwhile the traveling public was in difficulty. If a Boeing 747, by reputation the safest aircraft in operation, was now suspect, what confidence could passengers have in flying?

Finally, the NTSB determined that the probable cause of the accident was an explosion of the aircraft's central fuel tank. The capacity offered by this storage area was not needed to carry fuel for the comparatively short transatlantic flight being undertaken by TW 800. The fuel carried in the wings was sufficient to take the aircraft to Paris. The central tank was left almost empty, but it did contain a flammable mixture of fuel and air. This, the NTSB believed, had ignited, but their inspectors were unable to say why. The abstract of their Aircraft Accident Report carried the notation that "the source of ignition energy for the explosion could not be determined with certainty, but, of the sources evaluated by the investigation, the most likely was a short circuit outside the CWT [central wing tank] that allowed excessive voltage to enter it through electrical wiring associated with the fuel quantity indication system." Not a very satisfactory conclusion given that many hundreds of Boeing 747s, including models identical to the crashed aircraft, were in daily operation around the world. Equally puzzling was the suggestion that after nearly three decades of B-747 operations, a fuel tank should have exploded now. The empty tank scenario must have been enacted many, many thousands of times since the inauguration of the marque.

The conclusion of the NTSB left many people in doubt. Few challenged their determination, but many were less than satisfied with the explanation of how a spark may have ignited the explosive vapor. Could the prognosis of both agencies have been correct? Could an improvised explosive device have been positioned adjacent to the central fuel tank, set to go off at a predetermined altitude or time? A device small enough to leave little or no trace, especially after the debris had been submerged in the Atlantic, but sufficient to have caused ignition? This would suggest an act of sabotage by someone with access to the aircraft during its time on the ground. This could have been during its turn-round in New York or at a previous stopover. The aircraft had flown to New York from Athens. FBI investigators were sent to the Greek capital, suggesting that someone in the Bureau considered such a scenario possible.

Adding to the belief that a bomb had destroyed TW 800 were media articles on both sides of the Atlantic suggesting an Islamic group had claimed responsibility for the destruction. In England, just days after the loss of the aircraft, the *Daily Mail* and the *Mail on Sunday* reported that a facsimile message warning of an attack against America had been received in the Washington and London offices of *al-Hayat,* a leading Arab newspaper. It was alleged to have been sent by a group calling itself "The Movement for Islamic Change." They had claimed responsibility for a car bomb that had exploded at a U.S. military base in Riyadh, Saudi Arabia, killing several people. Their professed goal was to obtain the withdrawal of all American troops from Saudi Arabia. The message had warned, "America will be surprised by the size of the attack, the place of the attack and the time of the attack. The attack will come tomorrow morning and tomorrow morning is soon." In Washington the message was passed to the FBI. In London, the *Mail on Sunday,* which passed the copy of the warning they had obtained on to Scotland Yard's anti-terrorist squad, believed the facsimile message bore similarities to earlier ones sent by organizations funded by Osama bin Laden. Bin Laden's movements were already being monitored by the intelligence services on both sides of the Atlantic.

A group based in Pakistan claimed responsibility for the destruction of TWA flight 800. They said it was attacked in retaliation for the arrest of Ramzi Ahmed Yousef, who was on trial in America at the time. Evidence presented during his trial showed that Islamic militants had developed sophisticated bomb-making techniques. They had rewired a digital wristwatch for use as a timer. The explosive charge was a stable form of nitroglycerin that, they had shown, could be smuggled through existing airport x-ray screening devices. The power source was two nine-volt batteries. The detonators were hidden in the terrorists' shoes! This was five years before Richard Reid allegedly tried to bomb the American Airlines flight from Paris to Miami using a device secreted in his sneakers. Interestingly, one of Yousef's co-accused, Abdul Hakim Murad, was a qualified airline pilot. Also shades of things to come? Yousef had links to the Afghanistan-based bin Laden.

A final conclusion has yet to be drawn on what caused the destruction of TW 800. Unless and until the NTSB can ascertain that the spark that ignited the central fuel tank was down to "natural" causes, the possibility of a terrorist being responsible must exist. As the intelligence services in the Western democracies learn more about the activities of the al-Qa'eda network, perhaps an answer will emerge. President George W. Bush addressed a joint session of Congress and the American people following the September 11th attacks and talked of thousands of al-Qa'eda terrorists existing in more than 60 countries. He said: "They are recruited from their own nations and neighborhoods and brought to camps in places like Afghanistan, where they are trained in the tactics of terror. They are sent back to their homes or sent to hide in countries around the world to plot evil and destruction." The president understood the strength of the menace facing Western democracies. Given that al-Qa'eda has existed for some years, it must be assumed that some of the thousands referred to by the president will have been in the United States in 1996. Could they have been behind the loss of TWA flight 800?

SWISSAIR FLIGHT 111

The crash of Swissair flight 111 off the coast of Nova Scotia on September 2, 1998, was very different to the loss of TWA flight 800. There was little controversy and no suggestion of terrorist activity.

The Swissair MD-11 jet, a three-engine aircraft manufactured by Boeing/McDonnell Douglas had taken off from Kennedy Airport at 8:18 P.M. local time heading for Geneva in Switzerland. It carried a crew of 14, and there were 215 passengers on board. The largest single nationality group was American. SR 111, operating under a code-sharing agreement with Delta Air Lines, had begun its journey in Chicago, stopping over in New York before beginning its transatlantic crossing. Of those on board, 53 were Delta passengers. At 10:14 local time, Captain Urs Zimmerman radioed Moncton air traffic control (ATC) to tell them he had detected smoke in the cockpit and requested an immediate return to a convenient airport. He assumed this would be Boston. The control center offered the captain Halifax as an alternative. The Canadian airport was just 70 miles away, and Boston was 300 miles distant. Captain Zimmerman accepted Halifax, and he was directed to begin his descent. At this point the crew donned their oxygen masks. A British Airways jet operating in the vicinity broke into the transmission and gave Swissair details of the weather in the Halifax region. The air traffic controllers cleared the aircraft to descend to 10,000 feet.

At 10:18 Halifax air traffic control made contact with the Swiss aircraft, telling it to descend farther to 3,000 ft; the captain responded saying he preferred to go to 8,000 ft while the cabin was prepared for landing. Zimmerman was told he could go to 3,000 ft at any time and that he would be set up for landing on runway zero-six at Halifax. The flight had 30 miles to go. At 10:21 the aircraft still had fuel to discard in preparation for landing. At 10:23, it was still at 10,000 ft. A minute later, according to the transcript of the conversation between air traffic control and the aircraft, a message from the cockpit said the aircraft was between 12,000 and 5,000 feet. The pilot declared an emergency. They had to land immediately. At 10:25 the SR 111 crew repeated they were declaring an emergency. Air traffic control acknowledged the call and confirmed permission to dump fuel. They asked for confirmation when this had been completed, but there was no further communication between the aircraft and the controllers. Six minutes later the aircraft plunged into the Atlantic off the coast of Nova Scotia near to the tourist hamlet of Peggy's Cove.

The Transportation Safety Board of Canada (TSB) began the lengthy process of investigating the causes of the crash. Two years later no definitive cause had been discovered. A final report was expected in 2002, but in July of that year the TSB announced it was delaying production until 2003.

As in all aircraft crashes, great efforts were made to recover the flight data and voice data recorders, the "black boxes." These were discovered early on in the process of recovering the victims of the disaster and the debris from the aircraft. When the Canadians had completed this process, some 98 percent of the wreckage had been recovered. The cockpit voice recorder had no data for the last six minutes of the flight, the same period the aircraft was out of touch with air traffic control before it dived into the sea. It had stopped at the same time the flight data recorder, the second black box, had ceased to function. Cockpit voice recorders run on a continuous loop recording the last 30 minutes of conversation or cockpit noise. In this instance, it seemed that the power source for both boxes had been interrupted six minutes before the crash occurred. Cockpit voice and flight data recorders are powered from an aircraft's electrical circuit. They do not have an independent supply, although they do contain batteries that power an emergency transmitter. This sends out signals to help searchers locate the recorders following a crash in water or in difficult terrain. The power loss and the missing six minutes were to lead to recommendations by the TSB for future equipment design and operation.

Just as with the wreckage of the Trans World Airways and Pan American World Airways B-747s, the investigators sought to rebuild the relevant parts of SR 111. From the transcript of the conversations between the pilot and air traffic control, they knew they had to concentrate on the cockpit and front end of the aircraft. They did so, but no evidence was found indicating what had caused the crash. However, during the investigation a number of pointers had become clear. The TSB had found that parts of the debris had shown damage consistent with a localized high heat source or fire. Melted aluminium, electrical wires with melted copper and charred or missing wire insulation, and smaller fragments that were discolored from heat exposure were also identified. All had come from the area either immediately in front of or directly behind the cockpit bulkhead.

Although no cause has been attributed to the fire that is believed to have caused SR 111 to crash, several factors were identified that led the TSB in Canada and the NTSB in the United States to issue safety directives. The insulation, used to protect the cockpit from outside cold when at high altitudes and to reduce engine noise, was ordered to be changed. The Federal Aviation Administration issued an air worthiness directive in May 2000 requiring that where used, Mylar insulation blankets (used on the Swiss aircraft) had to be replaced within four years. The blankets fell below the standard now being set for such items. The existing material had been found to ignite more easily than other substances available and actually assisted in spreading fire. Boeing had issued a service bulletin in October 1997 advising airlines to replace their Mylar-clad insulation blankets with those covered in Tedlar, the trade name for an upgraded material. Such bulletins are not compulsory instructions and contain no deadlines. They are not air worthiness directives. The aircraft operating SR flight 111 had had its periodic heavy maintenance in August, just before the manufacturer's advisory was received. Requirements identified in service bulletins are generally implemented during major maintenance on an aircraft. Swissair began replacing the insulation material in their aircraft with the Tedlar in 1999. They acted ahead of the FAA directive.

A question arises from the instruction to replace the original insulation blankets with new fire-resistant material. Had the Federal Aviation Administration acted immediately following the issuance of the service bulletin, converting it into a mandatory air worthiness directive, would the fire on board SR 111 have destroyed the aircraft? Delays between the issuance of air worthiness directives following the distribution of service bulletins had caused multiple deaths in the past. In 1974, a DC-10 of Turkish Airlines (THY) crashed on a flight from Paris to London. All 346 persons on board were killed. The aircraft was unusually full as a result of an ongoing strike by British European Airways (BEA), which had caused many English rugby football fans returning from an international game in France to transfer to the Turkish flight. A cargo door parting from the fuselage as the aircraft was climbing through 11,000 ft caused the crash. Subsequent investigation showed that the locking mechanism on the doors had not engaged properly. There was a serious fault in the design, and *this had been known before the THY aircraft crashed.*

In 1972, an American Airlines DC-10 on a flight from Detroit was climbing through 12,000 ft when its rear port-side cargo door blew off. On this occasion, the pilot was able to land the aircraft without mishap. No one was killed. Crash investigators were able to prove that a ground worker had failed to properly secure the cargo door before the aircraft's departure. In the THY incident, the damage caused to the aircraft was greater than that which had occurred to American Airlines. The elevator and rudder cables were damaged as well as the engine thrust levers. The aircraft dived into a forest, killing everyone on board. The aircraft had been airborne for only ten minutes. Following the crash, the federal authorities issued an air worthiness directive requiring modification to the cargo door locking mechanisms, but it was too late for the THY flight and its passengers. Had the agency acted with greater urgency following the earlier discovery of the design fault in the aircraft, the Turkish aircraft may not have been lost. Some airline managers pondered the competitive position between the manufacturers of the DC-10 and the European-based Airbus Industrie consortium, builders of the rival Airbus. They wondered if commercial considerations had affected FAA decision makers. The often-criticized closeness between the Federal Aviation Administration and the manufacturers was again under scrutiny. Concern for bottom-line figures in company accounts may have put air passengers and crews at risk.

As the SR 111 post-accident investigation progressed, suspicion had focused on the wiring of the in-flight entertainment system. A number of wires had been found to have shown signs of arc-tracking. A month after the accident, Swissair voluntarily disconnected the in-flight entertainment system on its MD-11 and Boeing 747 fleets.

During the currency of their investigations, the Canadian Transportation Safety Board recommended that cockpit voice and flight data recorders be given an independent power source and be made to provide up to two hours of recording time rather than the mandated 30 minutes. In December 2000, they followed this proposal with five safety recommendations:

Review the adequacy of in-flight fire fighting as a whole, to ensure that aircraft crews are provided with a system whose elements are complementary and optimized to provide the maximum probability of detecting and suppressing an in-flight fire.

Review the methodology for establishing designated fire zones within the pressurized portions of the aircraft with a view to providing improved detection and suppression capabilities.

Take action to ensure that the industry standards reflect a philosophy that, when odor/smoke from an unknown source appears in the aircraft, the most appropriate course of action is to prepare to land the aircraft expeditiously.

Ensure that emergency checklist procedures for the condition of "odor/smoke of unknown origin" are designed so as to be completed in a time frame that will minimize the possibility of an in-flight fire being ignited or sustained.

Review current in-flight fire fighting standards including procedures, training, equipment and accessibility to spaces such as attic areas to ensure that aircraft crews are prepared to respond immediately, effectively and in a coordinated manner to any in-flight fire.

Three inferences might be drawn from the Canadian recommendations. Had the Swissair pilot's response to the emergency he faced on board SR 111 been different, the aircraft may have been saved. The checklist procedures following first indications of the fire took too much time to complete. The failure to land the aircraft immediately after smoke had been detected had contributed to the crash. No one can know if application of the recommendations, had they been standard at the time of the emergency, would have saved the aircraft, but clearly, the TSB considered them relevant.

In the year following the crash of SR 111, it was reported that the Canadian government had spent $63 million on the investigation. The figure was expected to climb much higher before any final conclusions are reached.

EGYPTAIR FLIGHT 990

A year after the loss of Swissair flight 111, on October 31, 1999, an Egyptair Boeing-767 en route from New York to Cairo crashed into the sea off the coast of Nantucket Island, Massachusetts. The crash cost the lives of 217 people. Aviation commentators immediately looked to sabotage as the cause of the crash. No one claimed responsibility for such an action, but this was not seen as contradiction of a terrorist act. Professor Paul Wilkinson considered that the lack of credible claims after major outrages was not unusual. "It's now quite common for state-sponsored terrorists to try to disguise their involvement. The point of their action is not publicity but revenge or damage to confidence in the target country." His words, spoken in November 1999, would have great relevance two years later when al-Qa'eda launched attacks on America.

The U.S. National Transportation Safety Board undertook investigation into the loss of the Egyptair flight. Under the terms of the International Convention on Civil Aviation (more commonly known as the Chicago Convention), investigation of aircraft crashes in international waters is the responsibility of the country of registry, in this instance, Egypt. However, the authorities in Cairo asked the American NTSB to take on this role on their behalf. Several bodies supported the U.S. safety agency, including the Federal Aviation Administration, the FBI, and the U.S. Coast Guard. Boeing, Pratt and Whitney, the engine manufacturers, and Egyptair also participated. Participation of airlines and aircraft and component manufacturers in NTSB investigations had been criticized earlier by the Rand Corporation of Santa Monica, California. They had conducted a study under contract from the safety agency. Rand believed participation by such entities could compromise the independence of the NTSB. "The parties likely to be named to assist in the NTSB investigation . . . are also most likely to be named defendants in the civil litigation that inevitably follows a major accident." Rand had urged the agency to seek any additional expertise required from other government agencies, universities, or others without an economic interest in the outcome of the investigation.

A search-and-recovery operation was begun in the immediate aftermath of the accident. By December 21, the initial wreckage recovery had been completed. Following the pattern of earlier crashes, the debris was taken to a single location, on this occasion an aircraft hanger at a former naval base at Quonset Point in North Kingstown, Rhode Island. By the beginning of April 2000, approximately 90 percent of the wreckage had been recovered. Long before then, however, leaks from the investigation were already suggesting reasons for the crash.

The black boxes—the cockpit voice recorder (CVR) and the flight data recorder, as noted earlier—were found on the seabed early in the recovery process. The transcription of the CVR took some time because of the need to translate into English the Arabic spoken by the pilots. This was a cooperative effort using interpreters contracted by the NTSB, an FBI language specialist, English-speaking members of the Egyptian investigating team, and a State Department representative. The usual 16 hours taken to develop a 30-minute transcript extended in this instance to 130 hours. Despite the attention given to the translation work, differences arose between the various participants, even to the extent of whether one or more persons had been in the cockpit throughout the incident. There was no recording of a distress call. Neither had there been one when TW 800 was destroyed or when AA 587 was lost two years later.

Review of the cockpit voice recorder tapes provided nothing to suggest there had been an explosion on board. Analysis of the flight data recorder gave no indication of a mechanical problem. But as early as December 10, stories were reaching the media suggesting that for unstated reasons, a relief pilot on the aircraft, Gamil al-Batouti, allegedly alone in the cockpit at the time, had deliberately sent the aircraft to its destruction. General Mohammed Fahim Rayan, chairman of Egyptair, dismissed the claim as "stories and dreams." There were other angry outbursts from Egypt. There, commentators believed that American investigators, with a lack of understanding of the cultural and religious differences between the two countries, were being influenced by the ownership of the aircraft and the nationality of its pilots. The State Department became concerned at the damage being done to U.S.-Egyptian relations, which might harm U.S. policy in the Middle East. Secretary of State Madeleine Albright, speaking following a meeting with Egyptian president Hosni Mubarak in Sharm el-Sheik, Egypt, told reporters, "No one should rush to judgement or make inferences based on partial and inaccurate information." Early in January 2000, the NTSB chairman, James E. Hall, declared, "No hypothesis for the cause of the accident has been accepted." He confirmed, "There is much still needs to be done before a determination of cause can be reached." Eight months later, when the NTSB released a 1,664-page preliminary report of their investigation, Hall reiterated his position. He said, "Speaking for the NTSB, I want to make it perfectly clear that no determination as to the cause of this crash has been made." For Hall, the circumstances of the crash and the scope of the human tragedy had made the crash of flight 990 very difficult to investigate.

Official Egyptian sources and the country's media rejected any suggestion that al-Batouti had crashed the aircraft. Egypt declined to have the NTSB hand the investigation over to the FBI. Reports began to circulate about rifts arising between the safety experts and the FBI similar to the differences which had been identified during the TWA flight 800 investigation. Now the FBI was being held responsible for the stories that had pointed the finger of guilt at the relief pilot. Early reports that the cockpit voice recorder had al-Batouti saying, "I have made my decision now," inferring some bad action, were no longer being repeated. A government source in Washington put the erroneous quotation down to confusion among the investigators. In London, where the crash investigation had been closely monitored, the *Sunday Telegraph,* in its November 21 edition, reported that the NTSB chairman, had attacked "unidentified sources" for fueling rumors that were "just plain wrong." The following day, *Associated Press* quoted Hall as saying that speculation about words captured on the cockpit voice recorder had "done a disservice to the long-standing friendship between the people of the United States of America and Egypt."

In Egypt, the magazine *Al-Musawir* referred to the transcript of the tapes and claimed that at least two other pilots were in the cockpit with al-Batouti when things started going wrong. They quoted the pilot-in-command, Captain Mahmoud el-Habashy as saying, "Pull with me. Help me. Pull with me." The magazine did not believe that that suggested an argument between the captain and the relief pilot. Earlier leaks from the investigators had suggested that the captain had previously left the cockpit and had returned just as al-Batouti put the aircraft into its fatal descent. A second magazine added its opinion: *Rose el Yousef,* a well-regarded publication and Egypt's most widely read weekly, asserted that the captain had never left the flight deck. He had remained in the cockpit throughout the sequence leading to the crash. Noises said to have been made by the opening and closing of the flight deck door were simply the door, left open, a practice common with many airlines, slamming shut by gravity as the aircraft maneuverd. The article's author stated that the cockpit voice recorder showed none of the struggle suggested by the leaks. The *Rose el Yousef* feature reported that the captain and the relief pilot had been joking with the co-pilot, Adel Anwar, about the latter's forthcoming wedding. The magazine concluded that either there had been a problem with the elevator flaps or there was a problem with the thrust reverser, a braking mechanism used to stop the aircraft once it has landed.

American investigators concentrated on al-Batouti partly as a result of cross-referencing the flight data recorder information with the transcript taken from the cockpit voice recorder. *Rose el Yousef* reported that the investigators had focused on al-Batouti uttering a prayer, "Allahoma, Fawadt Amri ellaika ya rab." The magazine suggested this could roughly be translated as "God Almighty, I delegate my destiny to you." It is a phrase, the writer suggested, that some might use when facing death and knowing they are powerless. Other reports suggested he had spoken the words "Tawalkilt ala Allah." This, it was suggested, translated into "I put my faith in God" or " I entrust myself to God." The *New York Times* quoted the chief spokesperson for the Egyptian government, Nabil Osman. He said the words uttered on the tape were a Muslim prayer "said in a time of crisis when a person is facing a difficult situation." He added, the "prayer would never be said in terms of suicide." The former U.S. ambassador to Egypt, Frank Wisner, Jr., said the utterances attributed to al-Batouti were commonly used by Egyptians in everyday settings. An Egyptair pilot, Ali Murad, suggested that in an English-speaking culture, the relief pilot might have said, "Oh My God" or "Jesus Christ." Ibrahim Hooper, the national communications director of the Council on American-Islamic Relations, was quoted by the *New York Times* as saying, "There's an information gap when it comes to Islam and Muslims, and this gap is easily filled with ignorance. If the inference was by a Christian pilot who said 'God help me' we wouldn't even be having this conversation [about al-Batouti]." The same November 18 edition of the paper reported that work by the multifaceted translation team, referred to previously in this chapter, would begin that week. The leaks had preceded any collective translation activity.

The speed with which stories referring to the possible self-destruct action of the relief pilot began circulating was in marked contrast to the periods required to investigate earlier accidents. The study into the loss of TWA flight 800 in January 1996 had still not been completed when the Egyptair aircraft was lost. Final conclusions had still not been reached in respect of SR 111. Yet within weeks of the loss of flight 990, the suggestion that a pilot had caused the crash was in circulation. This was a remarkably quick conclusion, and many observers, certainly in Egypt, believed far too quick.

Study of the very advanced flight data recorder that had been fitted to the crashed Boeing suggested that the aircraft's autopilot had been switched off and that the plane had been put into a steep dive. Analysis also showed that both engines had been switched off before the aircraft briefly pulled out of its dive before plunging again toward the ocean. Installation of a flight deck video recorder would have clarified most, perhaps all, of the disputed facts. Given the pressure to use such equipment within the passenger areas of aircraft cabins, their installation is likely to be only a matter of time, but too late to clarify what occurred in the cockpit of flight 990.

There was no doubt that a pilot disconnected the autopilot and put the aircraft into a dive. The flight data recorder affirms this. Not known was why. *Associated Press* reported the comments of General Issam Ahmed, head of Egypt's flight-training program and formerly head of the Ministry of Transportation's plane accidents committee. He believed that something had gone wrong in the aircraft's tail, possibly an explosion. The general urged the Egyptian authorities to look closely at what had happened in the rear of the aircraft and not to let the United States impose a suicide scenario on them—the tail carried "the mystery of the accident." He believed the two pilots had acted correctly in turning off the autopilot and the engines in an attempt to control the plane. When subsequent to the loss of flight 990 an American Airlines aircraft crashed on takeoff from New York, immediate focus was given to the possible malfunctioning of the tail unit.

On August 11, 2000, the NTSB released their preliminary report on the loss of Egyptair flight 990. The preliminary findings drew no conclusions about the cause of the crash, but the final report, presented on March 21, 2002, did. It went into great detail on events that had occurred on the flight deck of Egyptair flight 990 and confirmed the very early intimations that al-Batouti was to blame for the accident. The report's conclusion was that the crash had resulted from "the relief first officer's flight control input." The reason for the man's actions was not determined. The Egyptian Civil Aviation Authority (ECAA) challenged the findings, claiming that American investigators had "failed to consider a credible body of evidence supporting multiple failures in the aircraft's elevator control system as the probable cause of the accident." The ECAA said it would appeal the findings.

AMERICAN AIRLINES FLIGHT 587

American Airlines flight 587, an Airbus A-300, departed New York's Kennedy Airport at 9:13 A.M. on November 12, 2001. It was heading for the Dominican Republic. The aircraft began a climbing turn over Jamaica Bay when it encountered turbulence caused by the wake vortices generated by a Japan Airlines 747 that had taken off just one minute forty-five seconds ahead of the American service. Records from the flight data recorder later recovered from the crash site showed that the turbulence had caused movements of flight 587's rudder, part of which, together with the vertical tail fin, became detached from the aircraft. Control of the aircraft was lost and it fell from the sky. During the aircraft's fall, the engines came away from the wings. The main body of the aircraft crashed into a residential area of Queens. The rudder and tail fin were found first along the flight path, followed by the engines and then the main wreckage. Two hundred sixty people on board, including the nine crew members, died. Five more were killed on the ground by debris falling from the aircraft.

As in other accidents, there were variations in eyewitness accounts. Some claimed to have seen fire or smoke coming from the aircraft before it crashed. Others, the majority, had not. Early examination of the debris did not show any indication of an on-board fire. There was talk of an explosion before the aircraft lost height and before it began to disintegrate. There was more talk of a second explosion before the aircraft became engulfed in flame. Video pictures, which were thought to show the aircraft in flight and after it had begun to fall, failed to give any clear indication of what had gone wrong.

The NTSB became responsible for the crash investigation. The board is charged with conducting investigations of all civil aviation accidents that occur in the United States. It is independent of the Department of Transportation and its associated agencies such as the Federal Aviation Administration. Like aviation safety bodies in other parts of the world, the Air Accidents Investigation Branch in the United Kingdom and the Bureau Enquêtes Accidents in France, for example, the NTSB maintains "Go Teams." These are groups of special investigators able to respond to a crash incident at a minute's notice. Following the loss of flight 587, a 40-strong Go Team under an investigator-in-charge was sent to the site of the crash. As usual, their work was supported by other agencies and companies considered appropriate by the board. The NTSB used the American Airlines facility at Tulsa for a detailed examination of the aircraft engines. No evidence was found of a fire, bird strike, or other pre-impact malfunction. The auxiliary power unit (used to power the aircraft when it is on the ground) was sent to Honeywell, its maker. Nothing wrong was found with the unit. The tail fin and rudder assemblies underwent visual inspection in New York before being sent to the NASA Langley Research Center in Hampton, Virginia. Extensive preliminary tests at Langley sought to identify whether the vertical stabilizer and rudder had had any damage or faults before the accident. None were found. Although the flight data recorder was to indicate significant rudder movement before the crash, there was nothing to show why this had happened.

Concentration on the rear of the aircraft was understandable. The tail assembly was believed to have separated from the fuselage before the aircraft fell from the sky. The vertical stabilizer and rudder had landed in Jamaica Bay, from where they were recovered. In April 1999, another American Airlines Airbus 300 had experienced problems with its rudder assembly. As it was approaching Miami, Florida, the aircraft experienced multiple rudder deflections. The captain landed the aircraft safely without injury to any passengers. Subsequent investigation showed that the autopilot's wiring had been cross-connected by the airline's maintenance personnel in Tulsa, Oklahoma. This had caused the problem. Airbus Industrie called on all operators of the marque to inspect their aircraft for wiring cross-connections. The Federal Aviation Administration and its French counterparts issued air worthiness directives formalizing the manufacturer's advisory communication.

Close cooperation between the NTSB and their French counterparts saw members of the investigative team fly to France to work with experts from Airbus Industrie, the aircraft's manufacturer, at their headquarters in Toulouse. The purpose of their visit was to study at firsthand the mechanism of the rudder system and to simulate the pattern of the aerodynamic loads that may have affected the vertical stabilizer during the failure of flight 587. No early resolution of their work was promised. Preliminary reports from NTSB accident studies generally take up to nine months to produce. Final reports, with or without conclusions, can take two years or more; thus the public cannot expect to learn the outcome of the study into the loss of AA 587 until well into 2004. Until then the crash will probably remain unexplained, a highly unsatisfactory situation for airline passengers. As in earlier investigations, there may never be a definitive answer.

From the outset, investigation into the loss of the American Airlines aircraft was conducted on the premise it was an accident. There was no immediate indication it was anything else, and officials were keen to reiterate that there was nothing to suggest any foul play had been involved in the loss of the aircraft. Coming so soon after the September 11th outrages, another terrorist assault in America would have been untenable. Congress had been active in developing new legislation to contain the threat al-Qa'eda posed to civil aviation operations. The president had declared war on terrorism. Another strike within such a short space of time would have suggested their measures had been inadequate, and the damage to the confidence of the American public would have been immense. Every possible accident scenario had to be explored no matter how implausible. Even pilot error had to be considered. The latest loss had to be the result of causes other than aggression by forces opposed to the United States.

Yet for the air transportation industry in general and the traveling public in particular, a one-off terrorist strike might be the preferable option. The Airbus was a popular marque in operation around the world. If there were an unknown fault in its construction, many thousands of passengers would be at risk every single day. The same unknown fault may affect other makes of aircraft. A one-off terrorist strike might be down to the failure of an individual or a system that could be put right with minimum delay. Either way the need to identify what had caused the loss of American Airlines flight 587 was urgent. Eleven months after the crash, a public hearing conducted by the NTSB confirmed that the investigation was still ongoing. More work was needed before a draft final report could be produced. On November 1, 2002 in a closing statement to the hearing, the board of inquiry's chairman, the Honorable Carol Carmody said that "Spring [2003] would be the earliest that we could expect to receive such a draft, and circumstances could delay that further."

One difficulty of equating the loss of AA 587 with terrorism was the manner of its destruction. If the tail assembly did lie at the root of the problem, then sabotage when the aircraft was on the ground appears a more likely scenario than a suitcase bomb or a suicidal passenger detonating a device on board the plane. A mechanic, or someone else with access to the aircraft, might have created a scenario that ended with the destruction of the aircraft. Congress had recognized the potential danger emanating from airport workers with criminal intentions. The Aviation and Transportation Act required background checks on persons with access to restricted areas. Aircraft on the ground at airports are in such areas. The al-Qa'eda terrorists had learned to fly. Others could have trained as mechanics or obtained more mundane jobs such as aircraft loaders or cleaners, both jobs giving them access to aircraft. Terrorism is not restricted to a suitcase bomb, a suicidal bomber, or a hijacker.

That both engines separated from the wings as the aircraft fell from a comparatively low height posed another question: Could the engines have been sabotaged, if not by an explosive device, then by some other means so far undetected by the NTSB investigators? Finding answers to these and any other questions associated with the loss of the aircraft remains the task of the NTSB. One thing is certain, if the investigators cannot identify a possible mechanical or structural reason for the accident, they will be left considering the impossible. They may not find any indication of a terrorist's hand in the loss of AA flight 587, but in the absence of any other reason for the crash, terrorism would be back in the frame.

None of the accidents discussed has had a truly satisfactory conclusion drawn as to cause. The Canadian investigation into the loss of the Swissair MD-11 has come closest, with faults found in the aircraft's wiring and with ineffective insulation as a contributory cause. This seems the most likely to pass unchallenged as an accident. Perhaps, as action by the Canadian Transportation Safety Board and the Federal Aviation Administration might suggest, an avoidable one. The jury has to remain out on TW 800. So too with Egyptair. If the finger of guilt pointed at the relief pilot did arise from a lack of understanding of the cultural differences between Americans and Egyptians, there are lessons to be learned here. If a fault with the aircraft's manufacture lies at the root of the trouble, this has to be identified. It is too soon to expect additional commentary on the loss of the AA 587. The NTSB's preliminary and final reports will be awaited with interest.

CHAPTER 8

The Lessons: Past and Present

"Terrorism directed against civil aviation will not go away!" These words, cited earlier in this book, are extracted from the 1989 Beaumont Memorial Lecture given before the Royal Aeronautical Society in London. They represented then, and do so today, the primary lesson everyone has to take on board. Events of September 11, 2001, have shown that terrorism is very much with us in the third millennium. It has not gone away. President George W. Bush in his first State of the Union Address emphasized this fact. He told Congress that "tens of thousands of trained terrorists are still at large." Effective defenses against those evil men who perpetrate horrendous acts of airborne terrorism must be put in place. This has to be done and seen to be done if the traveling public, especially the American traveling public, is ever to regain its confidence in flying. It is a big task, but if the lessons of the past are learned and acted upon, it can be achieved.

Commercial airline CEOs must recognize their responsibility for protecting the traveling public. Ostrich-like attitudes ignoring the basic facts of international political and cultural scenarios will leave airlines, and thus their customers, vulnerable. Following the shooting down of the Iranian Airbus in the Gulf by the warship the USS *Vincennes,* non-American airline security managers recognized that an attack on a U.S. airline, on the simple eye-for-an-eye philosophy of the Middle East, was just a matter of time. Yet executives from U.S. airlines could not accept this would be a consequence of the Iranian loss. They reasoned that as the destruction of the Airbus had been an accident, the result of the navy gunners' mistaking the airliner for a warplane, the Iranians had no reason to seek revenge. It was a naive attitude. Ignored was the fact that the two countries were on a war footing and that Iran would inevitably see the destruction of the Airbus as an act of aggression. Retribution was inevitable. Now, in retrospect, U.S. carriers may accept that this was an obvious scenario, but they should have foreseen it. Security programs should have been tightened to minimize the potential for a revenge attack. The loss of Pan Am flight 103 was a direct result of the *Vincennes* incident. There existed FAA programs that would have protected the passengers and crew of the aircraft. They were simply not in place.

Commercial airliners are always likely to be used by terrorists as surrogates for the government whose flag flies on the aircraft's tail. The Popular Front for the Liberation of Palestine (PFLP) was making a political statement when it destroyed the Swissair, BOAC, Pan Am, and TWA aircraft in 1970. When, in 1986, a group of Middle East origins claimed responsibility for the bomb that blew a hole in the side of the TWA B-727 as it approached Athens, they said they were hitting back at American arrogance toward Libya. On September 11th al-Qa'eda used commercial aircraft to attack its chosen targets. None of the carriers attacked or used by the terrorists had done anything to offend those responsible for the outrages. The lesson is simple: Airline operations have to be protected against the possible ravages of terrorists who harbor hatred against an aircraft's state of registry. Such men, as President Bush rightly said, "embrace tyranny and death as a cause and a creed."[17] Civilian targets are as acceptable to such people as military ones. They may even be preferred. It must be expected that the prime target for terrorists in the new century, as in earlier decades, will be the United States. U.S. airlines and airport managements must be prepared. Congress has begun the process with its Aviation and Transportation Security Act. It is up to the Federal Aviation Administration and the air company managements to implement the legislation. Doing so will take time but time could prove costly should terrorists strike again in the interim. As suggested in an earlier chapter, many critics believe Congress has fallen short in its legislation, and so U.S. domestic carriers should exceed the demands of the legislative body. They must consider the lessons offered by past events and guard against any repetition in the future.

Although American targets figure on top of the hit lists drawn up by al-Qa'eda and others terrorist groups, countries allied with the United States must monitor the threat they face from such people. The danger may well transfer itself from the North American continent to other parts of the world. An example of just this scenario being enacted was played out in October, 2002 when Islamic fundamentalists detonated an explosive device on the Indonesian island of Bali killing more than 180 people. Fortunately, existing aviation security programs in most industrialized countries already contain and in many instances exceed the provisions called for by the U.S. Congress. The danger such countries face is complacency. Years of terrorist inaction can lull states into a false sense of security. Having spent many millions of dollars, pounds, or even Euros on the latest hi-tech defenses to keep weapons and explosive ordnance off aircraft, airport authorities may be tempted to leave too much to the machines. The tiered approach used by British airports still requires a human element. Operators of such equipment must be professionally managed and tested to obviate complacency.

The airline companies as well as governments worldwide must maintain and monitor airline and airport security programs. Company programs have to meet government demands and match—but preferably exceed—the minimum standards specified by ICAO. In 1988, the Federal Aviation Administration did not realize that Pan Am had dropped key elements of the federally mandated air carrier standard security program (ACSSP). The carrier had abandoned passenger and baggage reconciliation, a requirement at airports the aviation authority deemed to be at "extra-ordinary" risk. Pan Am was using untrained staff to undertake key security functions. It had insufficient staff on duty to protect aircraft left unguarded on the ground for long spells. The carrier was also using outdated screening equipment. For the federal administration, the lesson from this dark period is clear: They must ensure that carriers coming under their jurisdiction meet the ACSSP demands. To achieve this object, the administration must employ qualified inspectors capable of undertaking such a task. At the time of Lockerbie, the FAA inspector responsible for monitoring Pan Am's security activity at Frankfurt was misled: The company's wholly owned guard agency duped him into believing they had more staff on duty than they actually did. He failed to recognize that key elements of the ACSSP had been dropped, nor did he see that unsuitable staff members were filling the posts of security screeners.

The Aviation and Transportation Security Act has now given the Federal Aviation Administration the task of managing the line function of security screening at U.S. airports. Since FAA inspectors were already charged with monitoring this activity, they now have the added responsibility of inspecting themselves. Time will tell whether Congress has erred in handing this double function to a single agency. Should it prove to be so, then delegation of the screening function to the airport company would be a viable alternative. The federal authority would set the standards, and airport managements would be charged with meeting them. This would be a far better arrangement than that which existed before the Aviation and Transportation Security Act was passed. At that time the airlines were responsible for passenger and baggage screening, and they considered cost a significant factor. September 11th showed the system did not work.

The first time the world witnessed unlawful interference with civil aviation was in the early 1930s. A Peruvian aircraft on a domestic flight was hijacked and used to drop political leaflets to a surprised populace. There were to be no more aircraft seizures until the cessation of hostilities at the end of World War II. Then the division of spoils by the victorious allies left Europe divided. The Iron Curtain separated East from West. People young and old, as singles and in family groups, sought to escape from Eastern Europe to the West. Many in search of political asylum in the West hijacked aircraft as a means of escaping Communist control. The Western European governments were sympathetic, but later, people with different motives saw the ease with which aircraft could be seized. They realized aircraft could be used as a way to further their causes; thus from the 1960s, airlines have had to protect their operations from terrorists. British European Airways (with BOAC the founding partner of today's British Airways) conducted operations throughout Europe and so considered its aircraft vulnerable to hijackers. Airlines officials identified key locations and sent security officers and passenger service specialists to such places to close doors to those intent on seizing aircraft. They introduced passenger and hand baggage security screening. They had heeded the early lessons of the political refugee aircraft seizures—namely, that security in the air begins on the ground and that weapons must be kept off aircraft.

Many of the early lessons drawn from terrorist incidents were discussed in New Delhi in 1986 when an Indian High Court Inquiry considered the loss of Air India's *Kanishka,* the 747 bombed over the Atlantic the previous year. The aircraft had been destroyed when an improvised explosive device, hidden in an unaccompanied suitcase transferred from a Canadian domestic flight at Toronto, detonated in the cargo hold. Presiding judge Mr. Justice B. V. Kirpal developed recommendations for governments and the aviation companies from the testimony considered during the hearings. Not surprisingly, given the circumstances of the *Kanishka*'s loss, he focused on the danger of unaccompanied bags. He asked for "the baggage of interlined passengers to be matched with the passengers by the onward carriers before loading the baggage on the aircraft." He wanted all checked baggage, whether it had been screened by x-ray machine or not, to "be personally matched and identified with the passengers boarding an aircraft." Any baggage not so identified had to be off-loaded. The judge recognized the limitations of x-ray screening of checked baggage in 1986 and knew the lengths to which some people had gone to hide explosives in radios and other such items. He knew too that plastic explosives could be given an innocuous shape or form to avoid detection by a x-ray examination. Over-reliance on x-ray screening had to be avoided.

Concurrent with the Court of Inquiry sittings, ICAO too had considered what lessons could be learned from past terrorist incidents. The action taken by the world body following intensive review in Montreal led to a complete rewrite of Annex 17. Past incidents were used to develop strategies allowing effective defenses against acts of unlawful interference to be mounted. The work of the ICAO specialists, drawn from countries round the world and from key international bodies, including IATA, IFALPA, and the Airports Association Coordinating Council (AACC), was sufficiently pertinent to the problems posed by international terrorism that with the minimum of refining they are as relevant today as they were when first developed. This notion was endorsed during the preparatory work for the 2002 ICAO high-level ministerial meeting. Text of Annex 17 was revised and reorganized, but the basics remained unchanged. The Annex, built on a foundation of lessons learned in the previous decades, has stood the test of time. The specialists in 1986 had done their work well. The same can be said of those legal giants who penned the Tokyo, Hague, and Montreal conventions one and two decades earlier. Nothing had happened between the mid-1980s and the turn of the century to negate the earlier work The traumatic events of September 11th might well have been contained had effective passenger and hand baggage screening been in place at U.S. domestic air terminals. This had been an international security requirement for decades; indeed, it had been the first introduction in the fight against terrorism directed at civil aviation targets.

A lesson that too few administrations have learned is that rules and regulations, no matter how good they may be in principle, are ineffective unless implemented. The bitter example learned from the al-Qa'eda attacks was that screening operations at airports in the United States in 2001 were unacceptably poor. Congress focused on the ownership of security screeners at airports and on their recruitment and training. The legislators also proposed an expansion of the sky marshal program. The legislators intended that standards be raised sufficiently to prevent another series of tragedies such as those witnessed in New York, Washington, and Pennsylvania. The Federal Aviation Administration will have to decide how the program is to be managed. Research of passenger and hand baggage screening led ICAO to develop their recommendations for five-person teams. It will be interesting to see how the federal agency implements its new charge. Passengers will be able to monitor their performance for themselves.

To be effective, a security program, whether for an airport or an airline, has to be a mix of several elements. Good airport access control is essential. Only people authorized to enter sterile or restricted areas can be allowed to do so. As airports grow in size, so the methods of access control may need to become more sophisticated. At locations with just a handful of flights and where labor costs are low, this may be achieved by a guard force without the support of hi-tech machinery. At airports such as those in London, New York, Chicago, and Singapore, use might be made of biometric identification to reduce the reliance on human resources and to lessen the possibility of unlawful intrusion. As this text was being prepared, tests using biometric control for passenger clearance were underway, but the potential for using such systems worldwide is small. Most developing countries have still to adopt machine-readable passports, a 1980s development. Cost and lack of technical management have been major deterrents. In the industrialized West, where labor costs are high, machines reduce the outlay on staff wages. Elsewhere, where labor is cheap and money in short supply, administrators prefer employees to hi-tech machinery. Providing the staff are well chosen, well trained, and properly managed, this need not reduce the level of security.

Airlines have learned that a front line of defense at an airport is the check-in desk. Here, staff have shown an ability to sense behavior patterns that separate a potential risk passenger from the millions of law-abiding people who use air transportation every day. This has worked well for airlines in uncovering ticket and travel document fraud. What at first consideration may seem a daunting task has been less so in practice as has been proved, not least in the case of Richard Reid. It is at the check-in counter that the security questions are asked. The responses can help the agents assess the person standing before them.

At most international airports, the next security element travelers are likely to encounter after leaving the check-in counter will be passenger and hand baggage screening—a vital procedure in ensuring the security of aircraft. Until September 11th, screening was a procedure that was to all intents and purposes missing from the domestic scene in the United States. It is now a centerpiece of attention following the adoption of the Aviation and Transportation Safety Act. At most major international airports outside of America, somewhere in the baggage-handling system, hi-tech machines are being used to screen hold baggage. Congress has allocated funds to ensure that similar systems are introduced at U.S. airports. Their target is completion by the end of 2002. (This timescale may slip for the reasons given chapter 3, Governments Response to Air Terrorism.) At some airports, checked baggage is screened in the passengers' presence. At others, the procedure takes place deep in the bowels of the terminal building. Wherever it takes place, the screening will require a facility where passengers and doubtful bags can be brought together if bags have to be opened to identify items causing concern.

Access control applies inside airport terminal buildings as well as at the perimeter. Entry to sterile departure lounges has to be guarded, but the nature of the lounge makes this security element nonintrusive. Airport security management must ensure there is no uncontrolled entry or mixing of incoming, possibly inadequately screened passengers and those about to board outbound flights. New airport designs incorporate this physical separation into their blueprints. Older airports may employ a guard presence or even security screening for arriving passengers. The important lesson from past incidents is that "sterile" must indeed mean "sterile." An incoming passenger arriving from an insecure airport must not be allowed to pass weapons to a colleague already security screened and about to depart for a new destination.

Brussels International Airport had a problem with its original airport design. Incoming passengers did mix with departing ones, and at the time, Sabena, then the national carrier of Belgium, flew into Brussels from a number of African locations where security was known to be poor. The authorities decided to bus arriving aircraft passengers to a gate entry point where they could be screened before entering the main body of the airport. It was a brave decision because liberal thinkers saw the action as racist. It was also the correct decision because it eliminated the risk that a terrorist might hand over weapons to previously cleared passengers. In 1980, Switzerland created its own problem. At Geneva, there was no passenger mixing because security had been positioned at the gate lounge. Each lounge, housed at the end of a pier, served a number of departing aircraft, and so it was economic as well as customer-friendly to locate there a small newsstand and souvenir shop selling mementos. Among the items on sale were Swiss Army knives, considered memorable souvenirs of Switzerland. They sold well. But these can be deadly weapons. The Swiss argued that the knives were small with blades under 4 inches in length. But the blades were big enough and sharp enough, to inflict considerable damage, even to kill. Commercialism, sheer bottom-line profit, had got the better of the pragmatic Swiss.

A maxim that should have been learned very early in the growth of airborne terrorism is that passenger security on an aircraft depended largely on screening procedures undertaken on the ground. Yet the work of the ground-based staff can be undermined by the airlines themselves once an aircraft becomes airborne. Until very recently, passengers stripped of sharp objects, even in Switzerland, were handed replacement weapons in the shape of metal cutlery to use with their meals. Since September 11th, many airlines have exchanged metal knives and in some instance metal forks, for plastic ones, considered a less potential hazard. A customer service problem has arisen with this exchange, for no one has amended the menus. Steaks (on some carriers), chicken (more usual), or other meals requiring cutting are now often beyond the passengers' ingenuity to manage. Airline security chiefs and their company's chefs should get together. It cannot be beyond their ability to design menus that do not have constituents that require cutting. By now perhaps some airlines will have acted on this customer difficulty. If so, perhaps they will have considered another potential danger: Although many carriers were removing metal knives from aircraft cabins, drinks, especially wine, were still being served from bottles and drunk from glasses; these can make deadly weapons and are probably more to be feared than a blunt table knife. Security managers must think their programs through. Half-hearted gestures do not make for good security.

Lessons can, indeed should, be learned from incidents at major airports in the developed West as well as in the developing world. In 1983, a bullion robbery at London's Heathrow netted the criminals who carried out the raid £23 million (U.S. $32 million). By February 2002, this example of thieves' ingenuity had been forgotten. Nineteen years had passed and most of those affected by the great bullion robbery, as the media named it, had retired or had been replaced. The lessons they may have learned could not have been passed on since another audacious robbery was successfully mounted. This time, thieves waited for a shipment of U.S. $6 million in used bills to be unloaded and placed in an unprotected British Airways delivery van, then ambushed the lone driver and escaped with the money. This robbery had sinister possibilities.

For such a theft to have taken place, the men who hijacked the delivery vehicle had to have had prior knowledge of the shipment. Information could have been relayed from somewhere within the consignor's organization in Bahrain, from where the shipment had come or within the airline operation at the Gulf airport. Alternatively, the necessary arrival details could have been passed to the thieves from within the British Airways cargo operation at Heathrow or from U.K. customs. The latter receive data concerning incoming deliveries in advance of their arrival. Airlines send details of shipments to customs authorities by means of an electronic data interchange (EDI). This international facilitation arrangement, agreed by IATA and the Customs Cooperation Council, is intended to achieve a rapid clearance of consignments on arrival. Goods can be cleared while they are still in the air. The men who hijacked the money had had time to steal or prepare a vehicle in British Airways livery and obtain the airport security passes necessary to gain access to the controlled zone where the robbery had taken place.

The sinister potential of the robbery arises because the men who held up the driver of the original delivery van were described as Asian and the shipment had come from the Middle East. Lateral thinking suggests a possible al-Qa'eda hand in the theft. With the United States leading the way, restrictions had been placed on Osama bin Laden's assets and on the funds of his associated terrorist groups following the attacks on the World Trade Center and the Pentagon in the previous September. If these militants were growing short of money, their natural reaction would have been to look for other sources of income. Other terrorist organizations had robbed banks in the past and even traded in drugs to fund their operations. Taking money from British Airways might have been seen to be an easier option, as easy as taking candy from a baby. In practice, it clearly was.

Why al-Qa'eda? It must be assumed that Bahrain and its neighboring states, like the West, have their share of bin Laden's devotees. Bin Laden was born in Saudi Arabia just across the causeway from Bahrain. The United Kingdom is known to have cells and recruitment agents for his organization—U.K. recruits languishing in Guantánamo Bay and in a Boston jail at the time of the robbery were proof of this. Securing support for a currency robbery in England to finance the al-Qa'eda cause would not have been difficult. It would have required an intricate conspiracy involving a network of agents, but bin Laden's followers had shown themselves to be capable of such detailed planning.

The lesson that should have been taken on board decades earlier and must now surely feature high on all airline and airport managements' lists of priorities is that no place is secure against terrorists unless an effective, properly managed security program is in place. Airport managements have to ensure that access controls, including the correct use of identity documents (IDs) issued to staff and vehicles are enforced. The British Airways robbery may well hasten the introduction of biometric controls (fingerprint identification, retina and voice recognition) to safeguard entry to restricted areas. Doing so would overcome the potential for stolen or loaned IDs to be used for criminal purposes. In the meantime, where visual matching of ID cards with their owners is employed, those responsible for the process must be adequately supervised to ensure compliance with the rules.

There had been earlier examples of criminals using techniques comparable to those employed at Heathrow to physically attack aircraft. As described in chapter 4, Practical Airport Security, in the Pan Am assault in Karachi, terrorists had dressed themselves to resemble airport guards and had obtained a vehicle similar to those used by the airport authority. The attack on Pan Am could have been prevented or at least delayed, allowing security forces time to react. The gate guards had only to stop the vehicle carrying the terrorists to examine their security identification badges. Doubtless the perpetrators were well aware of the practice of simply waving vehicles through without even a casual glance at the IDs. Similar scenes can be witnessed in the developed countries, especially on rainy days at motor vehicle entry points. Access control guards prefer the warmth of a dry cabin rather than the discomfort of standing in the wet to check identifications. A method akin to the Karachi attack was witnessed again in 1994 when terrorists opposed to the Algerian regime seized an Air France aircraft at Algiers airport. Lessons must be learned and acted upon if aircraft security is to be maximized. Terrorists identify and exploit weaknesses in airport and airline security programs.

Wherever the system failed allowing British Airways to be robbed, it did so again at Heathrow just a few weeks later. On March 19, a second delivery of U.S. banknotes, this time valued at U.S. $3 million, arrived at the airport's Terminal No. 1 on an overnight South African Airways (SAA) service from Johannesburg. It was transferred to a security van, again driven by a solitary driver. Once more, it was two young Asian men who were reported to have ambushed the van. The similarity to the British Airways robbery was startling. However, this time the men hijacked the security vehicle itself and according to the driver, forced him at knifepoint to drive it out of the airport to where a getaway vehicle was parked. Once again the robbers had to have had advanced knowledge of the shipment. The source of the information could have been accomplices in Johannesburg, but given that a different airline had carried the money, attention focused, not surprisingly, on possible sources nearer to Heathrow.

Just as with the British Airways robbery, the South African Airways theft had taken place in a restricted, customs controlled area of an airport claiming and believed to be one of the most secure in the world. The thieves had gained access through the airport's security checkpoints, suggesting that they had either valid or very good counterfeit IDs. They were clearly familiar with the layout of the airport and its procedures. Everything pointed to insider information. Police investigators had to ascertain if the two incidents represented a double breach of the security operation at Heathrow, with fake or stolen IDs being used to fool the security guards at the access control point, or alternatively, whether the robbers were legitimate employees at the airport who used their right to be airside with such criminal success. Either way, the two robberies showed that people with criminal intent could access vulnerable areas of the airport unchallenged, posing a significant threat to airline operations. If goods could be hijacked from within a security sterile zone and taken out of the airport, other items could be smuggled in just as effectively. If those items were improvised explosive devices or weapons, all carriers operating from Heathrow would be at risk.

The cargo and security managements within the two airlines involved in the Heathrow robberies were clearly at fault. Their presumably routine performance was totally inadequate. British Airways had been caught unawares, although there had been precedents. South African Airways had had the opportunity to learn an important lesson anew only a few short weeks earlier, but their management had let the lesson pass unheeded. A professional, well-managed cargo-handling team working to predetermined guidelines and applying basic security controls could and should have made both robberies impossible.

Most airline security manuals contain detailed chapters covering the handling of high-value cargo shipments. These documents should require all personnel assigned to handle such shipments to be supervised. Unloading of aircraft, normally a function of baggage and freight handlers, has to be overseen by a cargo services supervisor when high-value goods are involved, and all movements of such cargo have to be escorted. Another requirement is that no unauthorized person be allowed access to the area where handling of high-value cargo is taking place or where such cargo is stored. Security patrols have to be mounted. Few of these provisions could have been in force at Heathrow when either robbery took place. Complacency appears to have been the norm. This has a familiar ring. The great worry generated by the double robberies was the possibility that the same lax attitude prevalent in the cargo-handling area had filtered through to other security activities at Heathrow. The airport had witnessed an expenditure of many tens of millions of pounds on upgrading passenger and baggage screening. Its standards in these areas are recognized to be among the best in the world. Of concern was the possibility that the human element in the screening process might be suffering from the same complacency evident in the British Airways and South African Airways cargo operations and in the airport's access control. If so, standards for personnel would be falling short of the standards set for machines. By the time this volume is published, whatever deficiencies allowed so much money to be stolen at the beginning of 2002 may well have been put right and any cross-contamination with other areas of security performance at the airport, if it existed, may have been eradicated.

The circumstances of the British Airways and South African Airways robberies caused the U.K. secretary of state for transport and the home secretary to commission a report on airport security. It was prepared by Sir John Wheeler. Dated September 13, 2002, it noted that "The Department [of Transport] is clear that its responsibilities do not include consideration of the threat at airports from serious and organised crime." The theft of U.S. $9 million clearly falls in this category of felony and while the DoT may believe it is not their responsibility, those who carried out the robberies twice defeated the security controls at Heathrow. As the report states, the DoT "is at the heart of the arrangements for aviation security," thus the breaches have to be a matter of direct concern to the department. It has to ensure that a coordinated response to the security failures is prepared and put in place. For the skies to be safe, Heathrow has to set and achieve high security performance standards. So too must other airports around the world, having taken notice and allowed the lessons learned from the double robberies to be applied at their facilities.

That a copycat crime should have been so expertly performed at the same airport within so short a time defies belief. The two robberies were almost romantic in their conception and execution. However, the consequences could be traumatic. If any of the stolen money is intended to fund terrorist activities, a great many people will be made to suffer from the security lapses at Heathrow. The lessons provided by the thefts must be taken on board by all airlines, everywhere. Care must be taken to ensure that an "it cannot happen to us" mentality does not take hold. This mentality leads to incompetence, laziness, poor threat assessment, inadequate training, and downright bad management. If it can occur in London, it can just as easily arise in New York or Boston. The U.S. Aviation and Transportation Security Act has mandated that background security checks must be undertaken of all individuals seeking to become airport security screeners. The same rule applies at London. This book has emphasized that similar checks should be conducted on anyone with access to sensitive areas of an airport. The protests of human rights activists who believe that such checks impinge on people's freedom must be put aside if maximum security is to be achieved at international and national aviation gateways.

Other lessons pertaining to security of aircraft while on the ground have been learned the hard way. A bomb destroyed a Lockheed 1011 aircraft belonging to Air Lanka, the national airline of Sri Lanka, while it was being prepared for departure from Colombo Airport. The explosion blew the aircraft in two. When the incident took place, 128 passengers were in the process of boarding the aircraft. Of these passengers, some 20 died. A customs officer with access to the aircraft's supplies and sympathetic to the Tamil separatist movement was arrested and charged with the sabotage. He had placed the explosive device in the aircraft's "fly-away" kit, a collection of essential technical items carried on each aircraft to facilitate emergency maintenance at overseas airports.

Access control at airports has to apply to every aspect of an airline's operation. It has to be in place at off-airport locations if the result of the activity being undertaken there impinges on a flight operation. For example, meals and catering supplies are often prepared away from the airport and transported by vehicles to a departing flight. Security applied at the airport must be repeated at such off-airport facilities and delivery vehicles guarded during their passage to the aircraft. The vehicles should be screened before being allowed to enter restricted areas of an airport. The better catering establishments have security guards and procedures in place already to ensure that no weapons or other illegal objects can get to an aircraft via a catering delivery. Attempts to do so have been made in the past. Similar efforts have been made to infiltrate engineering spares, as detailed earlier. It is a lesson learned with human lives.

Security policies in place today have been developed from incidents that have taken place in the past. The activity resulting from the deliberations in the U.S. Congress is proof of this. The learning process has often been long and hard and frequently littered with human lives, yet there are some who are reluctant to heed these lessons. Review of past incidents is vital if aviation security is to close the door to terrorists. But the task in this millennium must be for security executives to be proactive rather than reactive. For this to happen, the right people have to be employed to direct the security functions within airlines, at airports, and within governments. Security directors, whether within an airline or with an airport company, must meet the needs of the task delegated to them. Good aviation security depends on the caliber, the knowledge, and the experience of the personnel selected to manage the function.

The U.S. Congress has specified standards that security screeners at American airports now have to meet. They have stopped short of making recommendations for managers. In the past, airlines have had a tendency in some parts of the world to recruit retired police officers for the role of security director. It is an easy option. In the early days of airline security operations when protection of property was uppermost in managements' minds, this worked well. This does not necessarily bring success against the international terrorist. The skills essential for a successful airline director of security may not be found in a person whose experience has been confined within the parameters of a city or even a national or federal police force. Airline security directors should have experience and understanding of world geography and politics. They would benefit from personal exposure to a range of cultures. They need an understanding of people alien to their own environment. Most important, anyone heading an airline security department should have a deep understanding of airline and airport operations in order to translate security needs into effective carrier procedures. An airline is a commercial entity whose purpose is to make a profit for its shareholders. A balance has to be struck, one that ensures the security of the company's customers while satisfying the expectation of its owners. Security cannot be sacrificed to satisfy the accountant. A security director with an intimate knowledge of the carriers' operation is best able to plot the line that should be followed if everyone is to be satisfied.

Given that competence in risk analysis and an ability to identify cost-benefit potentials are musts for any successful executive, it would be an advantage for security managers to have a background in a numerate science. In the future, an airline director of security is as likely to have earned a master's degree in business management as to have had a career with a police force. Some European airlines have drawn their heads of security from within their own corporate structure, but with disparate backgrounds ranging from engineering, through airline operations management at an airport, to the legal profession. The best airline security is likely to be obtained when a balance of skills is available within the department. A broad appreciation of a company's operations may well explain why European support for procedures such a positive bag match was quickly forthcoming in 1985. It helped the major European airlines avoid traumas such as Lockerbie.

Hindsight is a great blessing. History provides an opportunity for turning hindsight into foresight. Hands-on experience gained in a variety of countries helps in the development of security defenses. All security executives should have this experience and be avid students of what has gone on before. It will help them predict and prevent incidents occurring in the future. It will also go a long way to making the skies safer for passengers and crews and for people on the ground. Security managers must always be open to innovative ideas and be unafraid to experiment in the interest of passenger security. The loss of Egyptair flight 990 led to discussion on installation of cockpit video recorders. Full understanding of that crash has still to be reached, but a video recording would have clarified most, perhaps all, of the questions surrounding events on the flight deck prior to its destruction. Perhaps a camera giving the captain a perspective on what is happening immediately outside the flight deck door would be beneficial. The use of passenger cabin video recorders has been debated for some time. Are there lessons to be learned here from the immediate past? Constant review of changing environments is always of value even if the conclusion drawn suggests there is nothing to be done.

Airport security directors with a responsibility for a fixed location have a different set of requirements. Here the advantages of a police or law enforcement background may well come to the fore. Even so, a sound knowledge of airline operations would clearly facilitate the task at hand. Unlike their airline counterparts, they will not have to worry about a myriad of national requirements that will differ from airport to airport. They will not have to negotiate with government authorities, sometimes seemingly unfriendly to foreign carriers. Nor will they have to massage their own companies' security programs into the requirements of a state whose ideas and culture may be alien to them. They will have to accommodate the needs of foreign air companies and understand the different behavior patterns of the various nationalities likely to use their facilities, but the only regulations of direct concern will be those of their own government.

It has been shown that measures developed in international forums with the benefit of multinational input, experience, and debate may be highly pertinent to domestic operations. Terrorists do not recognize national boundaries other than to identify security weaknesses that may exist beyond them. They cross borders to train in a variety of countries. Libya hosted training camps in the 1980s and early 1990s. Afghanistan succeeded the North African location. Civil aviation authorities and commercial managements should surely follow the example of the terrorist organizations: Senior security personnel from airlines and airports must be equally mobile. They should participate fully in their industry meetings, where they can exchange experiences and contribute to the development of new policies. It may well be that had Pan Am been in at the birth of positive bag match, the airline may have embraced its intent rather than fought against the policy with such dire results.

President George W. Bush believes the many thousands of al-Qa'eda–trained terrorists that exist are scattered around the world. Some are known to have based themselves in the United States. Jointly developed international programs to protect aviation against international terrorists will have great relevance to domestic operations, especially since U.S.-based terrorists have already recognized variations between standards applied to international operations from the United States and those pertaining to domestic flights. If the president is right and al-Qa'eda and others pose a threat within the United States, they will continue to seek out the weakest link in order to reach their objective. They may make repeated use of modus operandi that have worked for them in the past, but as the world witnessed in 2001, they are capable of using new, untried methods when this suits their goals. It must be expected that this new breed of militant whose objective Professor Paul Wilkinson identified as "revenge or damage to confidence in the target country," rather than publicity, will continue to be innovative. Security directors and government administrators must stay ahead of their enemy. They must act preemptively if the skies are ever to be made as safe as they should be.

It cannot be emphasized enough that commercial priorities, namely bottom-line figures in the company accounts, must not be allowed to override security requirements. This has application in the field of safety as well as security. Had the cost bullet been bitten when McDonnell Douglas first knew they had a problem with the cargo door on the DC-10, Turkish Airlines would not have lost its aircraft outside Paris. Had a change in the quality of insulation blankets on the MD-11 aircraft been ordered immediately when the current blankets were recognized as no longer adequate, SR 111 may not have been lost. Victoria Cummock's assertion that "history has proven the aviation industry's lack of sincerity and willingness to address safety and security on behalf of their customers" is documented fact. It must not be allowed to apply to aviation in the twenty-first century.

Other lessons have to be heeded by governments. They develop national and federal regulations and are responsible for ensuring that air companies implement them. Just as airlines and airport managements must pay attention to the individuals they hire as security managers, so too must governments ensure that the civil servants they use for monitoring civil aviation security are competent and sufficiently knowledgeable to perform their allocated function. How qualified were the personnel in the United Kingdom who devised rules telling airlines to put potential explosive devices in the holds of aircraft? How knowledgeable were those same people when they briefed successive ministers wrongly, providing them with inaccurate facts? Had any of the Department of Transport civil servants in the 1990s bothered to read the security circulars distributed by their forerunners, perhaps even by themselves, in the 1980s? How qualified was the FAA inspector who allowed the Pan Am performance at Frankfurt to go largely unremarked and who had not noticed that the company had dropped elements of a federally mandated program? A mix of the qualifications suggested for airline and airport security directors would surely not be amiss in civil servants working in the aviation security field.

The U.S. Congress gave the aviation administration additional functions following September 11th. The FAA administrator must now ensure that he has the right staff in the right places to perform in the best interests of the American people. The agency's success will spill over into the international arena, but for this to happen, the administrator has to have vision. He or she could do worse than study the lessons from Knut Hammarskjold's tenure as director general at IATA.

Hammarskjold knew the weaknesses in governments' application of effective security defenses against international terrorism. He knew his member carriers were vulnerable in many parts of the world, and he sought to have his own specialists eliminate security deficiencies wherever they existed. Because he knew that certain administrations would be unable to manage unlawful interference incidents, he persuaded the world's airlines to endorse a policy of post-incident activity. They agreed that "during and/or after actual incidents of air piracy," the association would "through the Director General intervene, as necessary, with individual states when such states fail to apply the conditions of the Conventions and where IATA involvement may result in a faster resolution of the situation." Airlines were to do the job of governments in their own interests and those of their customers. He understood why governments failed to act or why they acted incompetently following the hijacking incidents of the 1960s, 1970s, and early 1980s. Such a direction gained from the airline CEOs was highly innovative. It allowed IATA to establish teams of specialists to investigate incidents on-site following acts of unlawful interference. The teams determined where and how security breaches had occurred and identified lessons to be learned and applied in the future, and not just at the location where the incident had taken place but elsewhere on the commercial airlines' network.

Perhaps the boldest of IATA's proposals in the general field of airborne terrorism came after Hammarskjold retired. Drawing on the lessons from past incidents when hijackers had been provided with safe havens and allowed to go unpunished, the association outlined a plan to internationalize the response to acts of unlawful interference. President Bush did just this following the September 11th attacks, but on a much grander scale. He put together an international coalition led by America to mount a dramatic response to the ravages of al-Qa'eda. In 1988 IATA was looking to respond to hijackings. *The Times* carried a story on IATA's ideas during the currency of the Kuwait Airlines seizure.

> The world's airlines are to press for the creation of an international force to take control of any future hijack and for hijackers to be tried by a new international court (Harvey Elliot writes). Mr. Rodney Wallis, Director of Security for the International Air Transport Association, said last night that he would press for the force to be introduced at a meeting of the International Civil Aviation Organization in June.

The proposal was carried in greater detail in the *Financial Times.* It also featured on the leading BBC television journal *Newsnight* later that same week. The idea was initiated by the continued failure of smaller countries to honor their obligations under ICAO's conventions. The airlines had learned their lesson. Unless some organization, such as ICAO or its parent body, the United Nations, assumed responsibility when attacks against civil aviation targets occurred in territories smaller or less developed than the industrialized West, terrorism in its existing form would continue. The terrorists would know they could get away with their crimes. To prevent this happening, IATA proposed a five-point program:

The establishment of an international advisory group which would be immediately available to support governments when a hijacking occurs.

The establishment of an international team of experts who are qualified by practical experience to investigate acts of unlawful interference after the event, firstly to identify how the incident occurred and secondly, to recommend methods to prevent repetition, either at the airport where the security evasion occurred or at any other airport.

The establishment of an international force working in conjunction with the international advisory group and which would be able to provide a military response to an incident should such intervention become a necessity.

An international court which would try any captured hijackers or other criminals who have perpetrated acts of unlawful interference.

An international detention center where terrorists may be held while completing their sentence.

One surprising response to the publicity surrounding the proposals was a flurry of letters and telephone calls from individuals around the world to the IATA headquarters in Montreal. They were from men volunteering to serve on the intervention force. The applicants had misinterpreted the airlines' intentions. Intervention was to be by the United Nations with multinational input. A more valid response came from Washington and London. In the former, a House resolution was placed before the U.S. Congress favoring an international court to deal with terrorism. In London, the British foreign secretary, Sir Geoffrey Howe, adopted the first two of the five points. He incorporated them into a series of recommendations placed before his European counterparts. He went further. He had his representative at ICAO promote the proposals in the UN agency. Once there, however, the intent of the original proposals became diffused. For the proposal to be implemented successfully, any central organization taking up IATA's ideas had to initiate action immediately after an incident arose. The airline association's success with its intensified aviation security program had come, in part, from the airlines' making the first move. They approached the involved governments, but ICAO chose to go the passive route. Organization officials wanted any concerned authority to approach them. The organization proposed selecting team members from a list of volunteers offered by its contracting states. The airlines saw two problems with this approach. First, the incident would not wait while the niceties of an invitation procedure were followed. Terrorists have their own timetable. Second, volunteers offered to ICAO were likely to come from the very states the airlines believed lacked the expertise, strength, and willingness to combat terrorist incidents in the first place. These countries would need an intervention force to act on their behalf. Political posturing defeated the original concept. Perhaps the intentions of the Thirty-third Assembly of ICAO will fare better. Only time will tell.

The last two of IATA's five points were to see the light of day, but not in the aviation arena. Following the wars in the former Republic of Yugoslavia, an international court was established in The Hague to try criminals guilty of committing genocide and other atrocities during the conflict. Those found guilty were to be incarcerated in an international prison. There had been a precedent for such action, as IATA had elaborated in support of its own submission. After World War II, the Nazi leaders were tried in Nuremberg, one example of an international court. Those convicted but not executed were held in Spandau Prison in Berlin. The latter paralleled the idea of an international detention center. Despite these two examples from recent history, when al-Qa'eda fighters were captured in Afghanistan following the West's intervention in that country after the World Trade Center attacks, the United States chose not to continue down the international path. They took their prisoners directly to a U.S. marine base at Guantánamo Bay in Cuba.

There is another example of international judiciary cooperation reflecting, if only obliquely, the last two of IATA's five points. In the 1990s, following the indictment of two Libyans for the Pan Am Lockerbie bombing, Colonel Gaddafi consistently claimed he would release the men to a neutral court. In the event, it might be claimed that a variation on the IATA theme was played out. A nonpartisan venue, The Hague, was selected for the men's trial, but with a Scottish panel of judges. A prison was erected to house the men during the proceedings. Abdelbasset Ali Mohmad Al-Megrahi was found guilty and sentenced to life imprisonment in a Scottish jail. Al Amin Khalifa Fhimah, charged with Megrahi, was found not guilty and was freed.

Lessons come together in schools. Major airlines establish their own training establishments covering every aspect of an airline's operations, including security. Part of the curriculum will be those elements of the national or federal program mandated by governments. In the field of security, the air carriers have to exceed the requirements of their own governments because with international networks to manage, they will have to incorporate regulations pertaining to countries to which they operate. The giant airlines have always been able to do this, but smaller airlines had neither the resources nor the opportunity to match their larger counterparts. To meet their needs, in 1984 IATA created a residential security training course at Bailbrook College in the English city of Bath. Lecturers were drawn from the IATA Secretariat and from security experts within the major airlines, supplemented by government tutors in such subjects as explosives identification and threat assessment. Although originally intended as a service to the smaller airlines, several of the principal members of IATA quickly recognized the benefits of using the courses to train their newly appointed security executives. Governments too saw the advantages of using the facility to have their staff train alongside airline personnel and began sending staff members to the courses. The residential course continues today with regional locations now being used.

In Canada, a semi-government-sponsored organization, the International Aviation Management Training Institute (IAMTI), was established. This organization too included a three-week security management training course in the prospectus. It was broadly based and was aimed primarily at governments. The course objective was "to enhance the skills and knowledge of managers with respect to the planning and implementation of efficient and effective security programs in the aviation environment." Response planning and management featured in the syllabus, and this element in an airline's or airport's security program is highly important. If an aircraft is hijacked, or worse still, it is bombed, aviation managements must have a crisis management plan in place. Its features must be rehearsed and tested periodically. The absence of an effective reaction in smaller airports and in smaller countries to an incident was one reason the IATA "Internationalizing the Response" program was conceived. Students attend the IAMTI course from all over the world.

In America, the Federal Aviation Administration, has always been very generous to non-American airlines and to foreign governments, offering a wide range of training facilities and aids. Not surprisingly, the FAA programs have a more nationalistic approach to training than do the two international bodies; but FAA facilities are second to none, and theirs is a valuable contribution to the industry. Training is a truly vital part of air transportation's fight against terrorism, yet still too many governments, airport administrations, and airline managements fail to make sure that their staff are adequately prepared for their roles. ICAO-established training packages can be provided to the organization's contracting states. Whoever provides the training, adequate hands-on-exposure is essential. Once staff are posted to operational duties, monitoring on-the-job performance is the only way to ensure that lessons learned in the classroom are put into practice and maintained in the workplace.

This chapter set out to show that lessons from past incidents provide a basis for the development of sound security programs in the future. Better understanding of the 1970 coordinated aircraft seizures culminating in the terror spectacular at Dawson's Field may have prepared the intelligence services for events on September 11th. Adoption of internationally security programs that had evolved from the bombing of Air India's *Kanishka,* may have prevented the loss of Pan Am flight 103. Lessons learned from firsthand experience of terrorist activity at the outset of airborne terrorism in the early 1960s have led to many of the security procedures today's air travelers encounter every time they travel. The most notable of these is passenger and carry-on baggage screening.

All past incidents of aviation terrorism have something to teach today's airline and airport managers and those government administrators who have responsibility for commercial aviation operations. Lessons from the past must not go unheeded. The international aviation organizations, IATA and ICAO, seek to ensure that this does not happen and have based their security training programs on the eclectic, firsthand experiences of their multicultural membership. National bodies learn from their own past exposure to terrorism, but to maximize security for their citizens, they too have to incorporate into their national or federal programs the lessons drawn from the experience of others.

CHAPTER 9

Minimizing the Risk for Business and Holiday Fliers

As everyone connected with the airline industry is keen to point out, flying on a commercial aircraft is safer than driving one's car. In the opening chapter of this book, notables, including American presidents and vice presidents, have been quoted to underline this fact. Yet terrorist incidents do happen. However, these have to be seen in the context of the many hundreds of airlines operating to and from the many thousands of airports scattered around the world providing hundreds of millions of air journeys every year. Between the loss of Pan Am's *Maid of the Seas* over Lockerbie in 1988 and the attacks on the World Trade Center and other targets in 2001, there were no terrorist incidents affecting U.S. aircraft. This text has shown that had Pan Am applied mandated FAA rules, Lockerbie would not have happened. Had international security performance standards been applied to U.S. domestic services, the al-Qa'eda assaults might not have succeeded. Even so, nervous air travelers contemplating a journey on a commercial airliner will still want to have their fears assuaged. A good consultant at any travel agency will be able to help to a point. Carefully reading quality newspapers in print or via the Internet will keep potential travelers abreast of geopolitical events around the world. Most Western governments have an information bureau that includes an advice service for those planning to travel overseas. All these data sources can be harnessed to minimize the infinitesimal risk of personal exposure to terrorism while traveling by air.

There are three general categories of airline passenger. The first group consists of the business travelers. Their destinations are dictated by the nature of their work. They go where commercial interests take them. Simply because they have a business need, they might fly into locations others would consider insecure. The second category comprises those who travel to visits friends and relations. This group includes many who fly from the old world to the new and vice versa. From the United Kingdom, destinations include the United States, Australia, New Zealand, and Canada. From France, the destinations of family and friends include French Polynesia. Clearly, former colonial powers generate lots of "visit friends and family" passengers. Destinations are dictated to this group of passengers, who go where their hosts live. The third group comprises those individuals traveling for fun, taking a flight to visit new places or revisit favorite destinations. These passengers are going on holiday, and they have total freedom of choice as to where they travel. Their only restriction is likely to be one of cost.

BUSINESS TRAVELERS

Business travelers may work for companies with in-house security departments. Major international oil and construction companies, for example, employ specialists with wide-ranging security responsibilities. These specialists stay abreast of conditions in their colleagues' potential business destinations, where political turmoil might pose a danger to visitors. They remain alert to any government travel advisories. In the United States, the State Department provides such a service. In the United Kingdom, it is the Foreign Office. Both departments regularly publish travel advisories. Company security departments can lock into such administrative bureaus. Additionally, there are commercial companies that provide security information for a fee. These organizations have grown in number in the past decades, so one must be cautious when engaging their services. Security is a growth industry, and too many ill-qualified people have set themselves up as security experts. Simply having been a police officer, for example, does not qualify a person to offer an international security service. Nor does having a certain nationality qualify anyone automatically over someone else. Checking a company's credentials and those of its staff before committing to its services is an essential step—lives may depend on it.

The larger consultancy companies may be able to provide an online service with which an organization can become linked. The information available may vary from a general review of an area or a region to a detailed digest. The review may be refined to a designated city and perhaps be updated on a daily basis, but again care is necessary. The company may simply be rerouting information available from a government's foreign service, in which case the information is easily obtainable, free of charge, directly from the government. A security consultancy may have correspondents based in overseas locations who update the consultancy firm with routine reports. Such correspondents can provide up-to-the-minute reviews, but again, for them to have maximum value, the rapporteur will need to be located in the targeted country. Someone in Singapore, say, covering the whole of Southeast Asia and perhaps the Pacific Rim may be little better briefed than the travelers themselves.

Global corporations are probably best served by their own resources. The big conglomerates are able to obtain all pertinent information from their own staff in the destination country. Staff resident in an area have daily exposure to conditions of possible relevance for the occasional visitor. If a corporation operates regionally with a major city as a hub, frequent travelers from the area axis will likely be able to maintain a close watch on political events as they occur or threaten in the region. The key to preemptive personal security is the timely distribution of information to those who have need of it. Corporations operating internationally should establish within the corporate structure a security intelligence research unit into which data can be fed. There, an appropriate computer program can store all valid information on a real-time footing. Using this stored information, a security specialist can brief intending travellers, or staff members can tap into the data bank themselves. Such companies may have regional security managers whose job is not only to keep headquarters briefed on situations within their areas so that intending travelers can be advised of any local threats but also to protect ex-patriot staff resident within their regions. Although ex-patriot security falls outside the remit of this book, it is worth noting that many companies with overseas operations issue recommendations for such personnel and their families. A typical company guide for employees based overseas provides instructions on establishing safe and defensive driving techniques, garaging vehicles, managing house servants, maintaining communication channels, receiving mail and unsolicited packages, dealing with unknown callers, and the like.

The reference to house servants might be surprising to most residents in the West, but in Africa, the Middle East, and Asia, servants are part of an ex-patriot's life. In some countries, foreign residents will live in compounds, rather like small villages, with their own shopping and entertainment facilities. These compounds will have their own security procedures and guards in place, but many of the policies listed above will still apply.

Business men and women traveling to destinations where their companies have offices should be able to rely on company briefings to familiarize themselves with potential hazards they are likely to face. Even so, they would be well advised to ask questions for themselves. In 1997, four headquarters staff of an American company were murdered during a visit to Pakistan. They were in the wrong place at the wrong time. Their murders coincided with the arrest and trial of Ramzi Ahmed Yousef, which, in Pakistan, had led to an upsurge of anger toward the United States. Karachi is a city well known for political unrest and rampant street violence. This knowledge, together with the resurgent anti-American feelings in the country, should have warned against the timing of the men's travel. Had the men asked the relevant questions themselves, they may have decided against making the journey that led to their deaths. Business travelers should always satisfy themselves, perhaps through their security colleagues, perhaps independently, as to the conditions prevailing at their intending destination. Their lives may depend on it.

What questions might business travelers ask? They should certainly ask for a general briefing on the political situation in countries to be visited. Personal security demands they be aware of any hostility toward nationals of their country. An American business traveler especially will need to satisfy him or herself of this, for example, in respect of any Middle East territory or Muslim country. These are volatile areas where feelings toward the United States are often hostile. This was demonstrated most appallingly in March 2002. An American mother and her daughter, Barbara Green and Kirsten Wormsley, were killed in Islamabad, Pakistan. They died at the hands of terrorists who threw a grenade into their church while they were attending a service. Mrs. Green was an administrator at the U.S. embassy.

Intending travelers should ask for details of any recent incidents that might have increased the risk to visitors. Care should be taken when selecting a means of travel. Ascertain which airlines have good security programs and safety records. Are the carriers known to implement mandated procedures? Personal observation will provide some indication as to which air companies take security seriously. Discussion with colleagues and friends who use air services can also be helpful. The wider the information base, the better informed a traveler will be. It is very worthwhile asking if any carriers have been exposed to threats, perhaps originating from other areas of the carriers' operations? If these questions are answered satisfactorily, travel from their home base is unlikely to pose a threat. If sensible preparation for a journey has been made and care given to the selection of an air company, the average business flyer is unlikely to face exposure to risk from an act of terrorism while traveling.

Certain destinations may dictate the carrier to be used, for there may be only one carrier. Then the choice is simple. If there are alternative ways of reaching the destination, evaluate the opportunities carefully before deciding which to take. Generally, an airline registered in a developed country will offer better security than one from a third world nation. One reason is the probability that the developed nation's airline will have stricter security procedures mandated by its civil aviation authority, but as has been seen, this does not necessarily follow. Of course, for all the reasons discussed earlier in this book, the airline's nationality can influence the level of personal security afforded its passengers. Corporate security managers should have this data at their fingertips. Double-checking with the U.S. State Department, the British Foreign Office, or their equivalent in other Western democracies is always of value. Most definitely, intending business travelers should ascertain if these departments have issued travel advisories warning against flying to a particular destination.

Briefings on local conditions are essential for any business traveler. These briefings should be given before travel commences and updated, as necessary, on arrival. This will ensure that the visitor has the latest information. "Is it safe to walk in the streets unescorted?" "Is a taxi ride to the office or shopping district considered risk free?" Making normal enquiries regarding health matters—"Is it safe to drink the water," for example—is a common sense practice. So too are questions regarding precautions to be taken regarding cholera, typhoid, or other diseases possibly prevalent in the countries to be visited. Security questions should be asked just as routinely. Some companies formalize briefings for staff going overseas, providing them with travel leaflets covering routine matters, but it is well travelers ensure for themselves that the contents are up to date.

Small company's, even one-person businesses, without access to direct in-house contacts at overseas locations can use the various governmental information services to obtain up-to-the-minute reports on the status of the political and security environment in proposed destination countries. Anyone traveling on business to what is for them a first-time destination will have undertaken some form of economic or geopolitical research to ascertain market or client potential. Whoever undertakes that research should include in his or her study any relevant security indices. This does not require an executive with a security background. Any intelligent person with a general understanding of world politics and with access to quality newspapers and government information services is capable of undertaking the task. Keeping up to date through media sources should not be derided. In the early days of terrorism against civil aviation targets, ICAO security consisted of just one man, John Marrett. He frequently regretted the paucity of information received from member states and came to question the reliability of the data. He used news reports to obtain an understanding of those world events that had a potential bearing on aviation security. He followed up the newspaper stories with direct enquiries, often made through his airline contacts. This enabled him to develop a valuable database of information. Marrett oversaw the early development of Annex 17, including the work leading to the historic third edition following the loss of Air India's *Kanishka* over the Atlantic in 1985. He had previously conceived the idea for ICAO's Security Manual for Safeguarding Civil Aviation Against Acts of Unlawful Interference. Much of the work on the manual was undertaken by specialists from the major international airlines with a vested interest in improving security around the world, but John Marrett has to be credited with the effort that saw it into production.

Business travelers flying to unstable areas of the world should always carry with them certain key addresses. Details of the national embassy or consulate in the countries to be visited are important. Knowledge of local security contacts, the police or security forces, is a wise precaution. Selection of hotels has to be considered carefully.

It is wise to stay at a hotel that minimizes travel to the main place of work. In some countries it might be necessary to employ a security guard and perhaps a chauffeur trained in evasive driving techniques, even for the transfer from and to the airport. Countries where such heavy precautions are needed are clearly in the minority and will not concern many readers, but such locations are growing for certain nationalities. Airlines and international companies now have anti-kidnapping procedures in place in a number of areas to safeguard their staff against this scourge. In South America and in Asia, entire aircrews as well as individual businessmen have been kidnapped and held for ransom. Some air carriers no longer night-stop their flying crews in such locations. Pilots and cabin staff depart the country on the same aircraft in which they arrived. Of course, some business activities are more hazardous than others. In January 2002, Daniel Pearl, a *Wall Street Journal* reporter, was kidnapped in Pakistan while on his way to conduct an interview. He was later murdered by his terrorist abductors. Like many newspaper reporters, he was exposed to risk through his work. The average business traveler faces no such threat.

Business men and women fly to potentially unsafe destinations because their companies have operations there or clients and customers live there. Thus commercial travelers have little option. At times, such travelers are likely to have more difficulty avoiding risk than do other air passengers, but they can minimize their exposure to risk by careful pre-planning. A hazardous journey in one month may be less so in another. Timing can be everything.

VISITS TO FRIENDS AND RELATIONS

Passengers traveling to visit friends and relatives are more fortunate than their business counterparts. They will have close and trustworthy contact with the people they are planning to visit. Their friends and relatives will know all there is to know about local conditions. If there is any personal risk, such individuals can be warned of traveling at that particular time. "Friends and relations" passengers can, of course, still check with their government's information services. Nonetheless, their intending hosts are likely to know more than external government bodies about local conditions. Assuming all is well, the only consideration need be the routing selected for the journey. All travelers would be well advised to avoid war zones or areas of unrest. From North America, passengers flying to visit friends and relations in Europe will have no such concerns. Traveling westward from continental America to Pacific Rim locations, intending passengers should note that the Philippines and Indonesia have become difficult territories with terrorism rearing its head in the region.

The danger associated with the region was dramatically underlined in October 2002. Terrorists, believed to be Muslim extremists and allegedly linked to the al-Qa'eda, detonated a massive car bomb outside a popular night-spot on the Indonesian island of Bali. 188 people were killed by the blast and more than 300 injured. The majority of the casualties were young Australians but many British tourists, most in their early twenties, were among those who died. Within hours of the Bali atrocity, both Australia and the U.K. issued travel advisories warning their citizens against visiting Indonesia. Those already in the country were urged to leave. The advice came too late to save those who were maimed or killed. Subsequently both governments admitted they had prior, albeit non-specific warnings of possible terrorist activity in the region at the time of the bombing. This incident underlines the value of travelers researching the potential danger arising from political unrest in the destinations they have selected. Even before the Bali bombing, travelers from North America and Europe intending to visit friends and relations in Asia or Australasia, who might normally have considered Indonesia or the Philippines as a potential stop-over, would have been well advised to rethink their itineraries. Ramzi Ahmed Yousef's campaign of air terror was to have been centered in this area.

Passengers can bypass both sets of islands if the intended destination is Australia or New Zealand in the south or Hong Kong or Singapore in the west. Passengers traveling from Europe to Australasia at the present time, would do well to avoid routing through countries such as Iran, Pakistan, and even India. The threat posed by terrorism in so much of the region is likely to be long-lasting.

For Americans, traveling to visit friends or family poses minimal risk unless their closest and dearest live in a country engulfed in political difficulties. One country that generates heavy traffic of this nature and clearly does have political difficulties is Israel. The political and physical turmoil in the Middle East is discussed daily in the print media and in television newscasts. No one can fail to be aware of the daily hazards facing Israeli citizens and any foreign residents or visitors to that country. Decisions to travel to Tel Aviv from the United States or elsewhere in the world must be taken in the full knowledge of the unrest and risk that exists. El Al, the state airline of Israel, has been a sought-after target for many years for many groups of Middle East terrorists, but the carrier's well-publicized security program has so far proved to be too effective for militants to breach. On the rare occasions attempts have been made, they have always been thwarted. Similarly, security at Tel Aviv's Ben Gurion Airport for the return journey has been designed with the certain knowledge that complacency and incompetence would be measured in human lives. Despite the street and café attacks that occur with sickening frequency in Israel, the airport has to date maintained its successful defenses against terrorism.

HOLIDAY FLIERS

Holiday travelers have total freedom of choice when it comes to selecting a vacation destination and the carrier to take them there. A limiting factor may be cost. Vacations have to take their turn in the purchasing roster, which may include a range of desirable durable consumables. The purchase of a new car may figure high on a wish-list. School and college fees could eat into the disposable income pool, thus affecting holiday plans. A house move may cause a vacation to be postponed. Once these matters have been dealt with, the choice left to those going on vacation is where to go and how.

Until September 11th, American vacationers might have believed that a holiday confined to the mainland United States would let them safely avoid terrorist threats. Since al-Qa'eda brought terror to domestic U.S. skies, however, such a belief may be tinged with doubt. In any case, other hazards might be associated with domestic vacations. The opening chapter of this book quoted George Bush, who spoke of 18,000 persons being murdered each year in the United States. That was in 1986. Motorists contemplating a driving holiday have to reconcile themselves to the high death toll on U.S. roads. Yet such statistics do not confine U.S. citizens to their home. Nor should acts of terrorism, which account for far fewer deaths among U.S. citizens, stop Americans from taking an overseas vacation. In Europe, taking continental vacations by airplane increased in 2002 over the previous year. The destinations favored by Europeans are frequently the same cities, resorts, and mountain areas that figure in the itineraries of American vacationers. Since indigenous populations have deemed the destinations to be safe, the areas are equally secure for U.S. citizens. The advice to intending travelers, wherever they live, is to go to their chosen destination but take the same precautions one would in normal life. Pedestrians in major cities in their own country are careful not to wander into locations or situations where they might expect to become victims of street crimes, for example. It is no different when on vacation. Vacationers should not deliberately travel to countries where the risk of becoming exposed to an act of terrorism, either en route to the destination or while there, is a known possibility. This group of travelers has most of the world from which to choose; they should select somewhere safe.

Perhaps this philosophy, selecting somewhere safe, accounts for the rapid growth in cruising as a vacation plan of so many Americans. The cruise terminals on the Atlantic and Pacific coasts can be reached without leaving the boundaries of the United States. Cruise itineraries can be selected to confine the journey to American islands. Many other cruises are limited to the former British or French territories in the Caribbean or perhaps to Canadian ports, all considered safe locations. Yet cruising is just as quickly figuring in the holiday plans of Europeans. Southampton, made famous as the homeport of the great prewar liners plying between England and New York, now provides berths for the new generation of ships built purely for the holiday market. Barcelona in Spain, the Italian ports of Venice and Genoa (birthplace of Christopher Columbus, an old hand at cruising) and Piraeus in Greece are all starting points for sea-based holidays. For most Europeans, given the nature of their continent, any cruise terminal they choose to start the vacation from will almost certainly entail an air journey that crosses international boundaries. They are just as likely to board an aircraft to cross the Atlantic for a cruise departing from Miami or Vancouver as they are to fly to the Mediterranean to sail in that inland sea. Europeans are greater readers of international reports carried in the various media outlets than are most of their North American counterparts. Thus they will be cognizant of potential threats against carriers of a particular nationality and can select their airline accordingly. Should terrorists ever focus on marine targets, similar attention will doubtless be paid to cruise companies.

As has been suggested, cruising is almost invariably linked to air travel at the beginning and at the end of a vacation. The major conurbations from which the cruise companies draw their clientele are generally well away from the departure ports, and thus a decision to cruise is almost invariably followed by the necessity to select an air service to fly to the port of departure. Once a decision to fly has been made, it is just a small step to becoming more adventurous and to look for ports farther away as a starting point. These days, many Europeans and North Americans take an airline east- or westbound, depending on their starting point, to board vessels in Singapore or other Asian and Australasian ports. Thus although there is this expanding seaborne holiday market, much of it is dependent upon air travel. Wherever a vacationer decides to start his or her cruise, as much care should go into selecting the departure port, and therefore an air itinerary, as is given to a land-based vacation. In the main, the cruise companies take the necessary precautions when selecting their terminal locations. Certainly, few cruises originate in Beirut or Karachi.

There are several considerations to be included when deciding which air carrier to take. For vacationers going long distances, seating comfort may be a prime factor in their choice. In this regard, a chart published in the English *Daily Telegraph* is interesting. It gave the average seat pitches (the distance between a seat and the one in front) in the economy or coach cabins of selected airlines. It suggested that American Airlines is among the most generous, offering a seat pitch of 34 to 36 inches. Air New Zealand, Japan Airlines, Malaysian Airlines, and South African Airlines were all said to provide 34 inches between the rows of seats. Emirates came next with 32 to 34 inches. Qantas, Singapore Airlines, Thai Airways, Cathy Pacific, and British Airways were each reported to have seats with a 32-inch pitch. Charter companies generally have seat pitches ranging from 29 to 31 inches. Seat pitch variations will occur from time to time, of course. If one carrier is clearly attracting more customers as a result of improved comfort standards offered by larger distances from one seat row to another, competitors may seek to match the standards to protect their market share. If seat pitch is a concern, it is worth monitoring the marketing programs of the major air carriers before deciding which flight to take. The consultant at the local travel agency will be pleased to offer advice. If ever a traveler was to become embroiled in a lengthy aircraft seizure, a highly remote possibility, the additional leg room might assume an even greater value.

Selecting an airline will, of course, depend on more than seating space. As has been suggested earlier in this chapter, travelers to Israel often have an ethnic relationship to that country thus El Al becomes a natural choice for an airline. Yet the carrier is chosen not just because of its national origins but because it has earned a reputation for being the most secure airline flying to that part of the world. The additional time taken to check in for a flight and the more detailed passenger and baggage screening are considered an acceptable, even desirable, price to pay for the feeling of safety associated with the carrier. Confidence in an airline's security program is an important element in a passenger's feeling of personal security. During one notable interview, a former director of the Office of Civil Aviation Security at the Federal Aviation Administration said he would never voluntarily fly again with an American airline. This may sound like heresy, but he was speaking from the heart. He was truly concerned at the standards of security being afforded to air travelers at that time.

Billie H. Vincent headed the FAA Office of Civil Aviation Security from May 1982 until July 1986. At the beginning of Vincent's FAA tenure, he had to consider the two attacks against Pan Am services mentioned earlier in this book. Saboteurs had used improvised explosive devices to attack the airline. They had placed the devices underneath the passenger seats. Immediate reaction was to place the blame for the attacks at the door of Middle East terrorists—a reaction to be repeated years later when the Federal Building in Oklahoma was bombed. The methodology used, hand-carrying bombs intended to blow up aircraft in mid-flight, and the locations, well away from the customary theaters in which Middle East terrorists played out their wretched acts, created great debate within aviation circles. The attacks were considered turning points in airborne terrorism, suggesting the unpalatable fact that there existed persons and groups prepared to commit and capable of perpetrating acts of mass murder far away from their primary operating bases.

The first attack was against a Boeing 747 flying from Tokyo to Honolulu. The improvised explosive device used was a pressure-activated time bomb hidden underneath a passenger seat, where an unfortunate 16-year-old Japanese boy unwittingly activated the bomb's timing mechanism when he sat down. Fortunately, the terrorists made a mistake when they positioned the device. The explosive charge was placed so that when it detonated, the shock waves traveled longitudinally toward the front and the rear of the aircraft. This most fortunate of errors saved the lives of everyone on board, other than the youth occupying the fatal seat. His leg was blown off and he died instantly. Had the bomb been positioned so that the shock waves went sideways, they may well have ruptured the skin of the aircraft, causing results similar to those witnessed at Lockerbie. The list of fatalities would then have included everyone on board.

Two weeks after the Japanese youth was killed, an alert member of Pan Am's cleaning staff in Rio de Janeiro foiled a second attack. The cleaner found a bomb on an aircraft during a routine operation prior to takeoff. Recovery of the second bomb gave FAA and FBI experts an unprecedented opportunity to examine what was at the time the latest piece of terrorist technology. The improvised explosive device measured 12 inches by 4 inches by a half inch and incorporated sophisticated timing devices capable of being set many hours ahead of the selected detonation time. The construction showed that the device was intended to explode after takeoff, and hence followed the easily drawn conclusion that mass murder had become a tool of international air terrorism. The explosive charge was sheet plastic explosive of a type manufactured in Czechoslovakia and known commercially as Semtex. Power was provided by pencil-thin batteries attached to a detonator, an essential element of any improvised explosive. The timing mechanism was again intended to be activated by the pressure of a passenger's body weight when he or she sat down. A replica device was produced by the Federal Aviation Administration and the FBI working together at the former's technical center in Atlantic City, and controlled tests were undertaken. Explosive devices similar to the one found at Rio were detonated inside the fuselage of a DC 10 aircraft to simulate the effects of the blast. What was learned led to the introduction of new security regulations.

The need for new procedures to combat the threat posed by underseat bombs was emphasized shortly after the two Pan Am incidents. Similar improvised explosive devices fell into the hands of the police in Switzerland. These devices appeared to be linked to Abu Ibrahim, whose 15th May terrorist organization was based in Baghdad, Iraq. Intelligence services anticipated that the technology had been passed to other terrorists. Vincent acted. He published recommendations to combat the threat posed by underseat bombs. As a result, U.S. air carriers operating on international routes had to search the cabins of aircraft and, in particular, to lift the seat cushions and look under them before passengers boarded. Despite the fact that a second Pan Am disaster had been averted by such a procedure and the knowledge that other such devices existed, U.S. airlines voiced objections. The carriers wanted to avoid the cost penalties they believed would be incurred by such a process. Their lobby was effective, and the recommendations were rescinded. A New York court hearing charges against TWA following the 1986 detonation of an underseat bomb on their aircraft flying from Rome to Athens considered these decisions. TWA had failed to find the device during the aircraft's stopover in Rome.

Vincent laid the foundations for U.S. airlines' defenses against the checked-baggage bomber. In 1986, based on the work at IATA and ICAO, the Federal Aviation Administration called for positive baggage match to be performed by U.S. carriers at all European airports. The changes to the air carrier standard security program followed a declaration from Ahmed Jibril, who led a Palestinian terror group, that he would "no longer be responsible for civilians flying on Israeli and U.S. airlines." Positive baggage match was the key rule dropped by Pan Am at Frankfurt and London in summer 1988. Vincent believed, correctly, that adoption and implementation of the FAA rules would have saved lives. Failure to adopt proven methods of securing the safety of airline passengers left air travelers vulnerable, hence the strong position taken by the aviation authority's former director of security.

American air carriers have always demanded a level playing field in respect of aviation security rules. By this they mean they should not be disadvantaged financially or operationally by having placed on them regulations they perceive not to be applicable to their competitors. Ten years before the al-Qa'eda attacks, ATA (the American Air Transport Association) explained its position in a statement given by the organizations security spokesperson before a House of Representatives subcommittee on aviation.[18] Thomas C. Kelly told the members that the ATA had participated actively in the discussions leading to the development of the Aviation Security Improvement Act of 1990. He stated, "Our primary focus in the development of the legislation was to ensure that it would contain provisions imposing the same extraordinary security procedures on foreign flag carriers that the FAA currently imposes only on U.S. carriers operating in international routes." Kelly believed that putting security requirements on U.S. carriers unilaterally "places our financially distressed industry at a competitive disadvantage with the foreign carriers." The driving objective for the U.S. carriers had been the bottom-line figure in the accounts. The ATA had failed to acknowledge that its members were at greater risk.

THE CONTINUING THREAT

Much of the Arab and increasingly the Muslim world at large sees U.S. foreign policy as anti-Palestinian and anti-Muslim. Therein lies the basis of much of the continued threat to U.S. civil aviation. The events of Spring 2002, when Israel again sent troops into Palestine, exacerbated matters. The hatred such action generated in the region will be long-lasting, even if a peace can be negotiated. Residual anger is likely to encompass America, seen by many in the Middle East as the financial prop and thus the ally of Israel. Militants already consider American aircraft surrogate targets for the U.S. government and view them as easier prey than El Al. Thus U.S. airplanes will be under increased threat. The carriers have to level the playing field themselves; they have to institute security procedures to protect their services against an enemy that displays less anger toward other nationalities. The airlines must work with the Federal Aviation Administration to ensure adoption of carrier procedures that preempt possible terrorist attacks on their aircraft. Their first duty must be to protect their customers.

Wherever international airlines operate, all carriers must apply the rules of the country from which they are departing. Thus from London, U.S. carriers will have to meet U.K. passenger and baggage reconciliation standards as well as apply hold baggage screening rules. Basic security should therefore be the same on any carrier. Performance has to be monitored, of course. In this example, that would be the joint responsibility of the Federal Aviation Administration and the Department of Transport. The former must ensure the federal requirements are met; the latter has to make certain the national security mandates are correctly performed. Foreign flag airlines returning from the United States will have to meet FAA rules, but in addition they will have to satisfy their own national standards, which may, in the case of the major European countries, be higher than those of the United States. Yet the greater threat to date has been against the American air carriers. The shoe bomber was on American Airlines. The suitcase bomb that detonated over Lockerbie was on Pan Am. The underseat bombs discussed previously were on Pan Am and TWA. To level the playing field for their customers, U.S. air carriers must match and preferably beat the standards of their competitors. In this way, on-board personal security will cease to feature in a passenger's choice of carrier.

Air passengers can monitor aspects of a carrier's security performance for themselves. Even very occasional travelers will be able to gauge the competence of an airline's baggage-matching performance. If on reaching their destination airport passengers discover that their baggage has not arrived on the same flight, clearly the passenger and baggage reconciliation process has failed. This could be the result of carelessness by the baggage loaders, who may have put the bags on the wrong aircraft or simply forgotten to load them. Or it may simply be because a check-in agent placed the wrong labels on the bags (less likely to happen with fully automated check-in). Either way, the control mechanisms have not worked. There has been no effective matching process. If there is poor control or no matching, the potential for mischievous acts exists. Similarly, if passengers see unclaimed bags circulating on the baggage carousels while they are waiting for their own to arrive, again the probability that a mismatch has occurred somewhere in the system is very real. Without an acceptable baggage control system in place, the involved airline would be vulnerable to some form of malfeasance. Passengers would be at risk. If friends and colleagues exchange examples of baggage mishandling with each other, even casual vacationers will be able to build up an idea of an airline's security performance. Doing so will help them to decide which carrier to use for their next vacation.

After witnessing shortcomings in a carrier's or an airport's security performance, an air passenger would do well to write to the guilty party, forwarding a copy of the complaint to the civil aviation authority in the country concerned to give the authority an idea of what is happening at the grass roots of security. In the United States, this authority would be the FAA administrator. Civil aviation authorities have limited resources for inspection despite the importance of this function. If the identified weakness is at a foreign airport, a copy of the letter of complaint sent to the passengers' own aviation authority would help the latter develop a more sound database of performances overseas. Should an authority's answer fail to be satisfactory, the passenger's the next step would be to send a letter to his or her legislative assembly member or congressional representative, or Member of Parliament.

Once on board an aircraft, passengers should be able to relax. They and everyone else in the cabin will have gone through security controls and all should be bone fide travelers or members of staff. Security at the departure airport should have ensured that no one capable of causing damage to the flight has boarded the airplane. In the United States, security has tightened since September 11th, making a repeat of those terrible events unlikely if everybody does their jobs properly. If, however, the unthinkable happens and someone on an aircraft attempts to seize control, the flight crew will respond. They have been trained for just such an emergency. Any sky marshal on board will also have undergone contingency training. In addition, if airline personnel call for help, passengers in a position to assist will likely go to their aid.

It is impossible to lay down rigid guidelines for occasions that will alter with the circumstances, but before September 11th the general advice would have been against passengers' initiating action against hijackers. What happened on board United Airlines flight 093 remains uncertain. It is known, however, that the heroic action of certain passengers prevented an even worse catastrophe resulting from the seizure. Evidently, in their eyes, to have sat back and done nothing would have been wrong, unthinkable. That incident has changed the rules of in-flight responses. Suicidal militants have arrived and brought with them a new menace, but unless passengers are convinced that would-be hijackers of their aircraft are al-Qa'eda fanatics or their ilk, it is still best to leave matters to the captain in the hope that he can persuade the hijackers to let him land the aircraft safely. In these circumstances, passengers must remain low key, staying in their seats and avoiding making themselves conspicuous. They should avoid making eye contact with those now in control. Once the hijacked aircraft is on the ground, new criteria come into play. Security forces will certainly have begun to plan an end to the seizure long before the aircraft arrives. Well-rehearsed recovery programs will have been activated. Hard as it may be, passengers simply have to wait to be rescued.

During the Kuwait Airlines seizure, the young students on board mentally recorded everything that went on around them. As a result, when debriefed, they were able to relate to airline security specialists and special services personnel minute details of their time as hostages. Noting details of the seizure and pigeonholing incidents helped the students keep their minds focused during their time on board the aircraft. They deliberately sought not to draw attention to themselves—although for the young lady who had been in the washroom when the initial takeover happened, this had not been possible. The "polite" hijacker who had asked her to "please sit here" had been very attentive. He had noticed that the girl had kicked off her shoes during the flight and was now barefooted, so he fetched her a pair of airline slipperettes to put on. When she went to bow her head, as the other passengers had been instructed to do, he told her she need not do that. During her debriefing, the young woman told the special services captain that she had wondered what was coming next. When asked what would she have done had the hijacker sought "payment" for his attention, she simply said, "My intention would have been to get off the plane alive."

In this book we have examined various examples of terrorist attacks on aviation targets. Few of our readers, if any, will ever find themselves in similar circumstances. Even George Bush indicated, when he was vice president, how remote the possibility was that the average citizen would become involved in a terrorist act, whether in the air or on the ground. To ensure that such a possibility is indeed remote, the government agencies responsible for our safety must fulfill their charges properly. If they do, and if airline and airport managements turn the tables on history and show a sincere willingness to address safety and security on behalf of their customers, the chances of an airborne terrorist act will have been minimized, perhaps even eradicated. The skies will have become safer for us all.

Notes

1. The Vice President's Task Force on Combating Terrorism, 1985.

2. Report of the White House Commission on Aviation Safety and Security, 1997.

3. Commission on Aviation Security and Terrorism, 1989; White House Commission on Aviation Safety and Security, 1997.

4. Thirty-third Assembly of ICAO, Montreal, September 25–October 5, 2001.

5. Commission on Aviation Security and Terrorism, 1989.

6. Convention on Offenses and Certain Other Acts Committed on Board Aircraft, 1963.

7. Convention for the Suppression of Unlawful Seizure of Aircraft, enacted in 1970.

8. Convention for the Suppression of Unlawful Acts Against the Safety of Civil Aviation, 1971.

9. Thomas Hobbes (1588–1679), English philosopher and political theorist.

10. Commission on Aviation Security and Terrorism, 1989; White House Commission on Aviation Safety and Security, 1997.

11. Annex 17 (Safeguarding International Civil Aviation Against Acts of Unlawful Interference) to the Convention on International Civil Aviation.

12. The President's Commission on Aviation Security and Terrorism, 1989, recommended the appointment of an assistant secretary of transportation for security and intelligence.

13. Victoria Cummock in her addendum to the report of the White House Commission on Aviation Safety and Security.

14. Security Manual for Safeguarding Civil Aviation Against Acts of Unlawful Interference.

15. Investigation Findings: Explosion of Korean Air Flight 858, published by the Korean Overseas Information Service, January 1988.

16. Dick Shaw, Assistant Director General (Technical) of IATA.

17. State of the Union Address, United States Capitol, Washington, January 2002.

18. Committee on Public Works and Transportation, Subcommittee on Aviation, House of Representatives, July 24, 1991.

Index

Index

About the Author

RODNEY WALLIS led the international airline industry's effort to combat terrorism aimed against international civil aviation for eleven years (1980–1991). As Director of Security of the International Air Transport Association (IATA), he served on ICAO's Panel of Aviation Security Experts. He provided liaison between the international airlines and the International Criminal Police Organization (Interpol) on security matters. He made input to two U.S. presidential commissions studying airborne terrorism.